the
MARSHALL
reader

The life and contributions
of
Chief Justice John Marshall
[BICENTENARY EDITION]

SELECTED AND EDITED BY

ERWIN C. SURRENCY
Associate Professor of Law,
Temple University

DOCKET SERIES
Volume 3

Oceana Publications
New York City
1955

LC55011500

CONTENTS

CONTENTS

PREFACE

The purpose of this book is to present through articles by outstanding authorities, the life and contributions of Chief Justice John Marshall, who is recognized as being the great American Jurist.

The editor was faced with the same dilemma as a jeweler who wishes to make a valuable necklace. He has many more precious gems to choose from than he can use on the necklace. Anyone who has written on constitutional law must include a study of John Marshall's decisions and for this reason the literature about him is extensive. However, John Marshall was not a prolific writer and his only writings are opinions and official documents completed in various official capacities except for a few letters which have been preserved. This will explain why the editor has included articles about his life and work in the *Marshall Reader* rather than selections from his writings. The comments made by Marshall in his letters on some of his decisions are included to give some understanding of this man's personal thoughts.

It is the hope of the editor that this book will aid in effecting a better understanding of this jurist's contributions to American government, history, and law.

The editor would like to express his appreciation to the following publishers and authors for the use of the material reprinted in this book:

The Honorable Harold H. Burton, Associate Justice of the Supreme Court of the United States and *The American Bar Association Journal* for "Justice, the Guardian of Liberty"; The Honorable Felix Frankfurter, Associate Justice of the Supreme Court of the United States, and *The University of North Carolina Press* for "The Commerce Clause"; The Honorable Harold H. Burton and *The University of Pennsylvania Law Review* for "John Marshall the Man"; *The University of Michigan Press* and *The University of Michigan Clements Library* for "the autobiographical letter of John Marshall to Justice Story"; *The W. H.*

Anderson Co. for Albert J. Beveridge "John Marshall, His Personality and Development"; *The Maryland State Bar Association* for Albert J. Beveridge, "Maryland, Marshall and the Constitution"; *Columbia University Law Review* for Max Learner "John Marshall and the Campaign of History"; The Honorable Edward Dumbauld and *The University of Pennsylvania Law Review* for "John Marshall and the Law of Nations"; to *The American Bar Association Journal* for H. O. Bishop, "Chief Justice Marshall, Transportation Expert"; *The Massachusetts Historical Society* for Marshall's Letters; and *The American Bar Association Journal* for Robert B. Tunstall, "John Marshall: One Hundred Years After."

The editor would also like to express his appreciation to Miss Emily Drummond and Mrs. C. M. Boesch for their editorial help and suggestions.

PART I.

THE LIFE
OF
CHIEF JUSTICE MARSHALL

THE AUTOBIOGRAPHICAL LETTER OF
JOHN MARSHALL TO JOSEPH STORY[1]

Joseph Story requested his friend, John Marshall, to write a short autobiographical letter for his use in preparing a biography of the Chief Justice. The following letter was written in reply to this request. Marshall's letter illustrates one of his personal traits; namely, his modesty. Marshall makes no mention of the many important events in his life in which he played an important part, passing over them as though they were unimportant. The letter is printed with Marshall's original spelling.

The manuscript of this letter is in the William L. Clements Library, University of Michigan, and is here reprinted with the consent of the Library and the University of Michigan Press, who originally published this letter.

MY DEAR SIR:

The events of my life are too unimportant, and have too little interest for any person not of my immediate family, to render them worth communicating or preserving. I felt therefore some difficulty in commencing their detail, since the mere act of detailing, exhibits the appearance of attaching consequence to them;—a difficulty which was not overcome till the receipt of your favour of the 14th inst. If I conquer it now, it is because the request is made by a partial and highly valued friend.

I was born on the 24th of Septr. 1755 in the county of Fauquier at that time one of the frontier counties of Virginia. My Father possessed scarcely any fortune, and had received a very limited education;—but was a man to whom nature had been bountiful, and who had assiduously improved her gifts. He superintended my education, and gave me an early taste for history and for poetry. At the age of twelve I had transcribed Pope's essay on man, with some of his moral essays.

There being at that time no grammar school in the part of the country in which my Father resided I was sent, at fourteen, about one hundred miles from home, to be placed under the tuition of Mr. Campbell a clergyman of great respectability. I remained with him one year, after which I was brought home and placed under the care of a Scotch gentleman who was just introduced into the parish as Pastor, and who resided in my Fathers family. He remained in the family one year, at the expiration of which time I had commenced reading Horace and Livy. I continued my studies with no other aid than my Dictionary. My Father superintended the English part of my education, and to his care I am indebted for anything valuable which I may have acquired in my youth. He was my only intelligent companion; and was both a watchfull parent and an affectionate instructive friend. The young men within my reach were entirely uncultivated; and the time I passed with them was devoted to hardy athletic exercises.

About the time I entered my eighteenth year, the controversy between Great Britain and her colonies had assumed so serious an aspect as almost to monopolize the attention of the old and the young. I engaged in it with all the zeal and enthusiasm which belonged to my age; and devoted more time to learning the first rudiments of military exercise in an Independent company of the gentlemen of the county, to training a militia company in the neighbourhood, and to the political essays of the day, than to the classics or to Blackstone.

In the summer of 1775 I was appointed a first lieutenant in a company of minute men designed for actual service, who were assembled in Battalion on the first of September. In a few days we were ordered to march into the lower country for the purpose of defending it against a small regular and predatory force commanded by Lord Dunmore. I was engaged in the action at the Great Bridge; and was in Norfolk when it was set on fire by a detachment from the British ships lying in the river, and afterwards when the remaining houses were burnt by orders from the Committee of safety.

In July 1776 I was appointed first Lieutenant in the 11th Virginia regiment on continental establishment; and, in the course of the succeeding winter marched to the north, where, in May 1777, I was promoted to the rank of Captain. I was in the skirmish at iron hill where the Light Infantry was engaged; and in the battles of Brandy Wine, German town, and Monmouth.

As that part of the Virginia line which had not marched to Charleston was dissolving by the expiration of the terms for which the men had enlisted, the officers were directed to return home in the winter of 1779-80, in order to take charge of such men as the legislature should raise for them. I availed myself of this inactive interval for attending a course of law lectures given by Mr. Wythe, and of lectures of Natural philosophy given by Mr. Madison then President of William and Mary College. The vacation commenced in july when I left the university, and obtained a license to practice law. In October I returned to the army, and continued in service until the termination of Arnolds invasion after which, in February 1781, before the invasion of Phillips, there being a redundancy of officers, I resigned my commission. I had formed a strong attachment to the young lady whom I afterwards married; and, as we had more officers than soldiers, thought I might without violating the duty I owed my country, pay some attention to my future prospects in life.

It was my design to go immediately to the bar; but the invasion of Virginia soon took place, and the courts were closed till the capitulation of Lord Cornwallis. After that event the courts were opened and I commenced practice.

In the spring of 1782 I was elected a member of the legislature; and, in the autumn of the same year was chosen a member of the Executive Council. In January 1783 I was married to Miss Ambler the second daughter of our then Treasurer, and in april 1784 resigned my seat at the Council board in order to return to the bar. In the same month I was again elected a member of the legislature for the county of Fauquier of which I was only a nominal resident having resided actually in Richmond as a member of the Council. Immediately after the election I established myself in Richmond for the purpose of practicing law in the superior courts of Virginia.

My extensive acquaintance in the army was of great service to me. My numerous military friends, who were dispersed over the state, took great interest in my favour, and I was more successful than I had reason to expect. In April 1787, I was elected into the legislature for the county in which Richmond stands; and though devoted to my profession, entered with a good deal of spirit into the politics of the state. The topics of the day were paper money, the collection of taxes, the preservation of public faith, and the administration of justice. Parties were nearly equally divided on all these interesting subjects; and the contest concerning them was continually renewed. The state of the Confederacy was also a subject of deep solicitude to our statesmen. Mr. James Madison had been for two or three years a leading member of the House of Delegates, and was the parent of the resolution for appointing members to a general Convention to be held at Philadelphia for the purpose of revising the confederation. The question whether a continuance of the Union or a separation of the states was most to be desired was some times discussed; and either side of the question was supported without reproach. Mr. Madison was the enlightened advocate of Union and of an efficient federal government; but was not a member of the legislature when the plan of the constitution was proposed to the states by the General Convention. It was at first favorably received; but Mr. P. Henry, Mr. G. Mason, and several other gentlemen of great influence were much opposed to it, and permitted no opportunity to escape of inveighing against it and of communicating their prejudices to others. In addition to state jealously and state pride, which operated powerfully in all the large states, there were some unacknowledged motives of no inconsiderable influence in Virginia. In the course of the session, the unceasing efforts of the enemies of the constitution made a deep impression; and before its close, a great majority showed a decided hostility to it. I took an active part in the debates on this question and was uniform in support of the proposed constitution.

When I recollect the wild and enthusiastic democracy with which my political opinions of that day were tinctured, I am disposed to ascribe my devotion to the union, and to a government competent to its preservation, at least as much to casual circumstances as to judgement. I had grown up at a time when a love of union and resistance to the claims of Great Britain were the inseparable inmates of the same bosom;—when patriotism and a strong fellow feeling with our suffering fellow citizens of Boston were identical;—when the maxim "united we stand, divided we fall" was the maxim of every orthodox American; and I had imbibed these sentiments so thoughroughly that they constituted a part of my being. I carried them with me into the army where I found myself associated with brave men from different states who were risking life and everything valuable in a common cause believed by all to be most precious; and where I was confirmed in the habit of considering America as my country, and congress as my government. I partook largely of the sufferings and feelings of the army, and brought with me into civil life an ardent devotion to its interests. My immediate entrance into the state legislature opened to my view the causes which had been chiefly instrumental in augmenting those sufferings, and the general tendency of state politics convinced me that no safe

and permanent remedy could be found but in a more
efficient and better organized general government.
The questions too, which were perpetually recurring
in the state legislatures, aand which brought annu-
ally into doubt principles which I thought most
sound, which proved that everything was afloat, and
that we had no safe anchorage ground, gave a high
value in my estimation to that article in the constitution which imposes restrictions on the states. I was
consequently a determined advocate for its adoption,
and became a candidate for the convention to which
it was to be submitted.

The county in which I resided was decidedly antifederal, but I was at that time popular, and parties
had not yet become so bitter as to extinguish the
private affections.

A great majority of the people of Virginia was antifederal; but in several of the counties most opposed
to the adoption of the constitution, individuals of
high character and great influence came forward as
candidates and were elected from personal motives.
After an ardent and eloquent discussion to which
justice never has been and never can be done, during
which the constitution was adopted by nine states,
the question was carried in the affirmative by a majority of eight voices.

I felt that those great principles of public policy
which I considered as essential to the general happiness were secured by this measure & I willingly
relinquished public life to devote myself to my
profession. Indeed the county was so thoroughly antifederal, & parties had become so exasperated, that
my election would have been doubtful. This however was not my motive for withdrawing from the
legislature. My practice had become very considerable, and I could not spare from its claims on me so
much time as would be necessary to maintain such
a standing in the legislature as I was desirous of preserving. I was pressed to become a candidate for
congress; and, though the district was unequivocally
antifederal I could have been elected because that

party was almost equally divided between two candidates who were equally obstinate and much embittered against each other. The struggle between the ambition of being engaged in the organization of the government, and the conviction of the injury which would be sustained by my private affairs was at length terminated in the victory of prudence, after which the federalists set up and elected Colonel Griffin, who obtain rather more than one third of the votes in the district which constituted a plurality.

Colonel Griffin named me to General Washington as the attorney for the district, an office which I had wished, but I declined accepting it because at that time the circuit courts of the United States were held at two distinct places far apart, and distant from the seat of government where the superior courts of the state sat. Consequently I could not attend them regularly without some detriment to my state practice. Before this inconvenience was removed the office was conferred on another gentleman.

In December 1788 the legislature passed an act allowing a representative to the city of Richmond, and I was almost unanimously invited to become a candidate. The city was federal. I yielded to the general wish partly because a man changes his inclination after retiring from public life, partly because I found the hostility to the government so strong in the legislature as to require from its friends all the support they could give it, and partly because the capitol was then completed, and the courts and the legislature sat in the same building, so that I could without much inconvenience [leave?][2] the bar to take part in any debate in which I felt a particular interest.

I continued in the assembly for the years 1789 & 1790 & 1791, during which time almost every important measure of the government was discussed, and the whole funding system was censured; that part of it especially which assumes the state debts was pronounced unconstitutional. After the session of 1791 I again withdrew from the assembly, determined to bid a final adieu to political life.

The arrival and conduct of Mr. Genet excited great sensation throughout the southern states. We were all strongly attached to France—scarcely any man more strongly than myself. I sincerely believed human liberty to depend in a great measure on the success of the French revolution. My partiality to France however did not so entirely pervert my understanding as to render me insensible to the danger of permitting a foreign minister to mingle himself in the management of our affairs, and to intrude himself between our government and people. In a public meeting of the citizens of Richmond, some of the earliest if not the very first resolutions were passed expressing strong disapprobation of the irregular conduct of Mr. Genet, our decided sense of the danger of foreign influence, and our warm approbation of the proclamation of neutrality. These resolutions, and the address to the President which accompanied them, were drawn and supported by me.

The resentments of the great political party which led Virginia had been directed towards me for some time, but this measure brought it into active operation. I was attacked with great virulence in the papers and was so far honoured in Virginia as to be associated with Alexander Hamilton, at least so far as to be termed his instrument. With equal vivacity I defended myself and the measures of the government. My constant effort was to show that the conduct of our government respecting its foreign relations were such as a just self-respect and a regard for our rights as a sovereign nation rendered indispensable, and that our independence was brought into real danger by the overgrown & inordinate influence of France. The public & frequent altercations in which I was unavoidably engaged gradually weakened my decision never again to go into the legislature, & I was beginning to think of changing my determination on that subject, when the election in the spring of 1795 came on.

From the time of my withdrawing from the legislature two opposing candidates had divided the city, the one was my intimate friend whose sentiments were very much those which I had entertained, and the other was an infuriated politician who thought every resistance of the will of France subserviency to Britain, and an adhesion to the coalition of despots against liberty. Each election between these gentlemen, who were both popular, had been decided by a small majority; & that which was approaching was entirely doubtful. I attended at the polls to give my vote early & return to the court which was then in session at the other end of the town. As soon as the election commenced a gentleman came forward and demanded that a poll should be taken for me. I was a good deal surprized at this entirely unexpected proposition & declared my decided dissent. I said that if my fellow citizens wished it I would become a candidate at the next succeeding election, but that I could not consent to serve this year because my wishes & my honour were engaged for one of the candidates. I then voted for my friend & left the polls for the court which was open and waiting for me. The gentleman said that he had a right to demand a poll for whom he pleased, & persisted in his demand that one should be opened for me—I might if elected refuse to obey the voice of my constituents if I chose to do so. He then gave his vote for me.

As this was entirely unexpected—not even known to my brother who though of the same political opinions with myself was the active & leading partisan of the candidate against whom I had voted, the election was almost suspended for ten or twelve minutes, and a consultation took place among the principal freeholders. They then came in and in the evening information was brought me that I was elected. I regretted this for the sake of my friend. In other respects I was well satisfied at being again in the assembly.

Throughout that part of the year which followed the advice of the senate to ratify Mr. Jays treaty, the whole country was agitated with that question. The commotion began at Boston and seemed to rush through the Union with a rapidity and violence which set human reason and common sense at defiance. The first effort was to deter the President from ratifying the instrument—the next to induce Congress to refuse the necessary appropriations. On this occasion too a meeting of the citizens of Richmond was convened and I carried a series of resolutions approving the conduct of the President.

As this subject was one in which every man who mingled with public affairs was compelled to take part, I determined to make myself master of it, and for this purpose perused carefully all the resolutions which were passed throughout the United States condemning the treaty and compared them with the instrument itself. Accustomed as I was to political misrepresentation, I could not view without some surprize the numerous gross misrepresentations which were made on this occasion; and the virulent asperity, with which the common terms of decency in which nations express their compacts with each other, was assailed. The constitutionality of the treaty was attacked with peculiar vehemence, and, strange as it may appear, there was scarcely a man in Virginia who did not believe that a commercial treaty was an infringement of the power given to Congress to regulate commerce. Sever other articles of the treaty were pronounced unconstitutional; but, on the particular ground of commerce, the objectors believed themselves to be invulnerable.

As it was foreseen that an attempt would be made in the legislature to prevent the necessary appropriations, one or two of my cautious friends advised me not to engage in the debate. They said that the part which it was anticipated I would take, would destroy me totally. It was so very unpopular that I should scarcely be permitted to deliver my sentiments, and would perhaps be treated rudely. I answered that the subject would not be introduced by me; but, if it should be brought before the house by others, I

should undoubtedly take the part which became an
independent member. The subject was introduced;
and the constitutional objections were brought forward most triumphantly. There was perhaps never
a political question on which any division of opinion
took place which was susceptible of more complete
demonstration, and I was fully prepared not only on
the words of the constitution and the universal practice of nations, but to show on the commercial proposition especially, which was selected by our antago-
nists as their favorite ground, that Mr. Jefferson, and
the whole delegation from Virginia in Congress, as
well as all our leading men in the convention on both
sides of the question, had manifested unequivocally
the opinion that a commercial treaty was constitutional. I had reason to know that a politician even
in times of violent party spirit maintains his respectability by showing his strength; and is most safe when
he encounters prejudice most fearlessly. There was
scarcely an intelligent man in the house who did not
yield his opinion on the constitutional question. The
resolution however was carried on the inexpediency
of the treaty.

I do not know whether the account given of this
debate, which was addressed to some members of
Congress in letters from Richmond, and was published, was written by strangers in the gallery or by
some of my partial friends. Be this as it may my
arguments were spoken of in such extravagant terms
as to prepare the federalists of Congress to receive
me with marked attention and favour, the ensuing
winter when I attended in Philadelphia to argue the
cause respecting British debts before the supreme
court of the United States. I there became acquainted with Mr. Cabot, Mr. Ames, & Mr. Dexter
& Mr. Edgewic, of Massachusetts, with Mr. Wads-
worth of Connecticut and with Mr. King of New
York. I was delighted with these gentlemen. The
particular subject which introduced me to their
notice was at that time so interesting, and a Virginian
who supported with any sort of reputation the mea-

sures of the government was such a *rara avis,* that I
was received by them all with a degree of kindness
which I had not anticipated. I was particularly intimate with Ames, & could scarcely gain credit with
him when I assured him that the appropriations
would be seriously opposed in Congress.

It was about or perhaps a little after this time that
I was invited by General Washington to take the
office of Attorney General of the United States. I was
too deeply engaged in the practice in Virginia to
accept this office, though I should certainly have pre-
ferred it to any other.

I continued in the assembly though I took no part
in the current business. It was I think in the session
of 1796-97 that I was engaged in a debate which
called forth all the strength and violence of party.
Some Federalist moved a resolution expressing the
high confidence of the house in the virtue, patriotism,
and wisdom of the President of the United States. A
motion was made to strike out the word "wisdom."
In the debate the whole course of the administration
was reviewed, and the whole talent of each party
was brought into action. Will it be believed that the
word was retained by a very small majority. A very
small majority in the legislature of Virginia acknowledged the wisdom of General Washington.

When the cabinet decided on recalling Mr. Monroe
from France, the President invited me to succeed him.
But I thought my determination to remain at the bar
unalterable, and declined the office. My situation at
the bar appeared to me to be more independent and
not less honorable than any other, and my preference
for it was decided.

In June 1797 I was placed by Mr. Adams, then
President of the United States, in the commission for
accomodating our differences with France, and received a letter requesting my attendance in Philadelphia in order to receive the communications of the
government respecting the mission previous to my
embarcation. It was the first time in my life that I
had ever hesitated concerning the acceptance of

office. My resolution concerning my profession had sustained no change. Indeed my circumstances required urgently that I should adhere to this resolution because I had engaged with some others in the purchase of a large estate the arrangements concerning which were not yet made. On the other hand I felt a very deep interest in the state of our controversy with France. I was most anxious and believed the government to be most anxious for the adjustment of our differences with that republic. I felt some confidence in the good dispositions which I should carry with me into the negotiation, and in the temperate firmness with which I should aid in the investigations which would be made. The subject was familiar to me, and had occupied a large portion of my thoughts. I will confess that the *eclat* which would attend a successful termination of the differences between the two countries had no small influence over a mind in which ambition, though subjected to controul, was not absolutely extinguished. But the consideration which decided me was this. The mission was temporary, and could not be of long duration. I should return after a short absence, to my profession, with no diminution of character, &, I trusted, with no diminution of practice. My clients would know immediately that I should soon return & I could make arrangements with the gentlemen of the bar which would prevent my business from suffering in the meantime. I accepted the appointment and repaired to Philadelphia where I embarked for Amsterdam. I found General Pinckney at the Hague, and we obtained passports from the Minister of France at that place to secure our passage in safety to Paris. While at the Hague intelligence was received of that revolution which was effected in the French government by the seizure of two of the Directory and of a majority of the legislature by a military force acting under the orders of three of the Directory combined with a minority of the councils. This revolution blasted every hope of an accomodation between the United States and France.

On reaching Paris General Pinckney and myself communicated our arrival to Mr. Talleyrand & expressed a wish to suspend all negotiation till our colleague should be united with us. In a week or ten days Mr. Gerry joined us, and we immediately addressed ourselves to the minister. The failure of our attempts at negotiation is generally known. A journal which I kept exhibits a curious account of transactions at Paris. As soon as I became perfectly convinced that our efforts at conciliation must prove abortive I proposed that we should address a memorial to Mr. Talleyrand in which we should review fully the reciprocal complaints of the two countries against each other, and bring the whole controversy, at least our view of it before the French government in like manner as if we had been actually accredited. My motive for this was that if the memorial should fail to make its due impression on the government of France, it would show the sincerity with which we had laboured to effect the objects of our mission, and could not fail to bring the controversy fairly before the American People and convince them of the earnestness with which the American government sought a reconciliation with France. General Pinckney concurred with me in sentiment and we acted most cordially together. I found in him a sensible man, and one of high and even romantic honour. Mr. Gerry took a different view of the whole subject. He was unwilling to do anything, and it was with infinite difficulty we prevailed on him to join us in the letter to the minister of exterior relations. It was with the same difficulty we prevailed on him to sign the reply to this answer of the minister. We were impatient to hasten that reply from a fear that we should be ordered to leave France before it could be sent. We knew very well that this order would come and there was a trial of skill between the minister and ourselves, (Genl. Pinckney & myself) he endeavouring to force us to demand our passports, we endeavouring to impose on him the necessity of sending them. At length the passports came and I hastened to Bordeaux to embark for the United States. On my arrival in New York I found the whole country in a state of agitation on the subject of our mission. Our dispatches had been published and their effect on public opinion had fully equalled my anticipations.

I returned to Richmond with a full determination to devote myself entirely to my professional duties, and was not a little delighted to find that my prospects at the bar had sustained no material injury from my bsence. My friends welcomed my return with the most flattering reception, and pressed me to become a candidate for Congress. My refusal was peremptory, and I did not believe it possible that my determination could be shaken. I was however mistaken.

General Washington gave a pressing invitation to his nephew, the present Judge, & myself, to pass a few days at Mount Vernon. He urged us both very earnestly to come into Congress & Mr. Washington assented to his wishes. I resisted, on the ground of my situation, & the necessity of attending to my pecuniary affairs. I can never forget the manner in which he treated this objection.

He said there were crises in national affairs which made it the duty of a citizen to forego his private for the public interest. We were then in one of them. He detailed his opinions freely on the nature of our controversy with France and expressed his conviction that the best interests of our country depended on the character of the ensuing Congress. He concluded a very earnest conversation, one of the most interesting I was ever engaged in, by asking my attention to his situation. He had retired from the Executive department with the firmest determination never again to appear in a public capacity. He had communicated this determination to the public, and his motives for adhering to it were too strong not to be well understood. Yet I saw him pledged to appear once more at the head of the American army. What must be his convictions of duty imposed by the present state of American affairs?

I yielded to his representations & became a candidate. I soon afterwards received a letter from the Secretary of state offering me the seat on the bench of the supreme court which had become vacant by the death of Judge Iredell; but my preference for the bar still continued & I declined it. Our brother Washington was intercepted in his way to Congress by this appointment.

My election was contested with unusual warmth, but I succeeded, and took my seat in the House of Representatives in Decr. 1799. There was a good deal of talent in that Congress both for and against the administration, and I contracted friendships with several gentlemen whom I shall never cease to value. The great number of them are no more.

In May 1800, as I was about to leave Philadelphia (Though Congress was still in session) for the purpose of attending the courts in Richmond, I stepped into the war office in order to make some enquiries respecting patents for some of my military friends, and was a good deal struck with a strange sort of mysterious coldness which I soon observed in the countenance of Mr. McHenry, the secretary of war, with whom I had long been on terms of friendly intimacy. I however prosecuted my enquiries until they brought me into conversation with Mr. Fitzsimmons the chief clerk, who congratulated me on being placed at the head of that department, and expressed the pleasure it gave all those who were engaged in it. I did not understand him, and was really surprized at hearing that I had been nominated to the senate as secretary of war. I did not believe myself to be well qualified for this department, and was not yet willing to abandon my hopes of reinstating myself at the bar. I therefore addressed a letter to Mr. Adams making my acknowledgements for his notice of me, and requesting that he would withdraw my name from the senate, as was not willing openly to decline a place in an administration which was disposed cordially to support. After writing this letter I proceeded immediately to Virginia.

Mr. Adams did not withdraw my name, & I believe

the nomination was approved. I had not been long in Virginia when the rupture between Mr. Adams and Mr. Pickering took place, and I was nominated to the senate as secretary of state. I never felt more doubt than on the question of accepting or declining this office. My decided preference was still for the bar. But on becoming a candidate for Congress I was given up as a lawyer, and considered generally as entirely a political man. I lost my business alltogether, and perceived very clearly that I could not recove any portion of it without retiring from Congress. Even then I could not hope to regain the ground I had lost. This experiment however I was willing to make, and would have made had my political enemies been quiet. But the press teemed with so much falsehood, with such continued and irritating abuse of me that I could not bring myself to yield to it. I could not conquer a stubborness of temper which determines a man to make head against and struggle with injustice. I felt that I must continue a candidate for Congress, and consequently could not replace myself at the bar. On the other hand the office was precisely that which I wished, and for which I had vanity enough to think myself fitted. I should remain in it while the party remained in power; should a revolution take place it would at all events relieve me from the competition for Congress without yielding to my adversaries, and enable me to return once more to the bar in the character of a lawyer having no possible view to politics. I determined to accept the office.

I was very well received by the President, and was on very cordial terms with all the cabinet except Mr. Wolcot. He at first suspected that I was hostile to the two exsecretaries, & to himself, because they were all three supposed to be unfriendly to the President to whom I was truely attached. My conduct soon convinced him however that I had no feeling of that sort, after which I had the satisfaction of finding myself on the same cordial footing with him as with the rest of the cabinet.

On the resignation of Chief Justice Ellsworth I recommended Judge Patteson as his successor. The President objected to him, and assigned as his ground of objection that the feelings of Judge Cushing would be wounded by passing him and selecting a junior member of the bench. I never heard him assign any other objection to Judge Patteson [*sic*], though it was afterwards suspected by many that he was believed to be connected with the party which opposed the second attempt at negotiation with France. The President himself mentioned Mr. Jay, and he was nominated to the senate. When I waited on the President with Mr. Jays letter declining the appointment he said thoughtfully "Who shall I nominate now"? I replied that I could not tell, as I supposed that his objection to Judge Patteson remained. He said in a decided tone "I shall not nominate him." After a moments hesitation he said "I believe I must nominate you". I had never before heard myself named for the office and had not even thought of it. I was pleased as well as surprized, and bowed in silence. Next day I was nominated, and, although the nomination was suspended by the friends of Judge Patteson, it was I believe when taken up unanimously approved. I was unfeignedly gratified at the appointment, and have had much reason to be so. I soon received a very friendly letter from Judge Patteson congratulating me on the occasion and expressing hopes that I might long retain the office. I felt truely grateful for the real cordiality towards me which uniformly marked his conduct.

I have my dear Sir been much more minute and tedious in detail than the occasion required, but you will know how to prune, condense, exclude, and vary. I give you the materials of which you will make some thing or nothing as you please—taking this only with you, that you will be sure to gratify me by pursuing precisely the tract you had marked out for yourself, & admitting nothing which may overload the narrative according to the original plan. Do not insert any thing from the suspicion that I may look for it because I have introduced it into my narrative.

It would seem as if new and perplexing questions on jurisdiction will never be exhausted. That which you mention is one of the strongest possible illustrations, so far as respects the original act, of the necessity in some instances of controuling the letter by the plain spirit of the law. It is impossible that a suit brought by the U. S. can be within the intention of the exception. There is however great difficulty in taking the case out of the letter. The argument you state is very strong and I am much inclined to yield to it. As no private citizen can sue in a district court on a promissory note I am much inclined to restrain the exception to those district courts which have circuit court jurisdiction. But the difficulty is I think removed by the act of the 3d of March 1815 and by the decision of the last term. I speak of that decision however from memory as I have not yet received 12th Wheaton.

Farewell—with the highest respect & esteem

I am yours

J MARSHALL

1 Manuscript in the William L. Clements Library. Reprinted with the permission of the University of Michigan Press from John Stokes Adams, *An Autobiographical Sketch of John Marshall* (Ann Arbor, 1937).
2 A hole is torn in the page at this point.

JOHN MARSHALL—THE MAN*

Harold H. Burton

John Marshall is a favorite topic of orators at meetings of
bar associations and, for this reason, the literature of his life
and contributions to the law is vast. The following article
was written by Justice Burton of the Supreme Court of the
United States who has a professional interest in the work of
John Marshall. Justice Burton has published several articles
on this distinguished Chief Justice, one on the Burr Trial,
which is reprinted in this book, and another article entitled
"The Cornerstone of Constitutional Law: The Extraordinary
Case of Marbury v. Madison", which appeared in 36 A.B.A.J.
805 (1950). The following article entitled "John Marshall, the
Man" was prepared by Justice Burton for the John Marshall
symposium issue of the *University of Pennsylvania Law Review*, October 1955, and is here reprinted with the permission
of the author and the publisher.

"[H]ighly as he was respected, he had the rare
happiness to be yet more beloved." [1] This was said
of the late John Marshall, in 1835, in his home city
of Richmond, Virginia, by the bar and officers of the
circuit court over which he had presided as a circuit
justice for more than a generation.

Best known today for his creative opinions interpreting the Constitution of the United States as en-
dowing the federal government with powers adequate
for its effective operation, Chief Justice Marshall was
also a vigorous, courageous, warmhearted, and mod-
est man, exemplifying the best traditions of the
American Revolution.

Born in Virginia, September 24, 1755, he was the
oldest of fifteen children, nine boys and six girls.
Raised among the Blue Ridge Mountains, he received
his early education from local clergymen and his
parents. John's father, Thomas Marshall, built a home
at Oak Hill, and was one of the original subscribers
to the first American publication of Blackstone's
Commentaries. Thomas Marshall served in the Virginia House of Burgesses, at Williamsburg, was sheriff
of Fauquier County and later clerk of Dunmore

County. At 19, John was six-feet tall, straight and slender, with thick black hair and penetrating dark eyes.

He became a soldier of distinction. At 19, he was a lieutenant, commanding Virginia "Minute Men" fighting British Grenadiers near Norfolk. In March, 1776, he was a lieutenant in the Third Virginia Regiment in which his father was a major. Joining Washington's army, John took part in the engagements at Iron Hill, Brandywine and Germantown. At Valley Forge he shared the hunger and cold which tested America's fortitude and devotion. "[N]othing discouraged, nothing disturbed" John Marshall.[2] A champion at quoits, and generally a leader in athletic contests, he was nicknamed "Silver Heels" because of the white yarn that his mother had knitted into the heels of the woolen stockings in which he won many foot races. Later he fought at Monmouth, Stony Point, and elsewhere. Soon promoted to a captaincy, he was, by 1793, commissioned a brigadier general in the Virginia militia. In that capacity he commanded a brigade in the Whiskey Rebellion, and, until appointed Chief Justice, he usually was addressed as General Marshall.

John had little formal legal education. He attended but six weeks of law lectures by George Wythe at William and Mary College, where he was a member of the debating team of Phi Beta Kappa. At Valley Forge he had served as a deputy judge advocate. When 25, he received from his cousin, Thomas Jefferson, then Governor of Virginia, a license to practice law and was admitted to the bar in Fauquier County in 1780. In 1782, he was elected to the Virginia House of Delegates and then to the council of eight members chosen by joint ballot of the two Houses of the Assembly.

Eight times he was sent to the Assembly. When the new Federal Constitution was referred to the states for ratification, he urged that Virginia call a convention to act upon it. Such a convention met in 1788, with Marshall a member of it. His service to the Constitution dates from that time. In the convention he directed his principal attention to taxation, the militia, and the judiciary and stoutly supported ratification of the Constitution as a whole. This vital approval was secured by the narrow margin of ten votes.

While Marshall accepted these calls to public service, he declined others. In 1789, although named by President Washington as District Attorney of the United States at Richmond, he declined the nomination. The same was true when Washington offered him the Attorney Generalship of the United States in 1795, and the post of Minister to France in 1796. However, in 1797, when the need was pressing, President Adams induced him to join C. C. Pinckney and Elbridge Gerry on the XYZ Commission that attempted to adjust international differences with France in the days of Talleyrand. In that capacity he rendered high diplomatic service with widely commended integrity and skill. Throughout these years he was an active proponent of Washington's policies, although many Virginians were turning to the anti-Federalist leadership of Thomas Jefferson.

In 1798 he declined an appointment to the Supreme Court of the United States to succeed Associate Justice Wilson.[3] But in the same year, at the urgent request of George Washington, he ran for Congress from the Richmond district. He made a vigorous campaign. Unlike many Federalist candidates, he declared himself against the revival of the Alien and Sedition Laws, and, with the support of Patrick Henry, was elected, in April, 1799, to the Sixth Congress by 108 votes. Congress convened in Philadelphia, December 2, and, on December 18, Marshall performed the painful duty of announcing the death of Washington. December 19, he offered the resolutions, drafted by "Light-Horse Harry" Lee, which described Washington as "first in war, first in peace, and first in the hearts of his countrymen." These were precisely the sentiments of John Marshall.

In Congress, he pursued an independent course.

He cast a crucial vote, against his party, for the repeal of the most hotly contested section of the Sedition Law. He killed a Disputed Elections Bill that would have benefited the Federalists in the next presidential election. On the other hand, he ably defended the Jay Treaty and the administration's conduct in a *cause célèbre* as to an alleged mutineer who had been handed over to a British consul.

On May 12, 1800, President Adams named him Secretary of State and in June, he resigned from Congress to assume his duties in the cabinet. He declined to use his influence in favor of either side in the contest between Jefferson and Burr which resulted, on February 17, 1801, in the election of Jefferson as President and Burr as Vice President. He performed his duties as Secretary of State until late on the third of March, 1801, although he had been appointed Chief Justice in January and had been sworn in as such February 4, 1801. On March 4th, he administered the presidential oath of office to Jefferson.

Marshall's appointment to the Court terminated most of his activities in other governmental fields. To this there was one notable exception. In 1829, together with ex-President Madison and Monroe, he accepted election to the Virginia convention called to revise the constitution of that commonwealth. As a member of its judiciary committee, he helped to secure provisions for an independent judiciary.

The above activities would have constituted a full career for most men, but in Marshall's case his judicial career became so extraordinary that his earlier services are but little known. They are important, however, not only on their own account, but because they help to explain the breadth of his understanding of constitutional issues.

In the legal profession, he was the leader of his local bar as a trial lawyer. In 1786, his standing was such that when Edmund Randolph was elected Governor of Virginia, Marshall took over his practice. In May of that year, Marshall's name first appeared in the reports of the Court of Appeals of Virginia.[4] In about 1793, with the help of Robert Morris of Philadelphia, he and several associates contracted to buy the remaining Fairfax estates of over 160,000 acres in Virginia. This was his greatest financial undertaking. It caused him much anxiety but yielded substantial returns. In 1796, he made an impressive but unsuccessful argument in the Supreme Court of the United States.[5]

A disciple of George Washington, he undertook, while Chief Justice, to write a biography of Washington after the latter's death. It was primarily a labor of love and an expression of loyalty to Washington. Forced to early publication between 1802 and 1804, its five volumes contained valuable historical material, but were neither a financial nor a literary success. Many years later, he shortened the work to three volumes. One was published as a preliminary history of the colonial period and the other two as a *Life of Washington*. These were better received. Today they help to confirm the thesis that Marshall, to a substantial degree, succeeded to Washington's leadership in the establishment of a strong, representative federal republic dedicated to the preservation for the individual of the greatest freedom consistent with like freedom for all.

While Marshall's judicial career requires separate treatment for adequate demonstration of its monumental character, some reference to it is essential in any biographical sketch of him. He served as Chief Justice from 1801 to 1835. Such service is longer than that of any other Chief Justice of the United States, and all of it was rendered during the crucial formative period of the nation's history. Under his leadership, the loose stones provided for the nation's structure were built into a firm foundation.

While best known for the opinions he wrote for the Court in the exercise of its appellate jurisdiction, he also rendered outstanding service as a circuit justice. The most famous of his circuit cases was the trial and acquittal, in 1807, of Aaron Burr on a charge of treason.[6] Marshall's conduct in this case set an admirable example of judicial courage and demeanor.

While he was a member of the Supreme Court, it decided sixty-two cases on questions of constitutional law. In these he wrote thirty-six opinions for the Court. These are the foundation stones of our constitutional law upon which his fame and much of the stability of our federal structure depend.[7] In appraising this contribution and Marshall's part in it, it is important to emphasize the fact that these decisions were not his alone. However, to him as Chief Justice and author, there must go substantial credit for securing the support of a majority of the Court. Twenty-three of the decisions were unanimous. To appreciate this phase of his service, we should see him as the leader of those able judges who constituted "the Marshall Court." Together, they made, nurtured, and protected great precedents. Chief Justice Marshall served with fifteen Associate Justices. Seven were with him many years. They were: Thompson for 12 years, Livingston for 16, Todd for 19, Story for 23, Duvall for 23, Washington for 29, and William Johnson for 30 years. There has been no other period of comparable continuity, and none when continuity was so essential.

Returning to Marshall the man, he was a devoted husband and father. Brought up in a large family, he treasured family associations. On January 3, 1783, he married "Polly" Ambler, one of four sisters from a distinguished Virginia family. She was not quite 17, and he was 27. He had been in love with her for three years, since, as a young army officer, he first saw her in Yorktown. They had ten children, six of whom survived to maturity, five sons and one daughter. Although obliged to spend much time in Washington, he delighted to return to his home in Richmond. There he lived in the Georgian style brick house which he built on a two-acre plot. He was deeply affected when his wife died on Christmas Day, 1831. Thereafter, he constantly wore, on a chain around his neck, a locket containing a lock of her hair. He, himself, underwent a serious operation in 1831 but regained his health and lived until July 6, 1835.

The famous Liberty Bell that rang in Philadelphia to 1776 to announce the Declaration of Independence tolled to announce his death. His active service and that of the bell ended together, for, as the bell tolled, it cracked. Their voices were silenced, but they have never ceased to inspire the nation to seek to fulfill the high mission to which both Marshall and the bell were dedicated.

Marshall's judicial service is fittingly recognized in the excellent bronze statue of him, which faces the sunset on the lower west terrace of the Capitol. Appropriately placed near the place where Marshall presided over the Court, this statue is the work of W. W. Story, a son of the Chief Justice's friend and colleague, Associate Justice Story. It represents the Chief Justice, sitting in his judicial robe, expounding upon some subject of deep interest to him as he looks toward the towering monument erected to the memory of Washington, whom he so greatly admired.

In keeping with Marshall's devotion to his wife, his body is buried beside hers in Richmond. And in keeping with his modesty, the following simple inscriptions, written by him, appear on horizontal tablets above the graves. On his, we read: "John Marshall, Son of Thomas and Mary Marshall, was born the 24th of September, 1755. Intermarried with Mary Willis Ambler, the 3d of January, 1783. Departed his life the [6th] day of July, 1835." On hers: "Sacred to the memory of Mrs. Mary Willis Marshall, Consort of John Marshall, Born the 13th of March, 1766. Departed this life the 25th of December, 1831. This stone is devoted to her memory by him who best knew her worth, And most deplores her loss."

---

* Reprinted from 104 Univ. of Penn. L. Rev. 3 (1955) with permission of the author and publisher.

[1] Brockenbraugh, Reports of Cases Decided by John Marshall in the Circuit Court of the United States xviii (1837). This phrase is quoted also in Thayer, John Marshall 155-56 (1901).

[2] Lieutenant Slaughter said this of him at Valley Forge, as quoted in 1 Beveridge, The Life of John Marshall 118 (1916).

[3] George Washington's nephew, Bushrod Washington, received the appointment and later served on the Court nearly twenty-nine years with Marshall.

[4] As counsel in Hite v. Fairfax, 4 Call 42, 69 (Va. 1786). This was the first of more than 120 cases he argued in that court.

[5] As counsel in Ware v. Hylton, 3 U. S. (3 Dall.) 199, 210 (1796).

[6] United States v. Burr, 25 Fed. Cas. 2-207, Nos. 14692-a-14694a (C.C.D. Va. 1807).

[7] See Marbury v. Madison, 5 U. S. (1 Cranch) 137 (1803); Fletcher v. Peck, 10 U. S. (6 Cranch) 87 (1810); Sturges v. Crowninshield, 17 U. S. (4 Wheat.) 122 (1819); McCulloch v. Maryland, 17 U. S. (4 Wheat.) 316 (1819); Dartmouth College v. Woodward, 17 U. S. (4 Wheat.) 518 (1819); Cohens v. Virginia, 19 U. S. (6 Wheat.) 264 (1812); Gibbons v. Ogden, 22 U. S. (9 Wheat.) 1 (1824); Ogden v. Saunders, 25 U. S. (12 Wheat.) 213 (1827); Brown v. Maryland, 25 U. S. (12 Wheat.) 419 (1827).

JOHN MARSHALL—HIS PERSONALITY
AND DEVELOPMENT†

ALBERT J. BEVERIDGE

Albert J. Beveridge needs no introduction to the students of Constitutional Law because of his four volume definitive biography of John Marshall, which is still recognized for its excellence. The following article is taken from a speech delivered by Senator Beveridge before the Ohio State Bar Association in 1915 in which he analyzes the forces which shaped the thinking of John Marshall in his decisions as Chief Justice.

While the constitutional opinions of Chief Justice Marshall are more familiar to lawyers and, indeed, to the public than those of any other jurist, less is known of the man himself than of any other great character in American history. We have come to look upon John Marshall as a sort of legal Budda enthroned among the clouds and, by some mysterious process of genius, giving forth those immortal opinions which breathed into the Constitution the breath of life and made our nation a possibility. But of his personality and those epochal events which developed his ideas, little has been written.

And yet this character was peculiarly human and familiar and his career up to his appointment to the Supreme Bench more dramatic and full of color than perhaps any other man of his period except only George Washington and Alexander Hamilton. And without a knowledge of Marshall's life from early youth to middle age, it is much harder to understand thoroughly his fundamental opinions from the bench which now are and will always remain, the classics of American constitutional law. For every one of them were the fruits not only of powerful reasoning, but also and even more of a colossal human experience. In this address, of course, I can give only a few of these.

John Marshall was a child of the frontier. He was

† Reprinted with permission of the W. H. Anderson Co., from the Ohio Law Reporter.

born in a little log cabin in the unbroken wilderness, eleven weeks after Braddock's defeat, which was the most important military circumstance in our history vp to the Revolution. John Marshall was the eldest of fifteen children. His childhood and youth were spent thirty miles beyond his birthplace in a hollow of the Blue Ridge Mountains. Here the Marshall family lived in a small log house which is still standing. When he was seventeen years old his father built a somewhat larger house at another location. This is the famous Oak Hill.

While it is certain that there were not many books in the Marshall cabin, we know of one (Pope's Poems) much of which the boy committed to memory before he was twelve years old; and throughout his life he cared more for poetry and novels than he did for legal reports and text-books. When he was seventeen years of age his father subscribed to the first American edition of Blackstone; and, as his parents had desired that John should be a lawyer, it is certain that he read this work which was and remains the poetry of the law.

His father taught him to read, for he had no formal schooling until his thirteenth year. For a few months he was taught by a Scotch parson who lived in the crowded little Marshall house of logs. He had no further school instruction until he was about seventeen years old, when for a very short time he attended a tiny "academy" in Westmoreland county, some sixty miles east through the forests.

Seven years later he attended for two months the law lectures of George Wythe at William and Mary College, and this was all the instruction that John Marshall ever received at the hands of trained instructors. He took notes of Wythe's lectures in a blank book which still exists; but he was so much in love with Mary Ambler, whom he married three years later, that he wrote her name many times on the inside cover and on many pages of his note book and he was thinking of her more than of Wythe's lectures.

But slight, brief and scanty as John Marshall's formal schooling was, he received an education far more vital than any university could give. His father, who, as Marshall told Justice Story "was a far abler man than any of his sons" was a representative from the backwoods in the House of Burgesses when Patrick Henry made his wonderful speech and offered his historic resolutions on the stamp act; and was a member of the Virginia convention ten years later when Henry made his second epochal appeal, ending with "give me liberty or give me death," in support of his resolutions for arming and defense. Marshall's father supported Henry on both these occasions; and it was from the lips of the parent that the son learned from first-hand accounts of the beginnings of our Revolution against Great Britain and of the causes of that conflict.

Nine months before the Declaration of Independence, the Marshalls, father and son, as members of the Culpeper Minute Men, took part in the battle of Great Bridge, which was so bloody that it was called the "little Bunker Hill." The men wore wringed leggings, hunting shirt, with the words "Liberty or Death" sewed on the breast, coon-skin caps, and were armed with frontier musket, tommahawk and scalping knives.

Immediately after this John Marshall and his father enlisted in the Continental Service and became officers of Washington's army. Washington and Thomas Marshall (father of John Marshall) had been fellow surveyors, were long friends, and John Marshall's devotion to Washington never faltered.

For nearly four years young Marshall served in the patriot army. He fought at Brandywine, Germantown, Monmouth, Stony Point and in a very great many skirmishes. Because of John Marshall's cool-headed bravery he was often chosen as one of the picked men for extra hazardous services. He went through the winter of Valley Forge, where the starvation, nakedness and sufferings of the troops were so bitter as to be hardly credible in our day; and

John Marshall was the most cheerful person in that camp of misery and gloom. Throughout his life he loved fun and jokes; and although always with a native dignity, he was the most formal of men. He was also the best athlete in his regiment; and on account of the white heels of his blue yarn stockings showing when he ran races in his stocking feet, his comrades called him "Silver Heels" Marshall.

It was during these four years of fighting and privation that Marshall received his first great object lesson in the necessity for a strong national government and in the fatal inefficiency of the state governments. According to Washington, the militia was worse than useless. It would join the army one day and leave it the next. The states often failed to keep even the Continental Line up to their respective quotas. Sometimes a whole regiment had fewer than fifty men and a company would consist of one man. The officers were elected by the soldiers and until Baron von Steuben taught and trained them, not many officers had any more idea of discipline than the soldiers themselves. The equipment was so poor that the locks would often fall from the muskets, and there were few bayonets. Time and again Washington wrote to his brother and others that conditions were so bad that he had to conceal them from the public. One state would do one thing and another state would do another thing. Sometimes states actually assumed authority over troops of another state in the Continental Line.

So it is that the roots of McCullough vs. Maryland run back to Valley Forge and the dark and desperate days through which John Marshall passed before and after.

The second formative influence that shaped John Marshall's thinking toward nationality and conservatism was his experience in the Virginia Legislature and as a young lawyer between the end of the war and the adoption of the Constitution. Virginia planters owed a very great deal of money to British merchants. During the war laws had been passed sequestering these debts. While Marshall was in the Legislature bill after bill to repeal these sequestration laws was defeated on one pretext or another. The general conduct of the Legislature disgusted men like Mason, Madison and Washington. John Marshall was similarly impressed and said so in letters to friends.

Soon after the Revolution Washington lost his faith in the people's capacity for self-government; and the year before our Constitution was framed, Marshall wrote that he feared that the "people, when left to themselves, are incapable of any serious effort toward self-government." Thus a radical change had taken place in Marshall's opinions; for he went into the army with what he himself called "wild enthusiastic notions." Like nearly everybody else at that time, the young volunteer thought that a liberty, as vague as it was glorious, would make everybody happy and prosperous. What altered the views of the mature Washington and the youthful Marshall?

The conduct of the people during this period. And why did people so act to destroy the confidence of men who had fought for their freedom? The state of the country is the answer. There were few roads, and the best were difficult and sometimes dangerous to travel. It usually took four weeks and often eight weeks to send a letter from Richmond to New York. Frequently not more than two miles an hour could be made over the best roads. Even after he was elected president, Washington's carriage stuck in the mud on a main traveled road and had to be pried out with rails. It was eight days after Massachusetts ratified the Constitution before New York learned of that critically important event. Transportation between the then village of Pittsburgh and Philadelphia took five times as long as it now takes to go from New York to San Francisco. Before the Constitution was adopted there were very few newspapers and practically all of these were published in the three or four principal "cities," the largest of which was Philadelphia, with some forty to fifty thousand inhabitants. Country communities were almost completely isolated. Schools were very few and very poor.

Ignorance and a strange mixture of suspicion and credulity existed among a great majority of the people as a result of these conditions.

The historical evidences are overwhelming that a very large part of the people were against the very idea of government as such. The weak and ineffective state governments were the most that they were willing to endure. They looked upon a strong national government as an hostile and alien thing. On the one hand they felt that it was beyond their reach, and on the other hand they believed that such a government would make them discharge their debts; that it meant taxes which must be paid and laws which must be obeyed.

In broad outline these are the sources from which flowed that conduct of the people which made Marshall and Washington lose faith in them. If railroads, telegraph and telephones had then existed, perhaps these men would not thus have changed their minds.

The third of the principal causes of Marshall's nationalistic and conservative views was the chaos that existed under the Articles of Confederation combined with the struggle over the adoption of the Constitution. As everybody now knows, the Constitution grew out of the combined efforts of the country's commercial and financial interests. The convention that framed it had no authority to do more than to amend the Articles of Confederation. The proceedings of the convention were secret and the people knew nothing about the Constitution until it was submitted to the states for ratification.

There can be little question that the majority in Pennsylvania, Massachusetts, New York and Virginia were against the Constitution. It was ratified in Pennsylvania by very rough proceedings. Indeed, only one-tenth of the voters of Pennsylvania voted for the members of the state convention that, after a desperate struggle, ratified it. A majority of the Massachusetts convention were believed to be against

it; and barely enough votes were finally secured to
ratify it, by a deal with John Hancock in which he
was promised the support of Bowdoin's friends for
governor and possibly the presidency if Washington
were not chosen. Even at that it was only ratified by
a majority of nineteen in a convention of three hundred and fifty-five members.

In the Virginia convention the Constitution was
for the first time really *debated* on *both* sides by men
of great ability and high character and standing.
John Marshall, not yet thirty-three years old, was a
member of this convention and made three speeches
for the Constitution. It is generally supposed that
the great arguments of men like Madison, Pendleton,
Nicholas and Marshall secured Virginia's ratification.
As a matter of fact, the debates had very little effect
in changing votes. Votes were effected then as now
by personal lobbying, but not by corrupt practices.
When the vote finally was taken there was only a
majority of ten for the Constitution out of a convention of one hundred and sixty-eight members. One
or two of these who voted for ratification violated
their instructions and several of them voted against
the will of their constituents.

Speaking generally, it was an economic line that
divided the supporters and opponents of the Constitution. The creditor classes were for it and the debtor
classes were against it. The men who owed money
were opposed and the men to whom money was due
were for the new plan of government. The mercantile, commercial and financial interests were for and
the agricultural and most other interests against it.
Also, of course, there were, here and there, men
who believed that nothing but a strong central government could make the United States a nation on
the one hand and, on the other, about the same
number of idealists who felt that such a government
would destroy "liberty."

Still another of the commanding influences that
went to the building of the John Marshall who became Chief Justice was the influence of the French

Revolution upon American thought and action. The people were sympathizers with that bloody epoch and its doctrines. As the horrible atrocities of that savage upheaval went on, men like Washington, Hamilton, Adams Jay and Marshall feared that its philosophy would result in similar scenes in America and end in the overthrow of our own government. Next to the economic causes which divided the people before the Constitution and during the formative years after our national government was established, the influence of the French Revolution was the strongest force molding the opinions of men.

Following this closely, and, indeed, as a part of it, came the desperate attacks on Washington because of his proclamation of neutrality in the war between England and France and his steady impartial and just maintainance of that position. Next came the famous Whiskey Rebellion, where the laws of the United States were violated and defied by force of arms. And then followed the Jay treaty, which, bad as it was, kept this country out of war. In all these matters, in which are to be found the roots of American political parties, the majority of the people were against the government as administered by Washington, and showed their opposition in violent and dramatic fashion. In all of them, too, Marshall, who had now become the leading lawyer of Virginia, stood stanchly for Washington. He became Washington's political agent in Virginia. The President wanted to appoint him a district attorney, Attorney-General of the United States, Minister to France; but he declined them all.

From the time that Washington took the position that this country as a separate, independent and distinct nation, must be absolutely neutral in wars between foreign nations, the personal attacks upon him began and grew in bitterness and virulence until he went out of office. It is hard to believe the fierceness and brutality of these assaults upon the father of his country. When he retired from the presidency, the leading Republican paper in America said:

"The man who is the source of all the misfortunes of our country is this day reduced to a level with his fellow-citizens. * * * The name of Washington ceases from this day to give currency to political iniquity and to legalize corruption. * * * The day [of Washington's retirement] ought to be a *jubilee* in the United States."

Incredible as it may appear, there was literally nothing of which he was not accused.

During Washington's last year as president the Legislature of his own state, after a long and acrimonious debate, three times voted down the proposition that Washington was either wise, brave, or even patriotic. Marshall, in the Legislature, led the fight for his old commander.

When the French Republic was committing ravages on our commerce and outrages upon our seamen and citizens, President Adams sent Marshall to France as one of our ministers to patch up some kind of an arrangement by which French depredations could be stopped and peace between France and America could be restored and maintained. During these months in Paris, John Marshall saw the immediate results of the French Revolution in the rapidly rising autocratic power of Bonaparte. This confirmed him in the development of those views of government and society which I have been tracing. It was Marshall who, as the ablest of our commissioners, proved more than a match for Talleyrand; and Marshall wrote the famous dispatches relating the attempts to force the United States to pay a bribe, which, when published, gave a check for the first time to the triumphant progress of radical thought and action among the American populace.

His experience in Congress and as Secretary of State swept him still further upon the same strong current which, from the moment he marched under the flag of the coiled rattlesnake, as a Virginia Minute Man, to the fight at Great Bridge, until his appointment to the Supreme Bench had carried him steadily

toward that final national and conservative state of
mind which we find expressed in his opinions from
the bench.

Marshall's appointment to the Supreme Court was
a sheer accident, which nobody, and least of all himself, anticipated. Even President Adams had no idea
that he would appoint Marshall Chief Justice, a few
days before he offered that place to his Secretary
of State. When tendered, Marshall considered it some
days before accepting. President Adams had first
tendered the place to John Jay, who had been Chief
Justice under Washington, and who resigned that
office to go to England to negotiate the Jay Treaty.
From his experience on the bench Jay declined the
place because the Supreme Court, as then conducted
and considered, had little power and less dignity.
Most lawyers expected that Justice Patterson of New
Jersey would be chosen for the place, and, indeed,
he was the logical man. When finally the appointment of Marshall came, it surprised everybody and
was resented by some.

Thus it is that if anything in history can be said
to have been providential, the appointment of John
Marshall as Chief Justice of the Supreme Court of
the United States at the most critical period of our
constitutional history was an act of Providence.

And thus it was that all of his great opinions grew
out of history. His decision in *Marbury* v. *Madison*
was the direct result of the Kentucky and Virginia
Resolutions. The country faced a condition where
one state declared a law of Congress unconstitutional,
another state declared the same law constitutional, a
third said that it was invalid, a fourth that it was
valid; and the states denying the right of Congress
to pass a law asserted the states' right to disregard
the law.

Thus the Constitution was breaking to pieces; and
the chaos of the Articles of Confederation loomed
dark before us. Then came John Marshall with his
declaration that under the Constitution there was and
always would remain one great central body which

the fortunes of political parties could not affect, that alone had the power to tell the states and Congress and all the people whether an act of Congress is or is not constitutional. And so the Constitution was saved and the Republic endures.

McCullough v. *Maryland, Gibbon* v. *Ogden, The United States* v. *Burr,* and the group of decisions to which these cases belong were all assertions growing out of the teachings John Marshall had received from great and grim events that the blessings of life, liberty and the pursuit of happiness can only be secured and provided by a strong, orderly, national government.

PART II.

THE CONTRIBUTIONS
OF
CHIEF JUSTICE MARSHALL

MARYLAND, MARSHALL AND THE
CONSTITUTION

ALBERT J. BEVERIDGE[1]

Albert J. Beveridge was a favorite speaker before bar associations and his chief topic, of course, was the life and work of John Marshall. In the following speech, delivered before the Maryland Bar Association, the biographer of Marshall discusses the life of the Chief Justice and his constitutional contributions through the decisions of Marbury v. Madison, United States v. Burr, McCullough v. Maryland, and Cohen v. Virginia. No other author knows the life of Marshall as well as Beveridge and this sketch leaves the reader with a better understanding of the Chief Justice. This article is reprinted here with the consent of the Maryland State Bar Association, from their proceedings for 1920, beginning on page 174.

I should take as my subject the rather vague title of "Maryland, Marshall and the Constitution." I mean to cite those cases and tell, if I can, the story of those cases—so they will be comprehensible and not too dull to you—in which Maryland played the determinative part. I want first to say, so we can get a view of this whole thing, that, of course, as you all know, Maryland was against the adoption of the Constitution; and by far the ablest defense of the State rights idea that finally led to the Civil War, was made by Luther Martin in a report to the Legislature of Maryland, that great paper called "Genuine Information."

Luther Martin attacked, and ably attacked, the

Constitution on the ground that it did not establish
a Federal, but that it established a National, Govern-
men. Precisely the same point was made then, in a
broad, general way, that is now made and disputed
about concerning the covenant of the League of
Nations.

It was asserted on the one hand,—and that is what
led to all our amendments,—that the States created
the Constitution; that it was not a national government; that it was a mere league of States,—and that
phrase ran clear down to Marshall's death.

On the other hand, it was insisted that the Constitution created a Nation, that it came from the people
and that it acted directly on them and not on the
States. In order to get the Constitution adopted this
was denied by those who believed it and meant to
fight for it when the time came,—and it was never
urged again until the ratification was complete—that
it was a National and not a Federal Government
which this great instrument established.

But the penetrating mind of that marvelous genius,
Luther Martin, saw the truth,—that it was not a Federal Government but a National Government that was
really established; and because the State of Maryland
wanted a Federal Government—the Articles of Confederation merely strengthened,—he composed and
laid before the Legislature of Maryland, in accordance with the call of the Annapolis Convention, that
great document, "Genuine Information," in which he
assailed the Constitution. It is worth noting just here
that that profound argument of Luther Martin was
the rich quarry from which John C. Calhoun, more
than forty years afterwards, hewed out his powerful
argument for State rights. . . .

The next point is Marshall. I wish to make clear
here, so I shall not have to digress as I proceed, one
or two things about Marshall and his opinions. In the
first place, . . . these opinions of the great Chief Justice were not legal documents; they were great State
papers. Not one of them was addressed merely to
the case before the Court; all of them were addressed

to profound and determinative economic and social conditions, national in extent.

In fact, in two or three of the most important cases, three I think of at this minute, the mere record before the Court was either that of a moot case, as in Marbury vs. Madison, or else a feigned case; by which I mean an arranged case,—not genuine litigation. That is true of Cohens vs. Virginia and Fletcher vs. Peck. All of them, whether arranged cases or real litigation, were merely the occasions which this greatest jurist and statesman of all ages seized in order to give to the American people charts for their guidance in the future.

So when I refer to any opinion hereafter, bear in mind that it is not a legal document of which I am speaking, but a State paper, a "giving of the law" in the highest sense, ranking with the labors of Moses and other mighty law-givers of the world, and that the mere case Marshall passed upon was an incident rather than an occasion.

The second thing I would like for you to fix in your minds concerning Marshall is this: He was an uneducated man. He had hardly any learning in the law; and I am convinced if John Marshall had been a university man, if his mind had been cluttered with precedents, he never would have been the Moses of American jurisprudence. His teachers were events. The pen that wrote the opinion in McCullough vs. Maryland was dipped in the tears of Valley Forge and the blood of Monmouth. That is where those great fundamental ideas came from.

I wish to reinforce my statement, because you might credit it when I say that Marshall was not a man of learning and education. I will tell you why it was. There is a particular reason why the ladies may be interested in this. His father had designed him for the Bar. He was born in the backwoods and brought up in a little hollow in the Blue Ridge. I have often thought that every man who has been great enough to project himself across the centuries— not those men we call in commerce and politics

great and who last for a day and then are forgotten—
but those whose thoughts and works shine across the
years, every one of them has been born or brought
up in large and simple surroundings. None of their
nervous energy has been drawn away from them in
early youth by "society" and by the complexities that
divert the minds of men. All of them have had a
broad and simple outlook, so that throughout their
lives their minds become accustomed to deal with
any problem in a big and simple way. So with
Marshall.

He was designed for the Bar; and his father bought
the first copy of Blackstone in this country, a copy of
the first edition. John Marshall didn't read very much
of it because the Revolution was coming on. The
Marshalls were fighting men as all the yeomanry of
Northern Virginia were. So Marshall was studying
the manual of arms instead of Blackstone. He was
among the first to march under the rattlesnake flag
inscribed "Don't tread on Me," when the call came
from Patrick Henry.

He had no opportunity to learn law then. He went
in the army under Washington and there fought and
suffered for four years until the terms of the men
he commanded expired. He went back to Virginia
to await the recruiting of new men whom he might
take to the front. Thomas Jefferson being then Governor of Virginia, the men were not raised. Captain
John Marshall then visited his father at Yorktown.
His father, Colonel Thomas Marshall, was in command at that historic place. He had been elected by
the Virginia Legislature colonel of an artillery regiment, and Marshall went there to see his father,
whom he adored. The friendship that existed between Thomas Marshall and his son, John Marshall,
was very beautiful.

It happened that there lived in Yorktown the
Ambler family, Jacquelin Ambler and his daughters.
Mrs. Ambler was the celebrated beauty, Betty Burwell. She was one of the famous beauties of that
period. It was she who threw over Thomas Jefferson.

He was perfectly wild about her. If you look in the letters which he wrote at the time when he was a young man you will find his charming letter about Betty Burwell. But Jacquelin Ambler won her. There were three or four daughters. All but one had grown up to young womanhood. One, Mary Ambler, was only fourteen years old. They were always giving balls in those days; so when Captain John Marshall, his name glowing with his record in war, came down to visit his father, the young ladies gave a ball. Among them were the Ambler girls, one of whom afterward became Mrs. Edward Carrington, and wrote very informing letters about that period. In one of her letters she tells us about this ball and what happened there; so we do not have to depend on rumor. She said that their minds were chiefly concerned about Captain John Marshall. His name was very bright and high and the girls expected to see a handsome, dashing figure in brilliant uniform, and they all wanted to meet him, a young officer, as girls always do, and have a good time at the dance. He was the one on whom their minds were centered, —Captain John Marshall.

Mary Ambler had learned to dance but had not yet "come out," but having heard so much about Captain John Marshall, she said, "I am going to the dance, too, and set my cap at Captain Marshall and carry him off." So she went to the ball.

Mrs. Carrington said, "We were on the tip-toe of expectation. We thought we should see an Adonis, and this,—added to his fame as a hero and a soldier, —captivated our hearts in advance." After all had gathered at the ball, there came along a tall, guant, angular creature, with crude and rustic manners, whose clothes hung on him like a rack, and a slouch hat and unkempt hair;—that was John Marshall. "Instantly we lost interest in him—all except Mary," writes Mrs. Carrington. But John Marshall and Mary Ambler looked into each other's eyes; they fell in love with each other instantly; and then began that romance, the record of which lasted as long as she

lived and which constitutes one of the most attractive
and fascinating stories in all literature of affection.

Marshall thought that he would put in his time
going to William and Mary College, fourteen miles
from Yorktown. He went there and took law lectures
under John Wythe, one of the members of the Constitutional Convention. But he was thinking about Mary
Ambler all the time. I have a copy of his note book
that he kept at that time. It was found about fifteen
years ago in an outhouse on the place where he died.
There on one side are the notes he took of the law
lectures and we know from that exactly what lectures
he attended. At the beginning of the first page is
written out in the bold hand he had in his youth,
"Mary Ambler," on the cover inside "John—Polly,"
"Miss Mary—J. Marshall." Mary Ambler's name is
written all over the book, showing perfectly clearly
that he was thinking a good deal more of the girl
than of the law lectures.

Marshall was at college just five weeks. Jacquelin
Ambler, father of Mary, was appointed treasurer of
the new State of Virginia and went to Richmond
and took his girls with him, of course. On the way,
he stopped over night at Williamsburg, where Marshall was at college, and another ball was given.
John again met Mary there. The next morning the
Ambler family went on to Richmond; and two weeks
later John cut college. He could not stand it any
longer, and he went to Fauquier County, stopping
over in Richmond to see Mary Ambler. Thomas
Jefferson was then Governor and he signed Marshall's
license to practice law.

As I say he went to Fauquier County, where he
was born, and tried to get a law practice, but he
could not stay there on account of the girl, so he
went to Richmond where she lived. When she was
17 years old he married her. That is all the education
John Marshall had in the law. . . .

His appointment to that office was not expected by
anybody. He did not expect it himself. John Jay,
who resigned to become Minister to England to

negotiate a treaty, had the Chief Justiceship offered to him again, but he declined on the ground that the Supreme Court did not amount to anything. It was offered to William Cushing and he declined. When Washington was President he offered it to Patrick Henry and he declined. You must remember that this is one of the great things in the life of John Marshall, perhaps the sum of all the great things, that at the time that he became Chief Justice of the United States the Supreme Court held a very low place not only in the opinion of the Bar, but in public esteem.

To put dramatically before you the condition of the Supreme Court at the time the Government was founded and as it continued to be when Marshall ascended the Bench, perhaps this incident will be useful. In designing the Capitol so little was thought about the Supreme Court of the United States,—so small a place did it occupy in the minds of men,—that no room was provided for it in the Capitol. That is how it happened that, when the seat of Government was moved to Washington, the Supreme Court of the United States held its sessions in a room in the basement of the Capitol. It amounted to practically nothing.

The office of Chief Justice was finally offered to John Marshall, who accepted it with great hesitation. He was then Secretary of State under John Adams. The reason he accepted it was undoubtedly two-fold: One was that with his simple mind, his clear penetration, with his vision he saw how powerful that then feeble court could be made. He saw what he carried out in his life work. It was necessary if democracy was going to stand and endure that there must be some steadying influence that is above the reach of the people and above the control of administrations, and above all partisan influences,—some steadying influence which can say to all without partiality what is and what is not law under the Constitution of the United States. So he accepted.

In 1798, two years before this time, you will recall

that he returned from France as chief of our Embassy there after his successful intellectual duel with Talleyrand. That is the time the French Republic had tried to force the American envoys to bribe the Directory. That is the time of the great "X. Y. Z. Affair." Marshall came back at a most dramatic instant in our history. It was upon his return when our naval war with France broke out and on every hillside of the Republic were lighted fires of patriotism.

John Marshall was given a great reception in Philadelphia. There was a brilliant banquet given in his honor, and it was there that were spoken those words which have become famous, "Millions for defense, but not one cent for tribute," which were attributed by some to Charles Clotsworth Pinckney; but the words were first used at the Philadelphia banquet given to Marshall, and the author of them is unknown.

At that time there were great foreign propaganda in this country,—something which had been going on since the second year of Washington's administration. Immediately on the outbreak of the age-old conflict between France and Great Britain, this country was subjected to terrific foreign propaganda— which has continued to this day under other names. . . .

So it was a tremendous foreign propaganda began. Jacobin Clubs were formed all over the country. Verbal assaults were made on the President. Things were said, which now look rather innocent, but greatly excited those people, great men though they were. It was felt that the country was on the verge of a declaration of war. We actually were engaged in real conflict with France on the seas. So the heads of the greatest political party the world has ever seen, bar none, the Federalist party,—the party that gave us our Constitution, if it can be said any party that gave us our concept of nationality—those men of that party, in the midst of those strenuous times, lost their heads and passed the Alien and Sedition Laws, which provided, in a word, that the President might deport any person whom he thought dangerous to the country, and that anybody criticizing the Government and the President unduly might be indicted and punished by imprisonment or fine, or both.

That was a blow at the fundamentals of the American institution—free speech—and although the Republican party which had been formed by, and become strong under Thomas Jefferson, but which was almost dissolved at that time,—instantly that Republican party used this unwise legislation which had been passed by the greatest party the world ever saw, to assault that party; used it like a bludgeon and with it broke to pieces and destroyed the Federalist party, the greatest party of great men the world has ever seen. But when that great party overstepped the fundamentals of American freedom it had to perish, and did.

At that time the Judges on the Bench, especially the Federalist Judges, not all the State Judges, though some of them, were extremely ardent, let us say, were extremely zealous in the suppression of what they called "sedition."

More than that they made political addresses from the Bench. They would read sermons from the Bench. When cases came before them that involved sedition, treason, they became persecutors instead of judges. Their methods were abusive. Their manners were overbearing and not to be tolerated or endured.

Especially among the notable for, as I might say, ferocity, was one of the ablest men on the Supreme Court of the United States Bench, Samuel Chase of Maryland. At Philadelphia, in the case of John Fries which had gone to trial, he threw down three papers and he said, "These contain the opinion of the Court on the law of treason; there is one for the Government and one for the counsel for the defense and one for the jury." That is what occurred. William Lewis and Alexander J. Dallas, counsel in the case, promptly arose and left the Court room and said they would not stain their hands with a prejudged opinion.

Callender of Virginia was another case. The lawyers in that case were treated with contempt. Chase had a great gift of ridicule. He made the spectators laugh at them.

Justice Chase went up to Wilmington, Delaware, and, although the Grand Jury were farmers and the harvest season was at its height and there was no business to be transacted, he had them held there while the Clerk of the Court searched the files of the newspapers to find out whether or not any editor had printed anything he considered seditious. He was going to put down sedition, he said. He forgot they were not putting down sedition but suppressing free speech, to preserve which our institutions were framed.

Thomas Jefferson immediately wrote the Kentucky resolutions and Madison wrote the Virginia resolutions. These resolutions declared that when Congress passed any law that a State thought was unconstitutional, that State might disregard it; Jefferson went even further and said that no citizen is any more bound to obey an unconstitutional law than he is bound to bow down before the Golden Calf.

So the great question arose: Under our form of Government who can say what is and what is not law? Who can decide with final and determinative authority whether a statute is constitutional or unconstitutional? The Republican party in denouncing the Alien and Sedition laws had these resolutions passed, and, speaking by and large, they said this is a compact of States, and therefore any State could say when Congress has overstepped the terms of the partnership.

They sent the resolutions all over the country. Here is a curious thing to show how dangerous a little knowledge of history is and how essential a full knowledge is. If you will follow Elliott's Debates you will find the New England States, and the New York, Pennsylvania, Maryland, Delaware and New Jersey Legislatures passed resolutions to the effect that they disagreed with the Kentucky and Virginia resolutions, and asserted that the only power under our Constitution which can declare a law unconstitutional is the Supreme Court of the United States.

That is only partly true. A majority of these Legislatures did say that; *but the minority did not.* In the minority of every Legislature the Republicans fought with the determination of conviction for the theory that a State, and not the Supreme Court of the United States, has the right to say whether a national law is unconstitutional.

For instance, in New York the Federalist majority there declared the Supreme Court was the power to decide that question, but the majority was only five, fifty men voted for it *but forty-five Republicans voted against it.* The same was true in the other States. At that time the Federalist party, on account of its mistake in passing the Alien and Sedition laws, was on the decline and the Republican party, on account of its championship of free speech, was advancing.

So it was when John Marshall became Chief Justice of the United States and Thomas Jefferson was elected President of the United States, some of those States that had a few months previously declared in favor of the theory that the Supreme Court can declare a law constitutional or unconstitutional, had since gone Republican. Maryland was captured, and Pennsylvania and New York had an overrun, and even the New England ramparts of Federalism were crumbling. Thomas Jefferson said that the election of 1800 was a second revolution. The campaign of 1800 was fought out chiefly on the question whether or not the Supreme Court of the United States should decide what is or is not the law or whether that was the province of the States. So it was that the two great protagonists met, Thomas Jefferson for the rights of the States to declare what the law is, and John Marshall, Chief Justice of the Supreme Court of the United States, for the authority of that tribunal to make such a vital decision.

Now you have back of you the roots and beginnings of Marshall's first great state paper, the opinion

upon which American constitutional law rests, the one
original contribution from America to the jurisprudence of the world.

I must relate the case of Marbury vs. Madison to
you so you may comprehend its historical importance,
because it leads up to one of the greatest events of
Maryland's history, the Chase impeachment. That
is why I am taking time at this point. The last act
of the expiring Federalist Congress was a wise and
statesmanlike measure. It was the repeal of the
Ellsworth Judiciary Act of 1789. This was the law
under which our National Courts were organized, and
it has been lauded very highly. As a matter of fact
it was one of the most defective laws ever passed,
notwithstanding the eminence of the men who passed
it.

For example, under that Act the Justices of the
Supreme Court of the United States were compelled
to travel in pairs and sit in banc with the District
Judges, and because of storms, floods and so forth,
travel was very often dangerous. Many times the
District Court convened and the lawyers and litigants
and their witnesses would be there at great expense,
and sometimes wait weeks for the Justices to appear,
and sometimes they did not come at all. That is only
one incident of the defects of the law. Another de-
fect was even more important. If an appeal were
taken it was taken from the decision of the Court
below and it was taken from the very man who made
the decision below to the very same man who finally
decided the case above.

So the great Federalist party repealed that law and
passed instead the historic Federalist Judiciary Act
of 1801. That Act was so wise that in 1893 and 1895,
nearly a century afterward, it was re-enacted.

Under this Act many circuits were created and
other new features added. President Adams appointed Federalists as judges and that angered the
Republicans a good deal more than anything else
about the law. They determined to attack it and
they did.

It was the first thing that Jefferson did after he got in power. Among other places created by the Federalist Judiciary Act of 1801 were forty-two justices of the peace for the District of Columbia, and all the appointments were Federalists.

These justices of the peace were appointed the last day of the administration of President Adams. Marshall was Secretary of State as well as Chief Justice of the United States. The Senate confirmed them and the commissions were sent to Marshall, who signed them and affixed the seal; but, with his customary negligence,—he was the most negligent man in the world,—he did not deliver the commissions. When Madison became Secretary of State he found these commissions on his desk.

President Jefferson declared that he would not deliver these commissions and he said, moreover, that the District of Columbia did not need forty-two justices of the peace; and it did not. He said, "I will deliver only twenty-five, and seventeen I will not deliver at all." Four of the men whose commissions were refused were William Marbury, Dennis Ramsey, Robert Townsend Hoee and William Harper; and these four out of the seventeen whose commissions had not been delivered brought suit in the Supreme Court of the United States to compel James Madison, Secretary of State, to deliver these commissions. Madison, under Jefferson's orders, had withheld them.

There were seventeen whose commissions had been withheld, but thirteen of the men thought so little of the office that they did not join in the suit. It was a small office and the fees were inconsiderable. Even of the twenty-five men whose commissions Jefferson was ready to deliver, three refused to accept and one afterwards resigned.

The suit was before the Supreme Court of the United States for a mandamus,—that is, an order to compel James Madison, Secretary of State, to deliver the commissions. But before the Supreme Court could possibly hear the application the new Congress met, which was overwhelmingly Republican.

Then began the great Republican assault on the judiciary—which echoes in our ears to this day, and which I think you will find renewed in the desperate period on which we are entering. At once Senator John Breckenridge of Kentucky, acting for the administration, arose and moved to repeal the Judiciary Act of 1801, which, if repealed, would have restored the Ellsworth Act of 1789. A terrific debate ensued. I say deliberately that no man has a right to call himself a constitutional lawyer who has not read and studied that historic legislative engagement. The debate finally turned on the great question as to what power can determine what is and what is not constitutional under the fundamental law of our country. Every argument which had been advanced before or has been advanced since, why the Supreme Court shall have that exalted function, and every argument advanced before or since why the Supreme Court should not exercise a supervisory power over Congress was presented in that debate. . . .

Marshall was in Washington and undoubtedly read every bit of the debate which was well reported in the press. The Republicans were not content with merely repealing the Act and restoring the old one; that, of course, put all the Federalists out of office and they wanted to get the Federalists out of office—there were politicians in those days as well as now—but they were not content with that. They greatly feared these Federalists on the Supreme Court Bench, because, mark you, the Supreme Court was composed wholly of Federalists and there were no Republicans on the Supreme Court Bench, and they did not know but what John Marshall would have the nerve to declare that repeal unconstitutional. That question was debated. So the Republicans thought they would settle the matter by abolishing the Supreme Court for fourteen months, which they did. They passed a law that it should meet only once a year. This prevented the Court from meeting until February, 1803. Thus it was that the Supreme Court of the United States by Act of Congress was suspended for fourteen months. The reason that was done was based on human nature,—the weakness of human nature. The Republicans argued, and argued correctly, that if, for fourteen months the Federalist Circuit and District justices were out of office they would get tired and get over their wrath. It was like the managers of political conventions. They put things across and say there will be plenty of time for dissatisfied persons to get over their anger.

Just that occurred. During this period the Supreme Court of the United States being abolished, the new Federalist Circuit and District found themselves helpless. They said: "What is the use? we cannot do anything."

When the Supreme Court did assemble, the case of Marbury vs. Madison was before it. It did not amount to a hill of beans. As Jefferson said some years later, it was no more than a moot case. More than half of tho torm for which Marbury and his associates had been appointed had expired. The twenty-five justices of the peace did all the work there was to do. I doubt very much whether Marbury, Harper, Hooe or Ramsey were at all interested. I doubt if they even attended the hearing.

John Marshall was, therefore, faced with a curious situation. I have related all this that you may see with perfect vision the great daring and the mighty statesmanship of this man. Here was a little case before the Court, and he could readily suggest that it be dismissed. He might say: "Don't bother us with it, or leave it on the calendar. That could have been done. Or he could have said: This was an application which interfered with the political functions of the Executive Department and the Judiciary has nothing to do with it, and dismiss the case; or he could issue the mandamus and order Madison to deliver the commissions.

But if he took either course he was ruined. If he took the last course Madison would simply have refused to obey. Jefferson would have laughed at the Supreme Court of the United States and it would have sunk still further in public esteem. If Marshall took the first course and dismissed the case, then the Republican contention that the courts have no power over legislation, that Congress is as omnipotent as the British Parliament, that Congress, and not the courts, is the interpreter of the Constitution, would have been admitted.

It was one of the most crucial points of American history. No one knew when such a case would come before the Court again to enable it to speak. As a matter of fact, such a case did not arise again until half a century later in the Dread Scott matter, in which the Supreme Court of the United States could have declared a law unconstitutional.

So if Marshall had dismissed Marbury vs. Madison, a period of more than seventy years would have elapsed from the adoption of the Constitution, during which period the Jeffersonion theory that the Courts have no power over legislation would have been admitted, and the history of this country and the jurisprudence of America would have been exactly the reverse of what it was.

Under the circumstances, John Marshall resolved to act. He resolved to use his little case to declare from the Bench of the Supreme Court of the United States, by the unanimous opinion of the Judges, that the only power in America that can say what is or is not law is the judiciary; and that in the last analysis the Supreme Court of the United States can alone announce whether or not Congress or anybody else has violated our foundamental law.

There was not anything new or startling in the arguments used to sustain that point. All of them had been used before. What was original was the method by which Marshall reached his conclusion. It was audacity amounting to genius. He resolved to hold Section 13 of the Ellsworth Judiciary Act unconstitutional.

This section provided that the Supreme Court of the United States should have original jurisdiction to issue writs of mandamus and prohibition. The Con-

stitution provides that the Supreme Court shall have
original jurisdiction in certain cases, and appellate
jurisdiction in mandamus proceedings. So Marshall
argued that the Constitution and the Statute were in
conflict, and therefore, Section 13 of the Ellsworth
Act was unconstitutional. It was an audacious thing
to do, and this was the audacious thing about it:

Oliver Ellsworth, Chief Justice of the Supreme
Court, whom Marshall succeeded, was a member of
the Constitutional Convention and a Senator in the
First Congress; and he wrote the Judiciary Act.
William Paterson of New Jersey, who was then an
Associate Justice on the Supreme Bench with Marshall, had been a member of the Convention that
framed the Constitution; he had helped draft the
Ellsworth Judiciary Act; and afterwards, as a Judge,
had recognized its validity. It had been passed on
by Gouveneur Morris and Wythe of Virginia, and a
dozen men in the Senate and House, who also had
been members of the Constitutional Convention,
every one of whom was of infinitely more learning
than John Marshall; and not one of them imagined
that he was drafting a measure in violation of the
Constitution he himself had helped to write.

More than fourteen years the Government had
acted under this section. Four times the Supreme
Court itself had admitted directly or by inference
that it was constitutional. No human being suggested that it was not constitutional.

The Republicans did not think that Marshall would
hold it unconstitutional. What they thought was
that he would issue a writ of mandamus to Madison,
and they intended to impeach him if he did. That
appears in the newspapers at the time.

More than that, in this same session in the case of
Stuart vs. Laird (which was decided by Marshall
below, and therefore he said he would not take part
in the decision above), the Supreme Court decided
that the continuous practical construction for fourteen years fixed the meaning of the Constitution, and
established the validity of the Ellsworth Act.

Notwithstanding all these considerations, John Marshall actually persuaded his associates on the Bench that this section was unconstitutional, and that was the method by which he arrived at the place where he could give out his great fundamental opinion upon the supervisory power of the Courts,—that the Judiciary must look at the statute passed by Congress and the Constitution, and if they are in conflict then the Constitution, which is the supreme law of the land, must prevail over the statute, and the statute becomes null and void because it does what the Constitution says Congress shall not do.

For instance, suppose Congress shall by Act say that treason consists of advising the establishment of a soviet or of a monarchical form of government, and that treason might be proved by one witness or circumstantially. The Constitution says that treason shall consist only in levying war against the United States and giving aid and comfort to its enemies, and must be proved by two witnesses to the same overt act or by confession in open court. Suppose during the late war Congress should have passed an Act saying that treason shall consist of certain other things and that one witness is enough to convict a man. The Constitution says one thing and Congress says another thing. Which is the law? Marshall said that the Constitution is the supreme law and the statute must yield to it.

The second thing he did was this: If this law was constitutional, then this was a ministerial act and James Madison, Secretary of State, must carry out the law; that this is a Government of laws and not of men. When it becomes a Government of men and not of laws then any department can substitute its will for the general laws of the land, then anarchy has come and tyranny will result.

What was the outcome of that? Immediately the Republicans, under Jefferson's direction, resolved to impeach and remove from the Bench John Marshall and every Federalist on the Bench, and put Republicans in their places. Mr. Jefferson's plan was a very simple one,—it was one of the things that, for the moment, catch the people and that sometimes give thoughtful persons grave doubts about the soundness and wisdom of democracy.

Jefferson said, "We have been elected to effect great reforms. The Judiciary stand in the way; the Judiciary must be consistent with the will of the people so as to become an assistant instead of an obstacle to the great reforms the people want. Therefore, every man on the Bench the prevailing party does not approve of shall be removed, and those places be filled with those who are in accordance with the drift of the times."

So came that event which I consider one of the ten or a dozen determinative events in American history, and Maryland now again enters on the scene. The Republicans in the House led by John Randolph, on the orders of Mr. Jefferson written to Joseph Nicholson of Baltimore, impeached Justice Samuel Chase of Maryland for high crimes and misdemeanors. Do not forget that under the Constitution a person can only be impeached for high crimes and misdemeanors. That is *all* a person can be impeached for.

It was a very curious and remarkable bill of impeachment, and it was drawn with great political skill to capture the representatives from Virginia and Pennsylvania and everywhere else. But the principal excuse given for this action was the extraordinary charge which Chase delivered to the Grand Jury in Baltimore, where he said this thing of universal suffrage, the repeal of the Judiciary Act and all were going to imperil justice and civilization, and instead of being a democracy we would develop into a mobocracy.

Jefferson wrote to Joseph Nicholson and said the man ought to be impeached, and impeachment was brought.

The impeachment of Warren Hastings was still in everybody's mind. The hall where the Senate sat, which is now the Supreme Court room, was decorated, the Senators' chairs in crimson cloth and, where the members of the House sat, green cloth, and so forth. There appeared for his defense Joseph Hopkinson, who had written "Hail Columbia;" Philip Barton Key, the brother of the man who wrote the "Star Spangled Banner;" Robert Goodloe Harper, who had been in Congress, and Luther Martin, a man of the most amazing mind—all things considered—the American Bar has ever produced, with the possible exception of William Pinkney. The case for the House was managed by John Randolph of Roanoke, by Joseph Nicholson of Baltimore, and by Caesar Rodney of Philadelphia, and one or two others.

Just before the trial of the impeachment began there came up in the House the debate over the famous Yazoo frauds. This tremendously excited that strange person and genius, John Randolph of Roanoke, who threw himself into the debate with a ferocity little short of insanity. He assailed Jefferson's Postmaster General for lobbying on the floor of the House for the passage of the Yazoo plan. It was after this intense parliamentary struggle that he came to the impeachment trial of Samuel Chase, utterly exhausted physically; and but for that fact I have little doubt this impeachment, which failed, would have succeeded.

When the evidence was in, the great debate began. For what can an officer of the United States be impeached under our Constitution? The position of the Republicans was stated by Senator William Branch Giles of Virginia. How transitory is fame! How many know of William Branch Giles now? How many have even heard his name? Yet he was Jefferson's leader of the Senate at that time, and Jefferson said he was probably the greatest debater in the world. He was the master of Congress—he and Randolph—for years and years. Now his name is hardly known.

It is only when a man connects himself with mighty deeds and thoughts that he becomes immortal. Only when he does this is his name remembered.

Their position was,—and this is vital,—that impeachment is merely an inquest of office and that any Judge or any other officer whom the majority of the House and two-thirds of the Senate affirm is not a proper man for any place because he holds incorrect opinions, can and should be removed from office.

The position taken by Luther Martin and all the counsel for Samuel Chase was one which has prevailed since, the one which after a most extraordinary, profound, learned and brilliant debate, succeeded, viz: That under the Constitution an officer may be impeached only for an offense for which he can also be indicted; that high crimes and misdemeanors are technical words well understood when the Constitution was framed, and mean indictable offenses. That was their meaning when the Constitution was adopted,—that the Judge on the Bench, the whole judiciary, were not to be made the mere tools of a temporary partisan majority, but were to be permanent and to be removed only in case they committed such an offense for which they could be punished under an indictment.

Luther Martin made a great argument in that case. It was unanswerable. It even convinced Republican partisans under orders from Jefferson to convict Chase.

Do not forget that the significance is this: That this case, this impeachment of Samuel Chase, was the first step in the removing of all Federalists from the Supreme Bench, especially John Marshall. Giles said at the time he would not dare to send a mandate to Mr. Madison. He would not dare to say the laws of Congress are unconstitutional. If he did, let him be removed. Giles said to John Quincy Adams, the handsome young Senator from Massachusetts, "Our purpose is to remove them because we want the offices." And Marshall had dared to do what Giles asserted would result in his impeachment.

Marshall was frightened. He wrote a letter, which would be incredible if his well known signature were not attached to it. Chase wrote to Marshall to look up some evidence for him in Richmond, and he said he would. In this letter John Marshall actually proposed the most radical method for correcting judicial decisions that was ever made before or since that time. He proposed that, instead of impeaching judges, if anybody was dissatisfied with the opinion of the Supreme Court, there should be an appeal to Congress. Anybody, if he did not like the decision of the Supreme Court could appeal to Congress and Congress could have the final authority in the matter.

Marshall was not in any terror for himself; but he knew if the plan for the removal of the Judges succeeded that Jefferson would appoint Spencer Roane of Virginia to be Chief Justice. One of the reasons of Jefferson's hatred of Marshall was that he had expected to appoint Spencer Roane to that office. He did not imagine that Chief Justice Ellsworth would resign so soon. He did not imagine that John Marshall, of all men, would be appointed to succeed Ellsworth. Jefferson expected that he would have an opportunity to appoint the Chief Justice, and he intended to appoint Spencer Roane Chief Justice, of the Supreme Court of the United States. It shows on what small things great events turn. Had that happened, the opinion in Marbury vs. Madison would have been the reverse of what it was. It was because of what he knew was at stake that Marshall was terrified.

Finally the case was ended. The Senatorial Court voted overwhelmingly that the impeachment could not be sustained. Thus it happened particularly through the efforts of Luther Martin from Maryland, and other giants of the Maryland Bar, that the Judiciary of the United States was placed in an impregnable position. But for that decision your Federal Bench in Baltimore would not be the stable institution it is. It would be subject to the orders of a partisan majority of Congress.

The next case, equally fundamental, in which Maryland appears is the trial of Aaron Burr. I can give you only a sentence in regard to that. Alexander Hamilton had conceived the idea way back in 1796 of liberating—they were always "liberating" something—Venezuela. A few years before, Aaron Burr had the same idea with reference to the Floridas, Louisiana and Mexico, especially Mexico.

Burr went out of the office of Vice-President not knowing what to do. His money was gone and his law practice was gone. He was disgraced in the North and under indictment in New York and New Jersey; so there occured to him the project of years ago—the invasion of Mexico. He had intended to do it only in case we went to war with Spain. War was imminent. Mr. Jefferson in his message to Congress almost said a state of war existed. The people were talking about it. Everybody was eager for it.

So Burr started West. He went down the Ohio and Mississippi Rivers, and was received with triumphant acclaim everywhere he went—received like a conquering hero. Duelling in that part of the country was considered a matter of honor; and the fact that he had killed Hamilton in fair fight was not held against Burr in the West and Southwest.

Burr reached New Orleans, where enthusiasm for him reached a climax. All the time he had the idea, as I say, that it was certain that war was going to be declared against Spain, and he, Burr, being a soldier, as well as a lawyer and politician, wanted to lead the first division against Mexico. He started back to Nashville. An account of his journey is told in charming letters to his daughter Theodosia. When he was on the way, a secret agent of Spain, Stephen Minor, started the rumor that Burr was down there to separate the Union, the Western from the Eastern States. Burr and Blennerhassett had purchased several hundred thousand acres of land, and in case war did not break out, they intended to settle and attend to their land.

Some weeks after Joseph Hamilton Raveiss of Kentucky, thinking Jefferson was conniving at this thing, began a prosecution against Burr; and finally Jefferson, acting without evidence, but largely as a political matter, issued a proclamation about the expedition. He did not say they were traitors but that the expedition was illegal.

Instantly the popular mind took alarm, as it always does, when word comes from high quarters. The people said: "Dear me, what does it mean, this thing from the President of the United States. It does not mean he is going to invade Mexico because we want to do that. What does the President mean, then? Why, he must mean that Burr is a traitor."

Congress was tremendously excited. Nobody knew what to believe. Rumors flew fast and thick. John Randolph arose in the House and offered a resolution directing the President to send to Congress a statement of the whole thing. Jefferson had to respond, and he did so in the famous message in which he said that, while there was not any real evidence, yet these men were conniving to separate the Union and so forth; and finally ended up with the amazing statement that of Burr's "guilt there can be no question." Guilty of treason! The President of the United States had stamped on a citizen's brow the brand of treason.

The country did not wait to argue about it. The President had said this man was a traitor, and that was enough, and they clamored for his blood. Finally he was arrested and captured and brought overland East. He was brought to Richmond and the great trial began.

I think I can bring this matter to your eyes very easily as to how this thing worked. If the President of the United States during the late war had said specifically of someone, "that man is a traitor," I doubt whether any Judge in the state of mind in which the country then was, would have dared to consider a defense. I doubt whether the accused man would be alive.

Or during the Civil War, suppose Lincoln said specifically of any man "that man is a traitor," that man undoubtedly would have been killed, so excited do people become.

That is the experience that Marshall had. Richmond overflowed. Thousands and thousands of people came there, and there were not enough houses to accommodate the throngs. Washington Irving of New York was there, and people from all over the country. The passions of the multitude were violent, so violent that Marshall, during the trial, told Luther Martin that if the jury, at that moment, found Burr to be innocent they would not dare to bring in a verdict to that effect, because to do so would endanger their lives. Marshall understood all this. The popular feeling was terrific. I will not take the time to go over it in detail.

The trials lasted from May to October,—there were three trials in all. The Government was represented by John Hay and William Wirt. Jefferson's letters show that constantly he was directing the prosecution.

A drag net was thrown out over the United States. Printed questionnaires were sent to every justice of the peace everywhere, and anybody suspected of knowing anything was compelled to answer under pain of being imprisoned. Men were brought to Richmond from the most distant parts of the United States.

Money was spent which was never appropriated for that purpose in order to convict this man for whose blood the public were clamoring.

Constantly Jefferson himself, through letters, day by day directed the prosecution and said what should be done and what should not be done. All the power of the administration was brought to bear through every department of the Government to convict the man the President had said in his mesage was guilty of the crime of treason. That is what Marshall had to withstand.

Luther Martin, who in the Chase impeachment made the great argument I have referred to, came voluntarily to Richmond to defend Burr.

Luther Martin was a medium sized man, and there was nothing remarkable in his appearance. He had thin hair and broad shoulders, and he was the greatest drinker of his time. Everybody drank in those days, but nobody drank as much as Luther Martin. He drank on the Samuel Johnson maxim, "Wine for women, whiskey for men, and brandy for heroes." Martin tried to be a hero.

It is perfectly astonishing how Martin could drink the enomous amount of brandy he did, and yet be able to do the amount of work he did. He arose to heights equal to any that Erskine ever reached in the cases in which he made his fame. Such denunciation of executive authority I doubt has ever been surpassed in any country.

The final opinion of Marshall, and there were many of them,—the final opinion was delivered on the charge which Burr and Blennerhassett were indicted, —with having levied war against the United States on Blennerhassett Island in the jurisdiction of Virginia; that was the charge. The proof of the levying of war was the assembly there of sixteen to twenty young men who were to accompany Burr to the Washita land, which he had purchased, and they had a few rifles and fowling pieces which they used when they went out hunting in the woods. That is all the proof the Government had of the charge laid in the indictment.

They had no proof that Burr was there. Indeed Burr was not there,—he was 300 miles distant. They had a great number of witnesses to testify to collateral matters; but this is all the proved—although they had hoped to prove an overt act. Martin rose in defense, and moved the Court to arrest the testimony, on the ground that, if the remaining witnesses stated all that it was intimated they would state, it would really be immaterial, since it would not prove any overt act, and the Constitution required the proof of an overt act. That had not been proved, and it was conceded that all these witnesses who were going to testify would not testify to any overt act, and, therefore, they should not be heard, because there should first be proof to establish an overt act. That was the gist of the argument of Burr's counsel.

I have used the word "brilliant" so often that I dislike to use it again, but I must say it was one of the most brilliant legal encounters that ever occurred in any Court of justice. It lasted a long time. Marshall delivered his final opinion, which settled forever the American law of treason and overthrew the doctrine of constructive treason.

You must recall that the one article in the Constitution on which everybody agreed was that concerning treason; and the reason was that every man who had any part in the Revolutionary War was a traitor unless the Revolution succeeded. Under the law of constructive treason, Washington and every man engaged in the Revolution could have been drawn and quartered, and not only that, but every woman giving a patriot soldier a glass of water would have been guilty under the law of constructive treason. Not only that, but any person sitting silent where the patriot cause was being advocated would have been guilty under the law of constructive treason.

That is the reason why the provision defining treason was put in the Constitution. Everybody knew it at the time, but in the course of seventeen years, it had been forgotten, and so the populace clamored for this man's blood; but Marshall delivered his opinion that, under our Constitution, constructive treason cannot exist. Men accused of the blackest of all crimes, the accusation of which arouses the passions of men to the highest degree, must be indicted, and the offense clearly stated in the indictment, and the indictment must be proved as laid.

The proof must be under the Constitution, and that proof must consist of two witnesses to the same overt act, and not any circumstantial evidence. In this case it was said that Burr, who was accused of levying war at a certain time and place, was not there at all. Although the Government admitted that he was not there, still it was stated that he had procured treason and he was constructively there,—there by inference.

Marshall's answer was this, and I wish to say that

it was as true during the late war as it was then, and that it has stood for a hundred years and will stand—that if his presence constituted the overt act, his presence must be proved by two witnesses; but if, instead of presence, procurement was the overt act, that is, procuring the thing to be done,—then that also must be proved by two witnesses.

Thus it was that the law of constructive treason was overthrown. I haven't any doubt that during the Civil War perhaps hundreds of innocent lives were saved by that decision of Marshall. In the midst of passions terrificly aroused the judgment loses its bearings.

Instantly Marshall was assailed much more bitterly than any judge on the Bench was ever assailed in the whole history of the world. In the newspapers,—the Richmond Enquirer, the great Republican newspaper; the Philadelphia Aurora, and the Republican press throughout the country—he was denounced by men over their own signatures. William Thompson, in a series of letters which he published, said that Marshall and Burr were both traitors at heart. It was said that John Marshall had stained his name with infamy. Finally the people became so excited that in Baltimore, Maryland, a short time after his decision, Aaron Burr, Blennerhassett, Luther Martin and John Marshall, the Chief Justice of the United States, were hanged in effigy amid the howling execrations of the mob.

Thank God the founders of our Constitution placed one part of this Government above the fleeting impulses of the moment! Thank God that we had as our Chief Justice at this period a man who dared to brave the temporary passions of the multitude and declare that liberty and law should prevail no matter what the consequences to himself might be!

I had intended going into the case of Fletcher vs. Peck, but I must pass over that to the great case where Maryland takes a decisive part. I shall only say this with reference to Fletcher vs. Peck. It involved an extensive fraud, the most extensive fraud excepting that of the South Sea Bubble in the history of the world. Marshall's decision in it was pure statesmanship.

It was an arranged case, and on opinion from the Supreme Court of the United States would not have been admissible except as an act of statesmanship. But I must pass over that as I have not the time to go into it, and I must give some time to the vital case of McCullough vs. Maryland, which is as important, if not more so, than Marbury vs. Madison, in which Maryland was the impelling force.

Again I must remind you that none of these opinions of Marshall can be understood at all, unless you look at them from the point of view of statesmanship. You might as well read nothing at all as to read Marshall's opinions and decision as mere law opinions.

At this point I am going to talk about McCullough vs. Maryland. There now enters on the scene one of the most attractive and curious figures that ever overcame diplomats with address or overwhelmed courts with learning and logic, or ever held listening Senates spellbound by entrancing eloquence. It is the man whom I consider, perhaps, the first lawyer of the early part of American history; the equal of Webster in everything except appearance and political manipulation. I mean William Pinkney of Maryland. . . .

This man came into the case of McCullough vs. Maryland. As I said a moment ago, it is hard to understand the opinions of Marshall without understanding the events which produced them. Therefore, I shall take a moment or two to recall the history of the the times that led up to this opinion.

When the Constitution was adopted the great debate started, which ended at Appomattox—first, as to who might construe the Constitution, and second, as to what the Constitution meant. . . . When there is a conflict as to fundamental questions then that has got to be fought out. The Civil War could not be avoided because the question was a fundamental one. . . .

When the Constitution was adopted the question was, who should settle what it meant. For instance, Jefferson and his school, and some people say even yet, it must be construed strictly, and that it was a contract; that the powers given to the Federal Government were expressly given to it, and it could exercise no others. That question arose at once, when it was proposed to organize a national bank under Washington's first administration.

Everybody was in doubt and Washington called for opinions from Hamilton and Jefferson. Hamilton said that the Bank Act was valid, as an exercise of implied powers. Jefferson said that view would enable the National Government to do anything it pleased. Washington adopted Hamilton's view and the Bank was established.

In 1811, when near the end of the first Charter, a new one was applied for. It is a fact that the notes of the Bank of the United States were at par all over the world, and the only money in the world at that time at par. In some countries it was even above par. The Bank had carried out brilliantly everything that Hamilton, its projector, had predicted. But it made a great deal of money. It was called a "monopoly."

There were some State banks, and they began to stir up the people against the "central money power." Jefferson said that, in time of war it could overthrow the Government. You hear complaints now about the "money power." It began back there. There was a tremendous agitation against the rechartering of the Bank. Local banks stirred up the people everywhere. It was an ideal opportunity for the demagogue.

This was on the eve of our war with Great Britain. Incredible as the fact may appear, the Congress of the United States refused to recharter the First Bank of the United States and it went out of existence. Immediately State banks grew up all over the country.

They took advantage of everything. They grew to such an extent that turnpike companies issued money; saw mills issued money. These banks would have their "cappers" and agents who would go out among the people and try to sell the banks' bills at a discount. They would say, "Why, yes, they will be perfectly good; we will give them to you at a certain discount, and they will be good hereafter and you can give us a mortgage on your land." The first thing the investor knew the mortgage was foreclosed and his property was taken.

There was not only an economic breakdown but a moral breakdown as well,—all over the land. An economic breakdown is usually accompanied by a moral breakdown.

In the midst of this Congress was compelled as a matter of self-preservation to charter the second bank of the United States. Instantly all local and State banks, all local papers that were controlled by the State banks and all the local politicians who were under the control of the State banks, began to assail the great central money institution. It was an "octopus," they said, and was the cause of all the trouble. People suffered for money; they cried for more money and the National institution began to deflate,—something that we have got to do now in these times.

The golden age of the political mountebank came again. People were told that the cause of all the trouble was the "money power." What the people wanted the demagogues said, was more money. If the people owed debts they should not be compelled to pay them on time. In most States laws were enacted by which debts were suspended, or, through insolvency proceedings, altogether wiped out. The moral foundations on which economic civilization exists were being broken down.

Ohio, Pennsylvania, Maryland, Kentucky, Tennessee, Indiana and Illinois resolved to crush the monster, this "octopus," as it was called at that time. The way it was proposed to crush it was by taxation. Ohio put a tax of $50,000 on each of the two branches of the National Bank doing business in that State; Kentucky put a tax of $60,000 on each of its two branches; Illinois prohibited any bank not chartered under its State laws from doing business in the State. In Maryland, where the branch at Baltimore had been badly managed, perhaps criminally managed, there was passed a most extraordinary law, not only putting a tax on the branch, which it could well have paid, but providing that every piece of paper that went out of the bank should be stamped, and if it were not stamped then $500 must be paid for every offense. The result would have been absolutely confiscatory. The States said, in effect, to the National Government —You created your central bank but we will kill it; we will tax it out of existence.

The branch bank at Baltimore refused to pay that tax and the State Treasurer brought suit in the local Court at Baltimore against McCullough, Cashier of the Branch bank at Baltimore to collect the tax. The lower court decided, of course, in favor of the State of Maryland. It was taken to the Court of Appeals and, of course, the Court of Appeals decided in favor of the State of Maryland.

It was then taken by writ of error to the Supreme Court of the United States, and there, in 1819,—one of the great years in American history, for in that year John Marshall handed down those tablets of the law, the opinions in McCullough vs. Maryland, the Dartmouth College Case, and Sturgis vs. Crowninshield. Never in the history of the world have three such vital opinions been delivered by one judge in the same space of time. In one of these cases occurred that great argument, as important as any over the Constitution itself, which led to that fundamental State paper of John Marshall entitled his opinion in McCullough vs. Maryland. There are many lawyers, and I am one of the humbler among them, who think the opinion in McCullough vs. Maryland is second only to the Constitution of the United States itself.

The principal argument for the Nation, for national power, was made by William Pinkney, Joseph Storey sitting on the Bench at that time declared that it was worth going from Salem, Massachusetts, to Washington to hear that argument. The splendor of it! The majesty, the learning and sincerity! It was in that argument that the phrase of Lincoln, "Government of the people, by the people and for the people," was originated. I was reading it not long ago. It was put in a more diffuse form. In his opinion Marshall adopted it. Afterwards Webster in replying to Hayne condensed it still more; and finally Lincoln more tersely and in simpler form,—in a single sentence,— made it immortal.

If you read the opinion of Marshall you will see the argument of Pinkney stripped of his peculiar and florid rhetoric, which at that time was considered the height of eloquence. Marshall gave his opinion immediately. It was framed by him the year before under his trees in Richmond and in the Blue Ridge Mountains. Looking over the country, he saw the economic and moral breakdown, the chaos, the misery of the starvation of myriads of people all due to the disregard of our Constitutional foundations and economic law. So he gave that great chart of national well being. He said that ours is a Constitution designed to endure for ages to come—not a statute for particular occasions. Therefore, it has within it the power to meet rising situations and not merely the situation which existed when it was adopted. When anything is to be done which the Constitution authorizes Congress to do, it is in the discretion of Congress to select the means by which it shall be done.

It was at that point where he rose to that eloquence which attracted me as a law student when he said, "From the St. Croix to the Gulf of Mexico, from the Atlantic to the Pacific, armies must be raised and transported," and the business of the people done. This requires the transfer of money, and a bank is convenient for that purpose and therefore, the bank is authorized by the Constitution of the United States. The second point was that, since our National Government is supreme within its sphere of action, a

State cannot tax any agency of the National Government; and therefore, a tax such as that imposed by the State of Maryland and all the rest of them was unconstitutional.

That aroused the South tremendously. Hezekiah Niles in his "Weekly Register" published at Baltimore—by the way, Hezekiah Niles was the prototype of Horace Greeley and Niles' Register is our greatest historical source—in one of a series of articles said that the opinion of Marshall was more destructive to liberty than a foreign invasion. The "Register" was published at Baltimore, and it had more influence on American public opinion from 1811 to 1830 than any one other publication.

Down to Virginia the Republican machine, the foundation of which had been laid by Patrick Henry, and perfected by Thomas Jefferson, was triumphant under Spencer Roane. Spencer Roane, President of the Court of Appeals; Thomas Ritchie, Editor of the Enquirer, and that great man, statesman and soldier, now utterly forgotten, Colonel John Taylor of Caroline, were the triumvirate at the head of this machine; and they now began their attack.

Spencer Roane had great contempt for Marshall's learning. Colonel Taylor of Caroline wrote an extraordinary book called "Construction Construed; Constitutions Vindicated," in which he pointed out, as Randolph did later, that the principle announced by Marshall was destructive of State rights and that it gave the Federal Government power to free every slave in the Union—under Marshall's opinion the Northern financier would suck the life blood out of the people, and much more to the same effect.

Marshall was irritated. He was sensitive, and forgot himself so far as to reply in one of the longest, most verbose and dullest articles I have ever read in my life, published in the "Union," a Federalist paper of Philadelphia. I would not believe that he wrote that paper if I did not have the letters in his own hand saying he did write it.

Although civil war was inevitable from the moment

the Constitution was adopted, it may be said to have begun, in the clashing of irreconcilable views, when Marshall delivered his opinion in McCullough vs. Maryland. The Legislature of Marshall's own State passed resolutions coincident with the resolution on the Missouri question, in which it was said that Virginia would stand shoulder to shoulder with the people of Missouri in the defense of their mutually violated rights. A resolution, passed the same day, denounced the Supreme Court of the United States and proposed that, since there was no tribunal to settled disputes between the States and the Nation, a constitutional amendment should be adopted by which a new court should be created for that specific purpose.

So it was that Maryland entered into the determination of the fundamental nature of our Government. If it had not been for Marshall's opinion in McCullough vs. Maryland, this Nation could not have endured twenty years. But for that opinion of Marshall we could not have fought this last war. We could hardly have lifted our finger. So I called that opinion, as a young lawyer, in a speech delivered at the Bar Association at Pittsburgh, called it twenty years ago, "The Vitality of the Constitution," and I still think that a proper title for it.

The next case in which Maryland had a determinating voice was probably a feigned case. I again say you cannot understand the opinions of Marshall if you simply look at the legal points involved.

Cohens vs. Virginia was a police court case. Two itinerant peddlers of lottery tickets down in Norfolk, Virginia, sold eight half tickets in the Washington lottery. That was a lottery authorized by the City of Washington under its Charter from the National Government. You must remember that clear up to the last lottery decision, from way back in Colonial times, the lottery was a favorite method of raising money. When Marshall was in the Legislature of Virginia, he voted for many lotteries,—for churchyards, public schools and everything.

The City of Washington, in order to raise money
for municipal purposes, established the "Washington
Lottery." The two men who were arrested in Norfolk,
Virginia, I have always heard, although I cannot trace
it, were merely agents for the great bond house of
P. & J. Cohen of Baltimore, and they dealt in wild
cat paper and issued circulars which were sent
throughout the country. They were haled into Court
on information to the effect that they had been selling lottery tickets in violation of the law of Virginia,
which provided that anybody selling lottery tickets in
any lottery not authorized by the law of Virginia,
should be fined $100 for each offense. The case was
tried before the Burrough Court, consisting of the
Mayor and two or three justices of the peace, and the
Cohens were fined $100, the minimum. They could
have been fined $800; they could have been fined
the total amount of the lottery in Washington authorized to be raised, which was $10,000.

That was the Court of last resort, and an appeal
was taken from that to the Supreme Court of the
United States. That was in 1820, and the case came
up in 1821 for argument.

Two men appeared for the defense, Daniel B.
Ogden, the highest priced lawyer in the United States
next to William Pinkney, and William Pinkney himself, who at that time made more than $25,000 a
year, which would amount in currency today to
$250,000. They appeared for these two peddlers of
lotery tickets. The fee of either of these men would
have been a hundred times more than the sum involved. The fine of $100 would not have paid half
of Ogden's expenses from New York to Washington
and back. That is one reason for believing that the
case was feigned.

In his opinion, Marshall rose to heights of eloquence most unusual on the bench of justice. It was
magnificent. I used the words "Hebrew prophets" a
moment ago in trying to make a comparison. Sometimes his eloquence was almost emotional and if it
had been the mere case of the fining of two peddlers

in a police court case, if that was all there was to it, then his opinion was simply a piece of pompus rhetoric.

Let us draw back the curtains of history to a period twelve months before it was delivered. The men of the South—I honor the frankness and courage of those men of the South, although I am the son of a Union soldier; they were never bluffing; they meant what they said—rose on the floor of the House and the Senate and threatened war if the National Government exercised the power which Marshall said it had.

Senator Walker of Georgia said, "I close my eyes and I see by prophetic vision brothers' swords stained with brothers' blood." Another Senator said, "I see houses in flames and women and children in tears." In the House the language was still more violent,— spears, bludgeons and knives were springing up, they declared. When you listen to that terrible language you understand the stern passages, the exalted eloquence, of Marshall's opinion in McCullough vs. Maryland. You know to whom and to what his militant words were spoken.

You see embattled localism defying the power of the National Government, and then you realize the import of Marshall's tremendous passages in his mighty opinion in Cohens vs. Virginia, when he said that this is not a Government of States and sections, but a Government of and by and for all the people. It springs from them and it is made for them. In war we are one people, in commerce we are one people and in peace we are one people; and neither any section, nor any State, nor power, can defy or assail with impunity the Government of the Republic.

The case involved the question of whether or not the Courts of the Nation under the Constitution may revise the opinions of the Courts of the States. Virginia had said in her famous defiance in Martin vs. Hunters Lessees,—her whole Supreme Court had said,—that the Supreme Court of the United States, so far as Virginia was concerned, was a foreign tribunal; but William Pinkney in his argument crushed that and swept it away, as Storey said in describing his argument, "as with a mighty besom."

In short Pinkney's argument in that opinion, I repeat for the fourth time, was not merely a legal argument, but the outgiving of a great statesman whose mind was surcharged by patriotism and inspired with prophetic vision.

It may interest you to know something more about Marshall himself. We are interested in the personality of people who rise to eminence. We are interested to know what kind of clothes a great man wears and what he thinks and how he acts. Up to the time Fletcher vs. Peck was argued and his opinions delivered, Marshall's associates on the bench were fellow-partisans and had the same theories of government that Marshall so passionately maintained. But immediately after Marbury vs. Madison, the first vacancy on the Bench was filled by William Johnson of South Carolina, a powerful man and a Republican from the bottom up, a man placed there by Jefferson. The Associate Justices from that time on appointed by Jefferson, Madison, Monroe, clear down to the time of Jackson, were appointed for the purpose of checking John Marshall; at least that was one motive. Jefferson in one of his letters said, in urging an appointment to fill a vacancy caused by Justice Cushing's death, "It will be difficult to find a man who will be able to hold his own on the Bench with John Marshall."

So, after the case of Fletcher vs. Peck, Marshall was surrounded by men a majority of whom were of opposite political opinions to his own, and placed there for the purpose of overthrowing his views and statesmanship. Notwithstanding that weighty fact he continued to exercise an influence over his associates placed there for the purpose of checking him,—an influence as great as that exercise over his fellow partisans.

How did that occur? Here was the most extraordinary case in the history of the world where one man apparently hypnotized his powerful associates whose aim was not to be hypnotized. What was the reason? They called it "Marshall's court" in those days. What is the reason he was able to bring all of his associates on the Bench, some from the South, too, to his views in McCullough vs. Maryland? How was it he was able to bring his political opponents and associates on the Bench to agree with him and thus make his opinions unanimous in that mighty thunderbolt of his statesmanship in his opinion n Cohens vs. Vrginia?

In the assault on Marshall in Virginia and other States, Spencer Roane, Thomas Ritchie and Colonel John Taylor denounced as "apostate" these Republicans on the Bench with Marshall. They called them "those turncoats" on the Bench. Now what was the source of Marshall's amazing power? It was not his mentality only, because Storey was not much inferior to Marshall in that respect, and neither was Johnson. He had not much learning, whereas Storey and Johnson were learned lawyers. Neither was it Marshall's will power, because the writers of the times show that these other associates on the Bench were as determined as he.

What was it? His personality! That is what it was. In order to show the manner of man that he was, I think I can best do it by relating a little bit about his personal life. He was like Moses in this: The Bible said Moses was the meekest of men, and that was true of Marshall. There was no pretense about him. He had a great native dignity which exuded from him. You would not think he was common. He was gentle and tender and adored women. In that respect he was like Abraham Lincoln, as in many other respects.

If Marshall had lived in these days he would be for women suffrage. One of the most marked things about him was his devotion to his wife. It was most extraordinary and something which I like to speak about whenever I have an opportunity.

Within a year after their marriage Mary Ambler became an invalid, and although they lived together fifty years, she suffered all that time from a nervous malady; a disease of the nervous system which at times seemed to affect her mind. She was sensitive to any little noises, and they would tend to throw her into nervous distress.

I was told by an old citizen of Richmond, who was very well acquainted with men who used to see the Chief Justice frequently, that upon entering his house, he would take off his shoes and put on carpet slippers so as not to make a noise to disturb his wife. At night if a hog grunted or a cow made a noise or a dog barked, it would excite her very much, and Marshall would rise from his bed without putting on his shoes and go downstairs and drive the animal blocks away, in order that his wife might not be disturbed.

She was, of course, incapable of taking care of the house. He hired a housekeeper, Betsy Munkins, and his account book shows his payments by the month. When the house needed cleaning he would induce his wife to take a long drive with her mother or sister around the quiet roads of Richmond, and when the carriage was out of sight Marshall would throw off his coat and vest and roll up his shirt sleeves and place a bandana handkerchief about his head and gather the servants and help as well as direct them in the cleaning of the house.

There was no pretense about it. Marshall's reverence for women was remarked by all who knew him and it resembled more the manners found in the age of chivalry than anyone else.

The books he liked to read were novels and poetry. He wrote a letter to Storey that as soon as he resigned from the Bench, he was going to have fun reading poetry and novels and do nothing else as long as he lived. He hated to read law books.

He was a convivial man and he would drink cheering liquids—but then so did everybody else in those days. When we read of the performances of men like Jefferson in that line it can hardly be understood in these days. . . .

Marshall was very much addicted, as I said, to

having a good time even as a young man. I have Marshall's account book,—not very well kept—but it shows different items of his expenditures. It is the book in which Marshall wrote law notes when he was in college, and kept his accounts after he got married. It shows not a very brisk law practice at first. It shows money lost at whist and bacgammon; a good deal for wine, beer and whiskey. Convention might be shocked at the entry of the large quantity of wine and whiskey bought, but this must not be misunderstood, since at that time it was a universal custom.

When he was in the House, the Speaker of the House wrote a letter in which he said of this amazing young man from the South, 'We cannot do anything without him; he has tremendous power; is agreeable and of highly marked conviviality, and sometimes rather drowsy in the forenoon."

He was a great wit. People think Marshall drank a great deal more than was reasonable. Perhaps the amount would be considered excessive now; but it was nothing in comparison with what Washington or Jefferson drank. A young and brilliant Frenchman came over during the Revolutionary War, and he was with Washington while the war was going on. He tells what happened at luncheon—the toasts drunk and all that. The young Frenchman had to go up and lie down at half-past two o'clock. Then he visited Jefferson. He said that Jefferson after dinner had a bowl of punch brought out, and finally, after drinking of the punch they got to discussing Ossian. Chartellux tells about it without emphasis, just as you would say, It is a pleasant day. He seemed to think there was nothing remarkable about it. He said that "between the bowl and the book the night stole insensibly upon us."

I hardly understood how this punch could have the effect it was said to have had until I found out the recipe for it. It was the same punch that was used at the Quoit Club at Richmond to which Marshall belonged. The Richmond Light Infantry Blues used the punch for many years—clear down to the

Civil War. It was made of rum, brandy, whiskey, madeira, sherry and lemons—no water. A New England preacher attended one meeting of the Quoit Club as a guest. He said they were very abstemious; they had nothing but that punch, a toddy maybe,—but not a drop of champagne.

Here is a story given me by Senator McDonald. He said that it had been handed down through two generations of lawyers. It took me months to trace it. I did finally find the foundations of it in a letter from Storey to his wife.

The story is like this, and it has some historical foundation. It appears some talk got out about the Justices of the Supreme Court drinking too much. They all lived at the same house in Washington. They did not bring their wives to Washington with them, as the accommodations were frightful. They boarded together at 2-1/2 Street, called Marshall Place. That house still stands. They lived together like a sort of family and discussed their cases all the time; but they had every Saturday as "consultation day" at the Capital.

There came to be a little talk about the Justices drinking too much, even then. So Marshall said—I tell this to illustrate his quick wit—"Now, gentlemen, I think that with your consent I will make it a rule of this Court that hereafter we will not drink anything on consultation day,—that is, except when it rains." The next consultation day—I think the Court went on the water wagon during the week—when they assembled Marshall said to Storey, "Will you please step to the window and look out and examine this case and see if there is any sign of rain." Storey looked out the window, but there was not a sign of rain. . . . He came back and seriously said to the Chief Justice, who was waiting for the result, "Mr. Chief Justice, I have very carefully examined this case, I have to give it as my opinion that there is not the slightest sign of rain." Marshall said, "Justice Storey, I think that is the shallowest and most illogical opinion I have ever heard you deliver; you forget that our jurisdiction is as broad as this Republic, and by the laws of nature, it must be raining some place in our jurisdiction. Waiter, bring on the rum."

That also gives you some picture of the times. Marshall adored these social gatherings. He was invited one night to a social company at Philadelphia, which was held in a room at a tavern, and the place of meeting was across the hallway from the bar room. Marshall was late in coming in and when he came in they were playing an old game called Paradox. They give you a word and you must immediately make a verse on it, and this verse must be a paradox. When Marshall came in the bar room door was open. He merely looked in the bar room, and he saw in there some people whom he knew who lived in Kentucky, and he saw the fellows from Kentucky drinking whiskey and so on. He looked in, and then he walked into the adjoining room. The door was open and, instantly, he was told, "Mr. Chief Justice, your word is paradox." He had to make a paradox on it. Marshall looked across the room and saw the Kentuckians drinking whiskey in the bar room—this is the origin of that old doggeral you have heard before—and he said:

> "In the blue grass region of Kentucky,
>   This paradox was born,
> There the corn is full of kernels,
>   And the Colonels full of corn."

He was most social in his habits; but he wore very bad clothes. His clothes, Mrs. Carrington, his sister-in-law, said, often brought a blush to his wife's face. Sometimes he would not fasten his shoes. There is a description of him as Chief Justice sitting in the bar of the Court and talking, joking and laughing with the lawyers and telling stories. There he would sit, with his hair matted and uncombed, his clothes wrinkled and utterly unpretentious.

He was utterly negligent of his appearance wholly unconscious how he looked. And yet, how impressive and genuine was the man's profound dignity! He did not wear his heart on his sleeve,—no one ever dared to presume on John Marshall. The instant the time came for him to open Court, a transformation came over him and, clad in the robes of his great office, with the Associate Justices on either side of him, Charlemange on his throne never was more majestic than John Marshall.

Down at Richmond he liked to loaf around and go to market. He liked to find out what people were saying. There are several stories in regard to that, which I have spent a good deal of time in authenticating. One day a young man who had lately come to town and knew of Marshall but did not know him personally, saw an old and shabbily clad man hanging around the market. Everybody generally in that day had a negro to take the marketing home. This young man didn't see any negro, but he saw Marshall and said to him—he had purchased a turkey—"Old man, will you take my turkey home for me." Marshall said, "Yes," and when he got there the young man said, "Here is a copper for you, old man;" Marshall said, "Thank you." Of course, the story got around and the whole town roared with laughter.

Another time he called on the wife of a relative— she had never met him. She was expecting a butcher to call, as her husband wished to sell a calf. As she looked out she saw Marshall approaching, and she said, "Yes, that is the butcher," and she told the servant to send him to the stable in the rear of the house, where the calf was.

He was a person who made it extremely easy for people to agree with him; and if you agreed with him it pleased him. It was very hard to disagree with him. I tell you this to show to you the manner of man he was; for behind all this kindness, all this conviviality, all this apparent negligence, the mighty mind was as clear as sunlight and the unshakable will like a mighty rock.

At the boarding house where all the Justices who were associated with him lived, Marshall was as much the head of a family as he was the head of a Court. And that explains the influence which this amazing man exercised over his associates.

I have been struck by the resemblance between him and Lincoln. They were alike in mental qualities. Their method of reasoning was precisely the same. Take the Freeholder questions and answers when Marshall was a candidate for Congress and Lincoln's debate with Douglas, and put them down, and you would think the same hand wrote them. Both were managers of men. The process by which Lincoln handled his Cabinet was the same used by Marshall with his associates on the Bench.

They were physically alike except in face and eye. Lincoln's face was large and his eyes were blue; Marshall's face was small and his eyes were dark brown and very brilliant. If today you could see out here Lincoln and Marshall walking across the street—both were the same height, awkward, long and angular—you would say they were two brothers from the country. So if you can imagine Abraham Lincoln sitting on the Bench of the Supreme Court of the United States you will have a good idea of Marshall.

The great contribution which Marshall made to this country was the establishment of the principle of nationalism. The second was even deeper, and that was the creation of a steadying and stabilizing force in our democracy. We do not know yet whether the experiment of democracy will be a success. We hear laudation of the unwritten Constitution of Great Britain. Her perils are just ahead of her. We cannot say what her future shall be; but this we do know, that, according to the principles of mechanics as well as of human nature, unless there is a stabilizing influence as in the engine, a differential, unless you provide for that it will fly to pieces. It will fly to pieces unless there is a stabilizing force. There must be something which will enable the people to pause until their sober second thought operates, that will hold them away from the final irrevocable act until the period of emotion is over. . . .

Marshall died believing that all he had done had been destroyed. He saw, at the end, associates on the Bench who, it seemed, were determined to overthrow all the doctrines he had established. He saw his own mandate in the State of Georgia flouted and defied. He saw one of the most popular and one of the most dictatorial Presidents, Jackson, denounce and defy him. He went to the grave thinking that all his effort to establish order and stability in our democracy was destroyed. He could not see that he had set in motion mighty forces that no other man, except himself, had the vision to comprehend, no other man of his time.

[1] For an interesting account of the life of Albert J. Beveridge and a review of his life of John Marshall, see, Douglas H. Gardon, "John Marshall: The Fourth Chief Justice", 41 A. B. A. J. 698 (1955).

JOHN MARSHALL AND THE CAMPAIGN
OF HISTORY†

Max Lerner

The following article by the well known political theorist,
Max Lerner, evaluates the contributions of John Marshall
through his constitutional decisions primarily from an economic background. All footnotes, except for citations to decisions, from this article have been omitted by the editor for
lack of space, but this has in no way impaired this excellent
paper. This article is reprinted with permission of the Columbia University Law Review.

> Remembering that you cannot separate a man from his
> place, [I] remember also that there fell to Marshall
> perhaps the greatest place that ever was filled by a judge.

─────

1. *The Education of John Marshall*

John Marshall's first act when he became Chief Justice was at once characteristic and ominous. He
changed the established practise, borrowed from England, by which each justice in turn delivered his
opinion on a case, and he substituted for it "the Court"
or "the unanimous Court" speaking through a single
member, usually himself. He wanted to present to the
world the serried ranks of a united Court. And he
was for thirty-five years to cast over his associates on
the bench a spell whose persuasiveness seemed to his
contemporaries almost diabolical. The Supreme Court
had been in existence for twelve years before Marshall
came on the bench. It had had three chief-justices; it
contained able lawyers like Jay and Iredell; forceful
personalities like James Wilson. Yet Marshall might
well have said at his death that he found the Supreme
Court a straggling group of lawyers and left it an institution and a power.

The shambling but iron-willed Richmond lawyer
who was to preside over the Supreme Court from
1801 to 1835 did not seem earmarked by fate to play
his great role. He was a frontier boy, born in 1755 on

─────

† Reprinted with the permission of the publisher from
20 *Columbia Law Review* 396 (1939).

a small backwoods farm in western Virginia, but of
good proprietary stock. His education was a frontier
education; its economic horizon was bounded by the
self-sufficient backwoods plantation; his moral ideas
were those inculcated by upright parents, based on
self-improvement and steeled by the rigors of their
venture. On his father's side he came of humble stock,
but his father was a sturdy competent person who
stood out in the backwoods counties, served in the
Virginia Legislature and on his death left his children
large stretches of land. On his mother's side he came
of country gentry and tolerably high Scottish nobility.

A consciousness of property and of the owning
classes as the basis of social order came quite easily to
the alert mind of a normal boy, descended of proprietary stock and brought up in a high-minded home.
On the frontier the educational agency was not the
school but the family. Marshall's formal schooling
throughout his life amounted to less than two years,
including a year with a family tutor. He embibed
every homily that an idealistic family environment
could impress on him—of law and order, of moral
uprightness, personal loyalty and sturdy independence, of respect for authority and the identification
of authority with respectability. Being self-taught he
developed the resourcefulness and the wide sweep
that often characterize self-taught people, but also
their narrow self-confidence and dogmatism. To this
was added an innate sense of purpose and an unruffled
consciousness of stature that were to make of him the
dominating personality so magnetic to friends and
terrifying to opponents. His very insulation from formal teaching cut him off from influences that might
otherwise have crashed through the shell of his self-
sufficiency—separated him from the effective if rare
mind of the mature teacher or the iconoclasm of fel-
low-students. He never outgrew his provincialism. He
never acquired the cosmopolitan tastes of a Jefferson
or a Franklin. For the English mind, with its dour
insularity, he had some liking. But he found himself
ill at ease in French thought.

His reading was family-selected and re-enforced the compulsions of property and authority. By the age of twelve he had copied out Pope's *Essays on Man* and knew most of it from memory. At seventeen he read Blackstone's *Commentaries* assiduously with his father, who had subscribed to the volume less on his own account than that of his son. During the debates on the ratification of the Constitution he studied carefully the *Federalist Papers*, and we know him to have been greatly influenced by Hamilton's reasoning. While he was practising law at Richmond he read, as did every fervent Federalist, Burke's *Reflections on the French Revolution*, and in his *Life of Washington* he reproduces an essentially Burkian view of the impact of Jacobin ideas on the American mind. Marshall was not a man of extensive reading, although Story assures us in his *Memoirs* of his friend that he cared a good deal for literature and we know that later in life he liked Jane Austen's novels. But while his genius was not bookish, the three English writers he read in his formative years left an unmistakable mark on his thinking.

That they did so is of some moment. Pope's poem has a political content: it "depicts the universe as a species of constitutional monarchy"; from it Marshall could get his individualistic psychology, of a world ruled by egoism restrained by reason; his sense of "general laws" as governing human conduct; and an ethical bolstering for his authoritarian conservatism ("whatever is, is right"). Blackstone was of the tough and crabbed English tradition of a tenacious concern for property. He was the legal theorist of a landed aristocracy that felt its power slipping and sought to retain its hold by entrenching itself behind legal earthworks. As for Burke, he was a gigantic figure whose genius it was to translate a morbid hatred of change into undying political theory, and whose defense of the existing order was more compact of passion than any revolutionary attack upon it could be. In these writers—poet, lawyer, political theorist—was stored up the heritage of conservative English thought which was to pass through Marshall's mind into the fabric of American constitutional law.

In such an education the Revolutionary War was a curious interlude, a sort of shadow-play in which Marshall went gallantly through all the motions of a minor young hero, experienced Valley Forge, and came home to Virginia to be idolized by the girls. Marshall was young when the war came and scarcely more than stripling when it was ended. He had caught up the revolutionary contagion with the sensitive energies of youth; but he was quickly responsive to the ebbing of the revolutionary fervor in the leaders whom he followed—men like Washington and Hamilton, who were his archetypal heroes. It was natural in the turbulent years of the Confederation that he should, with them, be dismayed at the agrarian unrest; natural that he should be alarmed at the prospect of a military revolution becoming a social revolution—or worse, a Jacquerie; natural that he should be anxious for the creation of a strong constitutional government to keep it within bounds; natural that he should become a Federalist although a Virginian; natural, later in life, that he should repudiate "the wild and enthusiastic notions" of his youth and wonder that he should ever have entertained them.

His political career up to the time he became Chief Justice was solid and eventful if not distinguished. He settled in Richmond to practise law; became a member of the Virginia Legislature; fought valiantly for the Constitution in the Virginia ratifying convention; served a term in Congress; went to France on the unfortunate but eventually highly publicized X Y Z mission; was a member of John Adam's ill-starred cabinet, serving in the last years as Secretary of State and working heroically to rally the remnants of the badly beaten and demoralized Federalist forces. For a time it looked as if Marshall were only a second-string Federalist politician, caught like the other Federalists in a blind alley of history.

He had much in common with them. His class roots were theirs, although his disarming democratic ways, casting a spell over his biographers, have tended to obscure that fact. He was outwardly the frontiersman —a charming, gangling Virginian, rustic and unpretentious in his manner, simple in his tastes, careless and even unkempt in his clothes. An entire mythology has grown up around all the little tender and mildly heterodox ways in which the great Chief Justice half-outraged and half-titillated his friends by forgetting the dignity of his position. Remove this surface and we might with entire clarity view Marshall as we view Fisher Ames or Alexander Hamilton—as a conscious and clean-cut representative of the owning class, the aristocratic temperament and English political theory. Marshall, it is true, was no New England Brahman or New York fashionable. But he was actually a man of substance, with a deep personal and psychological stake in property. He stood heir, by descent, to a long proprietary tradition; he grew accustomed to regard himself one of the possessors of the earth; he continued this tradition, bought huge landed properties, and was always up to his neck in suits over land titles. By marriage too he had become related to landowners, speculators, and financiers. His business and political connections were with the men of funds and funded income, the lawyers and *rentiers,* the landowners and speculators, the shipbuilders, the merchants and manufacturers. Marshall's habits were molded in the back country of Virginia and among the impoverished farmers who made up Washington's ragged little army at Valley Forge; but his social theory was fashioned among the lawyers at Richmond, and the wealthy planters who travelled there to litigate land titles, and the Brahmans and tie-wigs of the New England financial aristocracy with whom Marshall threw in his political fortunes. You have here only the lag that you will find in many a man between his boyhood conditionings and his manhood maturities. The boyhood patterns linger on, outliving their utility or even their congruity, like the college-boy folkways in the chairman of a finance board, or a debutante whimsy in a dowager of fifty.

In several respects Marshall's career was a good preparation for his work on the Supreme Court. His political experience did him no harm: like Taney after him, he illustrated the general rule that the great justices have also been skillful politicians. He gained a sense of political realities and an adroitness in manipulating them. As the ranking member of the cabinet during the last demoralized years of the Adams administration, he practically ran the government and the campaign of 1800 as well. He grew accustomed to handling large political issues in an audacious way, he mastered the technique of the devious attack and the stretegic retreat, he learned the grand manner in politics. His talents were long in maturing. They proved substantial rather than brilliant. He was at his best, as he showed both on the French mission and in the Adams cabinet, in a small group where he could bring to bear the massive influence of his personality.

Much has been made of Marshall's nationalist feeling, especially by his biographer, Senator Beveridge, who uses it to pattern Marshall's entire career. For others as well it seems to be the far-off divine event toward which, as toward a fatality, the whole of Marshall's life moved. The logic goes somewhat as follows: Marshall as a boy lives in a backwoods region immune against the fierce localism of the Virginia planters; Valley Forge burns into his consciousness the heroic character of the national effort; in the Virginia ratifying convention his zeal for national unity is whetted by the attacks upon it and the hazardous margin by which it is saved; as a member of the French mission he is stirred to the depths by the contempt of Talleyrand for a weak and divided American nationality; as Secretary of State he bears the brunt of foreign negotiations, feeling keenly our inferior bargaining and coercive power; finally as Chief Justice he welcomes the chance to strengthen the Constitution as the symbol of national power against the claims of state sovereignty.

The pattern does not lack persuasiveness. In fact, it is a tribute to the ultimate triumph of Marshall's nationalism that we, who think and write in the shadow of it, accept it so unquestioningly as the rationale of his career. Coleridge once remarked that "every original writer must create the taste by which he is appreciated." Thus also every great figure in the history of political thought helps create the institutional and intellectual climate in which his thinking comes to be ratified.

Nevertheless we must not conclude that nationalism was the *primum mobile* of Marshall's being. It must be remembered that he was to show himself, on the bench, the best of the Federalist strategists. And nationalism, however fatefully it may have been rooted in his personality, was above all good strategy. Marshall learned this primarily from his experience on the X Y Z mission. He came home to find himself a national hero, toasted everywhere. The French had insulted our national pride, and the insult was skilfully publicized by the Federalists. Marshall learned that the common man, who would not respond to Federalist aristocratic theory, would respond to the same property interests when they were clothed in the rhetoric of the national interest. It was a crucial discovery and Marshall was to make the most of it on the judicial front, where in the name of nationalism he was to fight the battles of the properties groups.

Nor must we be confused by Marshall's apparent libertarianism. That too, like his nationalism, was probably sincere enough. Marshall carried over the English constitutional tradition. He thought of himself as a fighter for liberty, and drew his inspiration from the struggle against Tudor and Stuart despotism. There is in every man, even the inveterate Tory, a desire to associate himself with some ringing defiance, to attempt a Promethean struggle against the unjust ruling divinities. Marshall saw himself in combat against the legislative and executive tyranny of Jeffersonian democracy, and he must be accorded his vision of himself. He was full of forebodings about the future; his letters throughout his judicial career breathe a dark pessimism. It was his fate to come to the fore in the councils of the Federalist party in the declining years of the Adams administration. He must be seen symbolically as the dying Federalist who, out of the reckless strength of that dying, made the way safe for the path of American capitalism.

When John Adams in those fateful closing days of his administration looked about at the political terrain, he saw the Federalists defeated and fleeing everywhere before the new legions of Jeffersonian democracy. Only the judiciary remained. The Federalists "have retired into the judiciary as a stronghold," wrote Jefferson in what has become a famous prediction, "and from that battery all the works of republicanism are to be beaten down." There can be no doubt that Jefferson saw clearly. And there can be little doubt that Marshall was a party to the Federal councils and plans. Happily for the Federalists the Chief-Justiceship of the Supreme Court fell vacant. When Adams sought one man after another to fill it, he was playing perhaps unwittingly with American destiny. When finally he told Marshall that nothing remained but to send his name to the Senate that destiny was fulfilled. For Marshall, able as he was, never really found himself until he reached the Court. And the Court was where he belonged. The task before him was an unusual one, but he brought an unusual equipment. For his mind was not that of the great lawyers of history, with their heavy erudition, their tortuousness, their narrow legalism, but the mind of a man of action with its powerful concentration on a single purpose. He had mastered the art of finality. He possessed a large resourcefulness in the service of a singular tenacity of purpose. He was to be a magnificent dictator, dwarfing and uniting his colleagues, polarizing around himself as a dominant personality the forces that were later to be institutionalized in judicial review.

He seems miraculously to have turned up in history just at the point where a rising capitalism most needed him. So near a miracle does this seem I am ready to pardon Senator Beveridge his four volumes of ecstasy and hosannas. Yet Justice Holmes seemed nearer the truth. "A great man," he said of Marshall, "represents . . . a strategic point in the campaign of history, and part of his greatness consists of his being there." Marshall's role was to effect a nexus between the property interests under an expanding industrialism and the judicial power under a federal system of government. He was to be the strategic link between capitalism and constitutionalism. And for occupying that position in the campaign of history his education and the nature of his mind fitted him superbly. Rarely in American history has the exterior tension of events been matched so completely by an interior tension of preparation and purpose on the part of the exactly right man.

2. *Counter-Revolution and Judicial Supremacy*

There was a grim irony in the fact that Thomas Jefferson, riding the crest of the revolutionary wave of 1800, was sworn into office by John Marshall, his arch-enemy and the arch-enemy of his doctrine. That tense moment represented the climax of one struggle—the political-economic struggle between Federalists and Republicans, and the beginning of another—the judicial-economic struggle between the vested interests and the common man.

The owning classes were in a panic. Their defeat at the polls made it imperative for them to draft their best leadership for the crucial judicial battles to come. Marshall had been designated for the most strategic post. In 1798 he had refused to become an Associate Justice of the Court; in 1801, when the Federalists had been ousted both from the Presidency and Congress, he had no choice as a party-man but to accept the Chief-Justiceship. The necessity he yielded to was the last-ditch necessity of the Federalist propertied groups. As soon as he was on the Court he moved swiftly to his purpose. "The Democrats", he wrote to Pinkney on the morning of the inauguration, and the solemnity of the occasion should have made him weigh his words, "the Democrats are divided into speculative theorists and absolute terrorists. With the latter I am disposed to class Mr. Jefferson." This version of Mr.

Jefferson seems to have influenced the historians as
well, for the early part of Marshall's incumbency is
generally characterized as "Jefferson's attack on the
Judiciary." In reality it may with fully as much justice be called the judiciary's attack on Jefferson. Marshall's appointment was only part, if the most important part, of an extended Federalist plan embracing
the passage of the Judiciary Act of 1801, the creation
of new judgeships, and the eventual affirmation of the
power of judicial review.

Jefferson was no inconsiderate opponent. He had a
well-disciplined party machine, he controlled mass
opinion, and he was himself a supple and seasoned
warrior in this sort of battle. For all his revolutionary
talk he was no revolutionist. He had come into office
on a popular landslide. The enemy was beaten and
demoralized. Yet his Inaugural Address was an ad-
mixture of sweetness and light, and breathed a honied
humility. "We are all Federalists," he said, "we are all
Republicans." But before he had been half a year in
office he had determined to change his tone. Charles
Beard found among the Jefferson manuscripts the last
draft of his message to Congress in December 1801
before the final revision. It included a statement of
the doctrine of the separation of powers in as sharp a
form as was to be found in the Kentucky resolutions;
the right of each branch of the government to inter-
pret the Constitution after its best lights; his intent
to declare the Sedition laws of he previous administration unconstitutional and void. While admitting
that the Supreme Court as a coordinate branch could
check the power of the other branches of government,
the message would nevertheless have denied that the
Court had the exclusive right of construing the Constitution. Jefferson had already signed this draft when
at the last moment he lost heart, struck out the entire
passage, and wrote in the margin for posterity: "This
whole passage was omitted as capable of being chic-
aned, and furnishing something to the opposition to
make a handle of." Henry Adams, writing before this
draft of the message was known nevertheless lays the

blame for Marshall's victory on Jefferson himself and the fact that he faltered in his determination to crush his most dangerous opponent. He might, writes Adams, have had Congress declare the Alien and Sedition laws unconstitutional; he might have asked for an annulment of the dangerous Section 25 of the Judiciary Act of 1789. He might even, although that would have been more risky, have had a constitutional amendment passed giving the judges a fixed tenure of years—four or six—renewable by the President and the Senate. In fact, this was the suggestion that Jefferson finally made, desperate and defeated, four years before he died, when he understood more fully the extent of Marshall's victory.

Not daring the larger plan, Jefferson dared the lesser. He moved to have Congress repeal the Judiciary Act of February 13, 1801, which had reorganized the lower federal courts, creating additional circuit judgeships and filling them with staunch Federalists. He could count on a congressional majority. He could count even more on popular opinion, which was already militantly aroused against the highly partisan charges by the judges to the jury in cases involving the Sedition Act. It must be remembered that the excesses of the French Revolution had produced an anti-Radical scare, and that the Federalists had sought in the Alien and Sedition acts to use that scare as an instrument against Jeffersonianism. The victory of Jefferson at the polls showed how crude the Federalist tactic had been. The Jeffersonians now moved along two lines to undo the work of the Federalists. They sought the repeal of the Judiciary Act, and they moved for the impeachment of the more blatantly partisan judges. The first line of action reached its climax in the "Great Judiciary Debate" in the Senate, in January 1802; the second in the impeachment proceedings against Justice Chase in January and February of 1805. Between these two came the memorable decision in *Marbury* v. *Madison*[1] in 1803.

The Great Judiciary Debate of 1802 furnished the stage setting for *Marbury* v. *Madison*. The problem

of judicial review was no new problem when Marshall
came on the scene. It had been quietly volcanic since
colonial times. The Federalists, fearing the majority
sentiment, had hitherto not dared face the issue. Seeing themselves swept out of power, however, by the
"revolutionary" wave of 1800, there was nothing for
them to do but fall back on their last line of defense.
Of Jefferson it may be said that he did not so much
fear the judiciary as hate the Federalists. He saw that
the Federalists had retreated behind judicial entrench-
ments, had passed a last-minute act reorganizing the
judiciary, had created new circuit judgships and filled
them with the bitterest diehard Republican-haters
they could find in the country. When he saw this, he
knew what he wanted. He proceeded to move for the
repeal of the act and the offices. John Taylor of
Carolina, the official philosopher of the Jeffersonian
party, furnished him with a proper rationalization. It
is true, he said, writing to Breckenridge of Kentucky,
the leader of the Jeffersonian forces in the Senate, that
the Constitution guarantees judicial tenure during
good behavior. But that means only so long as the
office itself exists. Which Governeur Morris, with Federalist unkindness, rephrased as follows: "You shall
not take the man from the office but you may take the
office from the man; you may not drown him, but you
may sink his boat under him."

All of which on both sides, in the face of the actual
vote-counting, was only talk. In the debate the Federalists for the first time in our history openly and
insistently claimed for the judiciary the final and
exclusive power of interpreting the Constitution; some
of the Republicans restated the extreme states'-rights
doctrine of the Kentucky Resolution, others steered
shy of discussion. The Federalists did the best talking,
but the Republicans had the votes. The act was repealed and the stage was set.

The stage was set, but not even the Federalist claque
could have forseen the brilliance and audacity with
which their leading actor would play his part. John
Marshall hated Jefferson as he hated no other man in

the world: but he respected his strength. Jefferson had talked soft in his Inaugural, but he was willing to use the Big Stick and was obviously moving to dislodge the Federalists from the judiciary. Congress had repealed the Federalist act of reorganizaion; and, as if to twist the knife in the wound, had provided also that the Supreme Court was not to meet until February of the following year (1803). To be sure, Jefferson might have increased the Supreme Court and packed it with Republicans, and had refrained: but there was already talk of impeaching some of the more extreme Federalist judges. Marshall had to move swiftly and with daring. The Marbury case gave him his chance.

The case of poor Marbury (if he was poor Marbury; he may merely have been acting as a Federalist stooge) was raked by the cross fires of Federalist and Republican *Machtpolitik*. Marshall was faced at once by an opportunity and a dilemma. It was a God-sent chance which he had—to administer a rebuke to Jefferson, assert officially the judicial power that the Federalists had claimed in the debates, and place the judiciary in a position of control. This was the strategic moment: not to use it would be tantamount to defeat. Yet how to use it to advantage? If Marshall denied Marbury's claim to his office it would be an admission of judicial powerlessness. But if he upheld it, Jefferson (through Madison) would simply refuse to comply. He might say what Jackson is reputed to have said thirty years later, "John Marshall has made his decision, now let him enforce it," and thus make Marshall and the Court a laughing-stock.

Marshall solved his problem. By a maneuver he managed to administer a public spanking to the administration, assert judicial supremacy, yet leave Jefferson helpless to strike back. Marbury's commission, he said, was a valid one; even without the delivery of the document he had a vested right in it which it was the function of "a government of laws and not of men" to protect; having a right, he had also a remedy, which was mandamus. But the Supreme

Court, by its reading of the Constitution, could issue such a writ only where it has appellate and not original jurisdiction; and Section 13 of the Judiciary Act of 1789 which sought to confer original jurisdiction on the Court was therefore unconstitutional.

It mattered little to Marshall that if his conclusion was valid and the Court had no jurisdiction, everything before it was superfluous—a vast *obiter dictum* that was sheer political maneuver. It mattered little to him that none of the opposing counsel had argued that the section of the Judiciary Act was unconstitutional, and that in order to declare it so he had to wrench it beyond all principles of statutory interpretation. He was setting the classic example of what has since come to be called "judicial statesmanship." He made each of his purposes play in superbly with the others. He had disarmingly picked a portion of a Federalist statute to declare unconstitutional; and he had picked one beyond the reach of the Executive— one whose application depended upon the judiciary itself. There was, moreover, a movement afoot in the Jeffersonian Congress to capitalize on the popular feeling against the lower Federal judges, and abolish the lower courts entirely, parceling out their functions among the Supreme Court and the state courts. Marshall sought to quell this movement by asserting the finality of the Supreme Court's decisions on all matters of jurisdiction. There is no point in blaming him. It was the formative period of the American political structure, when every important move was decisive for later power configurations. Legalisms did not count: what counted was the daring, decisive *coup*.

From a legalistic standpoint alone, *Marbury* v. *Madison* has a nightmarish fascination. If ever the history of the Court is written with the proper cosmic irony, here will be the cream of the jest. Upon this case, as legal precedents, rests the power of judicial review. Yet every part of its reasoning has been repudiated even by conservative commentators and by later Supreme Court decisions, which none the less continue to exercise the power it first claimed. "Noth-

ing remains of *Marbury* v. *Madison,*" writes Professor
J. A. C. Grant, "except its influence." Everything else
has been whittled away. But its influence continues
to grin at us from the Cimmerian darkness like the
disembodied smile of the Cheshire cat.

It remains to ask how much *Marbury* v. *Madison,*
and through it Marshall, contributed to judicial review. Marshall did not originate it, nor did he single-
handedly succeed in establishing it beyond all dis-
lodgement. There are historians who give too much
credit both to the originality and the decisiveness of
his achievement. There are precedents for judicial
review, both in the colonial and the English decisions,
that stretch into the shadowy past. As for reasoning,
Marshall's argument added nothing substantial to the
argument of the Federalists in the Great Debate of
1802. Ultimately, the whole of the theory may be
found in No. 78 of the *Federalist,* written by Hamilton; in fact, much of Marshall's entire career may be
summed up as a process of reading Hamilton's state
papers and dissertations into the Constitution. And
yet his having translated these ideas into judicial
action is Marshall's decisive achievement.

As for the permanence of his work, I find much in
Louis B. Boudin's forceful contention that judicial
review as we know it is primarily a post-Civil War
creation, and that *Marbury* v. *Madison* decided only
the Court's power to determine its own jurisdiction.
And yet the permanence of Marshall's work is not to
be judged wholly in legalistic terms. The influence of
the case went far beyond its strict legal effect. Everything that the Court drew upon after the Civil War
in completing judicial review is already to be found
in Marshall's opinion. Marshall found judicial review
a moot question: he left it an integral part of the
constitutional fabric. And while the Court did not
again use judicial review against Congress ("national"
judicial review) until the *Dred Scott* case, more than
half a century later, it was because in all economic
matters the property interests favored expanding the
national power. Where judicial review was used ef-

fectively during this period was against state power
("federal" judicial review). In these decisions the reasoning of *Marbury* v. *Madison* and the increased
strength and prestige of the Supreme Court worked
powerfully. Marshall's role in this entire process was
to give judicial review a foothold, use it for the immediate interests of the capitalism of his day, tie it up
with the powerful appeal of nationalism, and entrench
it where a later stage of capitalism could take it up
and carry it further for its own purposes.

Marshall's decision has been described as a revolutionary *coup*. That it was daring and ultimately
decisive there can be little doubt. But it would be a
mistake to see it as an isolated act, or to see Marshall's
whole policy apart from the orientation of his class.
Marshall's decision was the high point of a counter-
revolutionary movement that stretched back to the
Constitutional Convention. The wheelings and turn-
ings of Federalists and Republicans were not only the
maneuverings of propertied groups and the agrarian-
labor masses for salvaging or hemming in the consequences of the Revolution: they were part of a world-
wide movement of social struggle fought out in France
and England as well as in America. For the history
of this period can be written adequately only if it is
seen as world history.

Marshall and his fellow-Federalists (and Marshall
was by no means the most extreme) viewed the Republicans as Jacobins, Jefferson as Robespierre, and his
letter to Mazzei as the sure mark of the Antichrist.
Jefferson, on the other hand, considered the Federalists
oligarchs and despots, and he feared Marshall's im-
placability and cunning. He was exasperated that his
victory at the polls should be frustrated by the judiciary. He never forgot that the Federalist judges had
used the bench as hustlings for election speeches. His
attempt to impeach these judges fell through: but it
was a characteristic part of the political tactics of the
day, as was also the united front that Federalist bench
and bar offered—a united front so complete that it was
difficult for the government to find counsel to prose-

cute the impeachments. It was class against class.

The whole situation was made far graver by the danger of war, either with England or France, and the threats of treason. War was one thing that Jefferson meant to avoid; his inaugural addresses and his annual messages are filled with eulogies of peace and of the joys of reproduction. Jefferson felt the American borders were being menaced by foreign invasion and internal disaffection. The Burr conspiracy was to prove how close that danger was, and the Burr trial proved how determined the Federalists were to embarrass the administration: while Marshall's own behavior was clearly partisan, Jefferson's moves behind the scenes were obviously those of a man determined to get a conviction.

Thus the first six years of Marshall's term—1801-1807—witnessed the battle of two giants in a setting of world revolution and counter-revolution. The Alien and Sedition laws (previously), the Judiciary Act, the Marbury decision, and the decision in the Burr case were the Federalist moves; the victory of 1800, the repeal of the Judiciary Act, the attempt to impeach Chase and the Burr trial were the Jeffersonian moves. Out of the whole melée there emerged as the great and enduring result the enunciation of the power of judicial review.

3. *Land Capitalism and Merchant Capitalism*

In Marshall's day the great threat to the property interests lay in the action of the state legislatures. Since colonial times the state legislatures had been the standing enemy of the creditor and moneyed class— they had even in colonial times sought to control business; they had been centers of focal infection, threatening both the ratification of the Constitution and the dominance of the moneyed groups in the new government. They had an unseemly habit of being responsive to the economic plight of the common man. What was needed now was a way of using judicial review to keep them in check.

Marshall found the answer in the "obligations of contract" clause in the Constitution: he seized upon it in a "higher law" theory to give a moral afflatus to sanctity of contract, and ended by creating the doctrine of vested rights as an implied limitation on state powers. To do this he had to stretch contract far beyond its contemporary meaning, but he was equal to the task. Sir Henry Maine once said that the progress of society is from status to contract: if that is true, Marshall must rank as one of the great heroes of humanity, for he gave contract a sanctity overriding every consideration of public policy or economic control. Next to judicial review itself this conception of contract—broadened into a doctrine of "vested rights"—is probably the most important invention in the history of the Court. It dominated the constitutional scene up to the Civil War, both in state and federal courts; it served as a model after which later doctrines of implied limitations on state power, such as due process of law and freedom of contract, could be fashioned.

The first of the contract cases to stir attention, *Fletcher* v. *Peck*,[2] has been described as "a cornerstone of legal structure laid in mud." Behind it is one of the most malodorous episodes in American history—that of the Yazoo land frauds. The Georgia Legislature of 1796, in what Beveridge has described as a "saturnalia of corruption," disposed of a strip of Indian land half the size of New England, comprising most of the present states of Alabama and Mississippi, to a land speculating company for about a cent and a half an acre. Every legislator except one had received a large bribe of land stock which could be disposed of for cash. The scandal broke; the people of Georgia, in a fury, wrote a new constitution, elected a new legislature and rescinded the corrupt act. But meanwhile the speculators had sold their stock to purchasers in New England and the Middle States. The latter proceeded to attack the legality of the rescinding act, and made many unsuccessful attempts in Congress to get compensation. Finally, on the basis of an opinion prepared by Alexander Hamilton, they contrived an obviously trumped-up suit and brought it before the Supreme Court. Joseph Story, later to become Marshall's *fidus Achates* on the Court, represented the New England speculators; but it is a safe guess that the opposing attorney did not trouble himself to present too formidable an argument.

Marshall's decision is breath-taking. He ignored the obvious collusion by which the case had been brought before the Court. He held that the Court could not concern itself with the alleged corruption of the Georgia Legislature, thereby inaugurating the Supreme Court tradition of maintaining when convenient a decent ignorance of events outside the Court. What counted was that the sovereign state of Georgia had, through the original legislative grant, entered into a contract the obligation of which could not be impaired by another act. As against the legislature's power to rescind its own act, Marshall argued that there was a higher moral duty to stand by the sanctity of contract. The moral duty flowed both from the sanctity of vested rights under a contract, and from more general considerations of "the nature of society and of government" which prescribed limits to the legislative power. Thus a decision which had started by throwing moral considerations out of the window ended by admitting them again through the back door.

It is not difficult to say why the framers of the Constitution inserted the "obligations of contract" clause. They had been distressed by the state legislation repudiating debts and placing moratoria on their payment, by paper currency legal tender laws, by installment and commodity payment laws. They were annoyed even more by "special acts", through which the legislatures had intervened in pending lawsuits and set contracts aside. To meet this problem of moratoria and other debtor relief laws, they counted on a sound and plentiful monetary supply, which would be achieved by giving the federal government a monopoly of coinage. But, as if to make doubly sure, they adopted also, at the motion of Rufus King, a clause probably suggested by the contract clause in the recently enacted Ordinance of 1787. The interesting thing is that the contract clause got little enthusiasm in the discussions at the Convention, but seems to have been the product mainly of an agreement within the Committee on Style. In the discussions attending ratification there was not much clarity about the meaning of the clause, except for a general agreement that it referred only to private contracts. The prevalent notion of contract at the time was a far narrower one than at present. In fact, contract as a basic concept of law was not developed until the period between the 1830's and 1860's. Little was thought about the contract clause until in 1796 Alexander Hamilton, retained as counsel by the New England purchasers of the land stock, submitted an opinion that for Georgia to rescind its act was a violation of the contract it had by implication entered into not to rescind the act.

This was the reasoning Marshall adopted, in a halting and hesitant way. His argument is even more rickety than that in *Marbury* v. *Madison*. He ignored what was the common understanding that the contract clause applied to private and not public contracts, and that it applied only when an obligation had been undertaken under a contract which the law protected and which had not yet been fulfilled. But having determined to assert his principle, Marshall went the whole way, and brought already executed public contracts within the scope of constitutional protection. He ignored also the fact that it was an established principle of the English common law that a legislature could rescind an act when fraud was involved, and the fact that British Parliaments had done so repeatedly.

Despite its logical weakness, however, Marshall's decision takes on meaning in the economic context of the day. Gambling in land values represented the principal financial activity in expansionist America at the turn of the nineteenth century, before industrialism came to overshadow everything else. Some of the most prominent men of the day had been involved in the Yazoo land scandal, including James Wilson, an Associate Justice of the Supreme Court, who was up to the neck in business: "When the deal was consummated," says Beveridge, "the Justice held shares to the amount of at least three-quarters of a million acres." Nor is this surprising. America was still an agrarian nation at the time, living by the soil and hoping to build its heaven from the soil. For the common people land meant a livelihood; for the landed squirearchy it meant a social position and a way of life; for a large intermediate group it meant easy profits. "Stock-jobbing" in land was much moralized over, and was considered one of the evils of the day; but it was an evil that involved wide circles in its participation. The great families of the day were landowning families, who had obtained their titles in some cases through fraud and in most cases through privilege. But their seigneurial estates could not be run profitably in the North with free labor, so they had turned to land speculation, where their political influence and their social and financial connections would be of account. The "aristocracy of patronage and paper," as John Taylor of Carolina termed the new banking and financial group, also found in land speculation a source of revenue. The fever spread to the workers in the northern cities; in fact, many of the people who had bought the Yazoo stock had invested the savings of a lifetime.

Land ate itself into the fiber of the period: but it was a speculative fiber that was involved. The economic fluctuations up to the Civil War were largely to be the history of land booms and land bubbles. The organizaion of the Yazoo land deal, in fact, foreshadowed the methods of later corporate promoting. The legislature was bought by "gifts" of stock; the promoters granted themselves large stock melons for promotion; northern men were hired as decoys in marketing the stock, and were paid by stock "gifts". This was agrarian capitalism, but it was the sort that was the spearhead of the emerging industrial capitalism. Marshall's decision was thus not merely the decision of a man who knew land and loved land—in whose circles of friendship land-speculation was the breath of life. It was also a decision in harmony with the progress of an exploitive merchant capitalism.

One other phase deserves mention. At the time the case of *Fletcher* v. *Peck* was being fought out, Marshall was himself involved in land litigation. Sometimes between 1794 and 1800 he had bought from the heirs of Lord Fairfax their claims to two or three million acres of Virginia land between the Rappahannock and the Potomac: these lands had been granted by Charles II in 1673 and had been taken back by Virginia after the Revolution and parceled out to returning soldiers as homesteads. The same had happened to the claims of the Penn heirs in Pennsylvania and the Granville heirs in North Carolina. Marshall, before he became Chief Justice, acting with his brother and Robert Morris—whom William E. Dodd, the Virginia historian, has called "a shameless speculator of Philadelphia"—bought the Fairfax claims and carried the litigation time and again to the Virginia Supreme Court, which decided unanimously against him. After he became Chief Justice, the case was carried to the Supreme Court. The issue involved in both cases was the same: the power of a state legislature to revoke a grant made by a previous sovereign body. The principle invoked was the same—sanctity of contract as overriding legislative sovereignty. When Marshall was deciding the case of the Yazoo land frauds, he was in effect setting a precedent for the decision of his own case. When that case came up for decision in 1813, as *Fairfax's Devisee* v. *Hunter's Lessee*,[3] Marshall quite properly refrained from sitting on it. The opinion of the Court was written by Justice Story, who had been one of the counsel for the land speculators in the re-argument of *Fletcher* v. *Peck*, and it was an opinion upholding the claim of the Marshall brothers on essentially the same grounds as the Yazoo case.

I am not urging a personal interpretation of Marshall's land decisions. Marshall was a man of stubborn integrity. He would undoubtedly have ruled as he did in *Fletcher* v. *Peck* even if his own land speculations were not concerned. But the fact that even he was involved in such speculations shows how deeply the substance of the issues reached to the economics of the period, how directly it was part of its ethos. And as the frontier of settlement moved further west and south after the Louisiana Purchase, the principle of *Fletcher* v. *Peck* and *Fairfax's Devisee* v. *Hunter's Lessee* was extended to the land claims of speculators based on flimsy and often corrupt Spanish titles. In *United States* v. *Arredondo*,[4] *Chouteau* v. *United States*,[5] and *Soulard* v. *United States*,[6] an exceedingly liberal interpretation was placed by the court on the power of Spanish officials to grant land deeds regardless of the written limitations of their authority, and on the validity of the titles based on those deeds. The result was that the bribing of officials and the forging of deeds became a common method of obtaining land titles, and the Supreme Court in accordance with its principle of not examining the ethics behind a contractual grant of a sovereign gave those titles authenticity.

Marshall and his Court felt no doubt that in thus placing the sanctity of contract above every adventitious consideration of policy or ethics they were encouraging economic stability. Actually they were encouraging the reckless development of American economic resources and the flagrant corruption of state politics which were to characterize the opening of the American continent throughout the nineteenth century.

The *Dartmouth College*[7] decision is one of the most famous that Marshall handed down. The little New Hampshire college, established in 1769 to educate and Christianize the Indians, found itself in 1815 without any Indians but with a Christian college community split to the center by a cleavage that ranged Congregationalist Federalists against non-Congregationalist Jeffersonians. The issue, as could have happened only in New England where politics was theology and theology politics, was fought out in a bitter state campaign. The Republicans won both the governorship and the legislature, and they proceeded in 1816 to pass an act amending the college charter, increasing the number of trustees and thus taking control away from the Federalist Old Guard. Jefferson, from his Monticello retreat, applauded: to do otherwise, he wrote, would be to hold "that the earth belongs to the dead and not to the living." The case was fought out before the highest court in New Hampshire, which held the law valid, on the ground that the college was a public corporation, devoted to public purposes, and that its charter could therefore be amended as public policy shifted. *Fletcher* v. *Peck*, it was held, did not apply; that related only to legislative grants involving the property rights of individuals, and not to grants of power for public purpose.

The case went to the Supreme Court, where it was argued with eloquence for the college by Daniel Webster, at that time (at thirty-seven) reaching the height of his powers. Every schoolboy knows Webster's reputed eloquent plea ("it is, Sir, as I have said, a small college. Yet there are those who love it") and how Marshall, whom the Yazoo land scandals had left cold, found his own eyes suffused with tears as Webster, overcome by the emotion of his words, wept. But few schoolboys know that the case had ultimately less to do with colleges than with business corporations; that sanctity of contract was invoked to give them immunity against legislative control; and that business enterprise in America has never had more useful mercenaries than the tears Daniel Webster and John Marshall are reputed to have shed so devotedly that March day in Washington in 1818.

The mechanics by which the decision was arrived at are almost as interesting as the decision itself. After the argument the judges found they could not agree. The case was continued. Webster, who had ways of knowing, guessed that at least three of the seven judges were safe. Justice Livingston was crucial. Since he leaned heavily on the advice of Chancellor Kent of New York, whose learning was as well known and almost as greatly admired as his conservatism, steps were taken to argue Kent out of his view that the New Hampshire court was right in holding the college a public corporation. There were letters, whisperings, conferences. When Court met again the following February, Marshall read the opinion of four of the judges. It held that the charter was a contract, that it was a "private" contract in the sense that the trustees represented the original grantees, whose vested rights to the money and effort they had put up had to be protected; that no one would give money to found a "private eleemosynary institution" such as the college was unless he could be certain that the charter that was granted him in return for his money would run in perpetuity.

There were holes in the argument, especially where Marshall agreed that Parliament, which granted the charter, could legally (not morally) have amended or revoked it, and that with the Revolution the state of New Hampshire had succeeded to the sovereignty. Marshall's sustained assurance, however, could bridge any gap in logic. While his opinions did not even mention *Fletcher* v. *Peck* (the concurring opinions of Story and Washington did), that case was assumed. What the *Dartmouth College* decision did was to apply *Fletcher* v. *Peck* to corporate charters. The question of whether they were public or private was actually of small moment historically, whatever may have been its importance in the case itself: for, once it was clear that a charter was a contract within the meaning of the contract clause, the exemption of public contracts could not have exempted the charters of business corporations from the operation of the rule. What was important was the ruling that a charter of incorporation was a contract: this Marshall scarcely discussed, although Story and Washington did; yet this was the new impetus given to the extension of the contract clause, and it was in this sense that the *Dartmouth* decision went a step beyond *Fletcher* v. *Peck*.

A step beyond it not only in constitutional terms,

but in economic terms as well. *Fletcher* v. *Peck* threw the protection of vested rights around the capitalism of land speculation, and allowed it to operate on any terms it chose. The *Dartmouth College* case did the same for corporate business enterprise. I am not speaking in terms of specific intent. The corporation in Marshall's day was not the unit of business enterprise and was not to become so until after the Civil War; although it may be said in qualification that already it was not entirely unimportant, and that it was to become increasingly important with the grant of charters for turnpikes, canal companies, railroads, bridge construction companies. In its consequences the decision operated to make an initial grant of power, of tax exemption, of government lands a permanent one. Later developments, principally Chief Justice Taney's decision in the *Charles River Bridge*[8] case, have stripped the decision of some of its starkness. Taney rules that while charters are contracts, they must be strictly construed in favor of the public interest, and no power exercised that was not expressly granted in them. State legislatures also learned how to insert "reservation clauses" into constitutions and statutes—provisions reserving to themselves the right to "alter, amend, or repeal" the charters they granted. But the overmastering fact is that the *Dartmouth* case set up an inviolability of corporate charters that has had slowly to be qualified, instead of starting at the opposite pole with a rule of legislative discretion and control. And by putting all the burdens on the original wording of the charter, it encouraged a tie-up between corporate interests and legislative greed that has been one of the peculiar marks of the American capitalist spirit.

The contract cases made Marshall the best hated man in the country. State bankruptcy laws, squatter laws, tax laws fell under the interdict of "vested rights." The decision which aroused the bitterest feeling was *Sturgis* v. *Crowninshield,*[9] ruling that a state bankruptcy act violated the contract clause as it applied to contracts already entered into ("retrospective"). Marshall's opinion, however, sought to go further and apply this even to contracts made after the passage of the law. This was too much even for Marshall's usually obedient colleagues, and acting in response to a storm of popular protest they repudiated this obiter dictum eight years later in *Ogden* v. *Saunders*.[10] Marshall, however, held out to the end. For once he found himself a solitary dissenter. His dissenting opinion in this case gives the clearest statement of his whole philosophy of contract as the basis of the doctrine of vested rights: it breathes a weird Rousseauist natural-rights mysticism, and represents perhaps the most explicit statement we have of the transcendental sources of sanctity of contracts which he finds to be "original and pre-existing principles," "anterior to, and independent of society." The obligation of contract, he says is a moral obligation, dictated by reason or nature. In short, in the words of a commentator, "it is not the state that gives validity and force to the contract, but, conceivably, a contract which gives validiy and force to the state."

Marshall was clearly riding an obsession. His primary drive was to protect private property from governmental encroachment. His struggle against the powers of the state legislatures was an instrument for this purpose. But the pursuit of even a secondary objective over a long period of time may transform it eventually into an independent objective. States' rights finally became Marshall's bugbear. He came to believe that every concession to the states' regulatory power sapped the Constitution. He began his Supreme Court tenure in the shadow of Jeffersonian democracy: he ended it in the shadow of Jacksonian democracy. Increasingly his letters and conversation were filled with dark forebodings about the future.

Yet he had done his work. Vested rights remained an operative doctrine in state judicial review until the Civil War, especially in such industrial states as New York. And after the Civil War, the due process clause of the Fourteenth Amendment more than took the place of the contract clause. But the interpretation which the Supreme Court was to place on the due process clause would not have been possible without Marshall's establishment of the power of judicial review, and the calm audacity with which he had transformed the genius of business enterprise into a set of implied limitations upon state power.

4. The Uses of Nationalism

It is, however, not with the states but on the national judicial-economic front that Marshall's greatest meaning for today lies. In a series of decisions beginning with *McCulloch* v. *Maryland*[11] and *Gibbons* v. *Ogden*[12] extending through *Willson* v. *Black Bird Creek Marsh Company*,[13] he evolved a broad interpretation of the "necessary and proper" and commerce clauses of the Constitution which was at once tough-minded in its understanding of contemporary economic reality and bold in its vision of the economic future of the nation. This is the nationalistic phase of Marshall's career: it is also the most brilliant and—if the progressive forces of the Court win in their present struggle for power with the reactionary forces —it is likely to prove the most enduring.

I can say this without succumbing uncritically to the elements of sheer rhetoric in Marshall's nationalism. That rhetoric, like the rhetoric of sanctity of contract, serves to conceal the shaping forces of Marshall's decisions, and is best cleaved by the sundering blade of the logic of business interests.

Taken simply as rhetoric, its hallowness is most shockingly revealed by Marshall's serious negotiations with the New England secession movement on the eve of (and even during) the War of 1812, his efforts to sabotage the war, his non-too-concealed willingness in 1812 to stand for the Federalist presidential nomination on a New England program. Nothing in American history is as short-sighted and illiberal as the Federalist party policy from 1807 to 1815, and Marshall for the most part shared it and helped shape it. "The record shows," Beveridge admits, "that John

Marshall was as bitterly opposed to the war of 1812 as was Pickering or Otis or Lowell," to name the Federalist leaders for whom a split from the rest of the American nation had become an obsession. In the face of a war that was being fought for the agricultural rather than for the industrial and mercantile groups, Marshall's principles of nationalism were dangerously shaken. For Marshall had little of the deeper national consciousness of the common man, based on national expansion and democratic adventure and the promise of American life. His was a strictly judicial nationalism, on a base of economic realism.

Its guiding logic was the relation of the national power to the scope of industrial development. The upswing of a rising capitalism made it necessary that congressional jurisdiction be strengthened as against the power of the states with reference to the two main lines of business expansion of the period—a national banking system and a national transportation system. The first, Marshall accomplished in the famous decision in *McCulloch* v. *Maryland*.[11] What was involved on the surface was the constitutionality of the Second United States Bank, and the question whether a Maryland state tax on its bank notes was valid. What was involved below the surface was the question whether the government would use every force at its disposal to ensure favorable conditions for the newly emerging capitalist class and a free field for its operations.

Marshall made the Maryland bank case the occasion of his most resounding opinion. He had two questions to answer. Did Congress have the power to charter a national bank? Did Maryland have the power to tax it? The first question had been moot for years. It turned on the interpretation of the "necessary and proper" constitutional provision. When, at Alexander Hamilton's instance, the first bank had been chartered in 1791, it was only after a heated discussion of constitutionality—the first general discussion of what the new Constitution meant. When an attempt was made in 1811 to recharter it, there was again a sharp debate on the meaning of the "necessary and proper" clause. When, under stress of monetary chaos and state wildcat banking, a Second United States Bank was created in 1816, it did not lay the ghost of the constitutional problem. The Maryland tax case brought it up again, amidst wide interest.

The Bank had already begun splitting the opinion of the country—a process which was to come to its climax in the Bank War of Biddle, Jackson, and Taney. Already in the North and East it was the bulwark of the Republic, in the South and West the "great monster". In the three years of its establishment it had first expanded credit and then contracted it—a policy which had not helped its popularity; its branches had been guilty of fraud, peculation, and mismanagement of funds. In those three years eight states had passed laws taxing the branches: and while the *McCulloch* case was being argued a bill was in Congress for repealing the charter. It was imperative that swift action be taken—imperative both for the bank and for the Supreme Court, which was so thoroughly in sympathy with it. A case was "arranged"; how much collusion there was in it is difficult to say, but after the decision the Ohio Legislature declared that "many of the strongest grounds were relinquished or not brought into view" by Maryland counsel. The case was pushed through expeditiously, and three days after Pinkney finished his argument, Marshall had a ten thousand word opinion ready.

The opinion was pretty much a condensation of Pinkney's argument, and yet it was more than that. It was a brilliant essay in the philosophy of government, bold in its logic, uncluttered with learning. There was, it is true, little new in it—little that had not been said in the debates over the "necessary and proper" clause, or that Marshall had himself not said in his first opinion on that clause in 1805. But Marshall showed how old materials gathered from various sources could be welded by a burning passion into a new weapon for new struggles. *McCulloch* v. *Maryland* struck the first resounding blow for a broad construction of the Constitution.

There have been some commentators, and Charles Warren is a good instance, who have deplored the "accident" that the strictly legal struggle over broad or narrow construction should have got tangled up with the excitement over the United Bank. But to take this view is to miss the integral connection between law and economics. The importance of the controversy over broad and narrow construction lay exactly in the uses to which it could be put by the economic interests. The newly emerging industrial capitalism of the time needed the Bank, and the Bank for its very existence needed a broad construction of national power: and Marshall came smashing through with exactly that. He built on the "necessary and proper" clause a doctrine of implied national powers which could be used not only to justify the chartering of a central bank as part of the power to regulate coinage or issue currency, but could also be used to justify a national system of internal improvements. "We must not construe the Constitution," cried Henry Clay in the 1818 Congressional debate on internal improvements, "as one would a bill of indictment." Marshall's decision was like a clarion response to Clay's cry: "Let the end be legitimate, let it be within the scope of the Constitution and all means which are appropriate, which are plainly adapted to that end, which are not prohibited but consist with the letter and spirit of the Constitution, are constitutional." [14]

This was brave doctrine. The Federal party was dying, unable to survive the sectarianism it had shown during the War of 1812. A new cluster of property-interests was arising, and Henry Clay of Kentucky was a good spokesman for them: a new passion for prosperity was showing itself in the West as in the East. Clay and his group looked to the national government to exert itself to send money circulating through all the channels of trade. Marshall's nationalism was as welcome to them as to Landon Cheves, the President of the Bank, and to the corrupt and interlocking monied interests of New England, New York, and Pennsylvania.

There was, of course, an outcry against the decision. But it was primarily against the second part of it, rather than the first. For Marshall, after deciding that Congress had power to charter the Bank, waved away Maryland's attempt to tax it with "the power to tax involves the power to destroy." He thus showed himself master of the two-way stretch, interpreting national powers broadly and state power narrowly. Ohio refused to recognize the decision as going beyond the case itself or relevant to her own Bank tax, and for five years carried on a guerilla warfare against Court and Bank. Spencer Roane, Chief Judge of the Virginia Court of Appeals and Marshall's *bête noire,* attacked the decision in a series of letters in the *Richmond Enquirer,* which so nettled Marshall that he published in the *Philadelphia Union* under a fictitious name a lengthy defense of the decision. Jefferson, writing to Roane from Monticello, must have looked back to the days when the "necessary and proper" clause had been used by the courts in upholding the Alien and Sedition laws, and when he had himself spoken with a bitter vision of the national powers to which this "filiation of necessities" might lead. He wrote now: "After twenty years . . . we find the judiciary on every occasion, still driving us into consolidation. In denying the right they usurp of exclusively explaining the Constitution, I go further than you do." And Madison, far more amenable than Jefferson and Roane to the drift of events—Madison who had said in 1811 that regardless of what we might have thought originally of the constitutionality of the Bank it had been settled by twenty years of acquiescence, now wrote: "It was anticipated I believe by few if any of the framers of the Constitution, that a rule of construction would be introduced as broad & as pliant as what has occurred."

In taking this position, it does not follow that the Virginia dynasty was (as Warren has suggested) either blaming Marshall for not declaring the Bank unconstitutional or implying that the Court had the exclusive power to pass on its constitutionality. Their reasoning was as follows: the Bank is unconstitutional, whoever does the interpreting; Congress has chosen to charter it, but that is Congress's affair; certainly the Court does not have the exclusive power of interpreting the Constitution; in any case, Maryland's power to tax the Bank is a part of its sovereignty as a state.

Two years later the question of state sovereignty was raised in even sharper form when two lottery vendors, the Cohen brothers, had sold in Virginia tickets for a lottery authorized by Congress in the District of Columbia. They were convicted under a Virginia anti-lottery law and appealed to the Supreme Court. The only question the Virginia counsel were willing to argue was that of jurisdiction: could an appeal be to the Supreme Court from a criminal case in a state court, even where a federal question was involved? Marshall held that it did; and then, by a tactic similar to that of *Marbury* v. *Madison,* held that Congress had not intended to authorize the sale of the lottery tickets in Virginia. Thus Marshall was again willing to cede the smaller if he could gain the larger.

One result of these decisions was a renewal of the popular hostility to the Court. Jefferson, who after the 1819 term had called the judges a "subtle corps of sappers and miners constantly working underground to undermine the foundations of our confederated fabric," now wrote bitterly: "the battle of Bunker Hill was not fought to set up a Pope." Virginia, Ohio, and Kentucky were in full revolt; there was talk of a movement in Congress to repeal Section XXV of the Judiciary Act of 1789, which granted appellate jurisdiction to the Supreme Court over state courts and on which the Cohens' decision rested. This failed. But for the next ten years the Democrats in Congress did not cease to attack the exercise of the judicial power.

That they were unable to do anything about it was due to several causes. First, it was not clear what would take the place of the Court in the function of finality of Constitutional interpretation. Secondly, the judicial nationalism of Marshall was mixed up with too many issues that were already splitting the country—the money power as represented by the Bank of the United States; the slave power as involved in the Congressional attempt through the Missouri Compromise (1820) pending when *McCulloch* v. *Maryland* was being argued and discussed) to regulate slavery in the territories; and government interventionism through subsidies, which meant a good deal to the Western states. These were the controlling issues—these and the constant upswing of capitalist development and national expansion. It was Marshall's good fortune to float his nationalist judicial doctrines on this tide, when the whole tempo of economic development was in his favor, and when an attack on the Court would immediately founder on the rocks of these issues.

Marshall's handling of the commerce clause cases best stamps the Golden Age of the Court's history. Article I, section 8, clause 3 of the Constitution gives Congress power "to regulate commerce with foreign nations, and among the several states." That this has become probably the most hotly contested clause in the Constitution is not at all strange, for "to regulate commerce among the several states" is a clause that reaches directly into both the nature of our economic system and the nature of our federal system. Scarcely a word of that clause but has given rise to a mountain of learned and fine-spun discussion. What does "regulate" mean: does it involve only aid, or may it mean to restrain or prohibit? What does "commerce" mean: does it mean merely transportation, or does it include the essentials of the economic process? What does "among" mean: does it mean that the power stops at the states' boundaries, or does the power extend beyond those boundaries into the state itself? Casuistries like this do not grow up of their own accord. In Marshall's and Taney's day they were part of the battle of the capitalist and industrial versus the agrarian and slavery interests: later in the days of Fuller, White, and Day and in our times they were part of the struggle between a planless and a regulated capitalism.

Marshall hammered out his commerce clause doctrine in three principal cases—shrewdly, carefully, pragmatically. When the case of *Gibbons* v. *Ogden*[12] came up for settlement in 1824, the commerce clause was practically untrodden ground. What was chiefly available, as Walton Hamilton has pointed out, was a body of verbal and business usage clustering around the word "commerce". Marshall made ample use of this. But above all else he was aiming at the sure establishment of national supremacy, and he chose his own methods.

Gibbons v. *Ogden* involved a steamboat monopoly granted by the Republican Legislature of New York to Robert Rivingston, a powerful member of the Republican machine, and Robert Fulton, the inventor of the steamboat. An attempt was being made by an independent steamboat company to break up this monopoly, and it had behind it the hearty concurrence of other states and of popular opinion as a whole. Only the extreme states' rights men of Virginia and other southern states were jealous of what Marshall might do, not out of concern for navigation but because of the possible effect of his doctrine on attempts by states to set up fugitive slave laws. Marshall had to move with discretion. He listened to a brilliant array of counsel pour their eloquence out to a more than usually crowded court-room. Webster had sat up all night to prepare his argument against the monopoly. He afterward looked back with pride on the effect he had on the Chief Justice: "I think I never experienced more intellectual pleasure than in arguing that novel question to a great man who could appreciate it, and take it in; and he did take it in, as a baby takes in its mother's milk."

But Webster was claiming too much. Justice Johnson, in a concurring opinion, did hold to Webster's view that when Congress was given the power to regulate commerce, it had the exclusive power whether it exercised it or not, and any state act of regulation was void. According to this view the fact that the independent steamboat company had a federal license to navigate under the federal Coasting License Act of 1793 was not essential to the case. Marshall's opinion, in the words of Mr. Justice Frankfurter, "was either unconsciously or calculatedly confused." In his actual decision he rests on the Federal Act as supreme over a conflicting state act; but the main part of his opinion is an essay on the commerce power as exclusively federal. No doubt he was testing states' rights opinion; he was fearful of saying too openly that state authority would henceforth be limited by the commerce clause, whether or not the federal government had acted legislatively.

What has remained, however, is not Marshall's decision but his essay; not his caution, but his daring. He had created the doctrine of the "dormant" power of the commerce clause—a doctrine that was to make of the clause a powerful engine for narrowing the scope of state power and increasing the scope of federal power.

This decision, however, and that of *Brown* v. *Maryland*[15] and *Willson* v. *Black Bird Creek Marsh Company*[13] which I have discussed in the previous section. For Marshall was not concerned here primarily with limiting state authority; he was concerned with increasing federal authority. And it is significant, therefore, that while his states' rights decisions dwell on judicial supremacy, these nationalist decisions do not. It is true that these cases were actually building up the Court's power, and that through them the Court, as well as Congress, became the arbiter of vast questions of national policy. But there is a difference of emphasis. So anxious was Marshall to uphold the congressional power to rule exclusively in its domain, as against the state power, that *Gibbons* v. *Ogden* contains what is, at least by implication, one of the most forceful arguments against judicial review of congressional legislation that we have in the literature.

First Marshall had defined the three crucial terms of the clause. Commerce, he said, "undoubtedly is traffic, but it is something more, it is intercourse." "The word 'among' means intermingled with . . . commerce among the states cannot stop at the external boundary line of each State, but may be introduced into the interior . . . comprehensive as the word 'among' is, it may very properly be restricted to that commerce which concerns more States than one." And the power to "regulate" is "to prescribe the rule by which commerce is to be governed." After these definitions, Marshall is anxious to make it clear that the states cannot set up their own ideas of the wisdom of the congressional exercise of this power. That is absolute: the only restraint upon it (within the Constitution) is the self-restraint of Congress: "The wisdom and the discretion of Congress, their identity with the people, and the influence which their constituents possess at elections, are . . . the sole restraints on which they have relied to secure them from its abuse. They are the restraints on which the people must often rely solely, in all representative governments." [16] Thus Marshall, in defending congressional power over commerce, was adopting a position of national legislative supremacy which could even be used against judicial supremacy.

I am convinced that Marshall did this because the legislative power he feared was not that of Congress, but of the states. And the irony of his position is that the doctrine of vested rights (later applied to due process) and the doctrine of judicial supremacy, which he had developed in the state-power cases, combined eventually to whittle down his concept of national supremacy in the domain of the commerce power and the "necessary and proper" clause, and defeat it.

5. *With the Stream*

We must not construe Marshall's nationalistic decisions in terms too noble and high-flown. The actual circumstances of the commerce cases which came before his Court were such that Congress was using the clause to aid and not restrain business enterprise. The two main lines of business expansion of the day were a national banking system and a national transportation system. To allow the states, always suspicious of business enterprise, to interfere with either would have been, Marshall saw, fatal for the unimpeded development of business. To remove such obstructions, to ensure favorable conditions for business, was in the early stages of industrial capitalism the prime function of a central government. Here Congress and the Court were not yet at war with each other: it was not necessary to emphasize the Court's role of constitutional guardian as against Congress.

Marshall had here the advantage of working with the stream of history. He had vision enough to see that political power had to be coterminous with the scale of economic activity. He saw it dimly and confusedly, and it was all tangled in his mind with a hatred of states' rights and of the common man, and with a protective obsession about the rights of property. But his chief historical meaning for us lies none the less in this dim insight of his.

The position of his opponents, the Virginia dynasty —Jefferson, John Taylor, Spencer Roane, Madison, and Monroe—embodied an archaic economic vision, whatever the merits of their political views. Jefferson at 82, writing in 1825, a year before his death, was bitter not only about the judicial power but the whole centralizing tendency in the national government. "Take together the decisions of the Federal Court, the doctrines of the President and the misconstructions of the Constitutional Compact acted on by the Legislature of the Federal branch, and it is but too evident that the three ruling branches of that department are in combination to strip their colleagues, the State authorities, of the powers reserved by them. . . . Under the power to regulate commerce, they assume indefinitely that also over agriculture and manufactures, and call it regulation to take the earnings of one of these branches of industry—and that, too, the most depressed—and put them into the pockets of the other—the most flourishing of all." With this one must take Monroe's veto of the Cumberland Road Act of 1822. With it one must take also John Taylor's *Construction Con-*

strued and Constitution Vindicated, his *Tyranny Unmasked,* and his *New View of the Constitution.*

Taylor was the political theorist of the Jefferson school, as Roane was its constitutional theorist. Together these men were setting their faces against the future. However able (and Taylor was probably with Calhoun, the ablest anti-capitalist theorist in America until the generation of Henry Demarest Lloyd, Daniel De Leon, and Thorstein Veblen), they were dreamers. They dreamt the Physiocratic dream of a society that was even then beyond recall—a republic of small farmers. They failed to see the technology was settling that question for them. They were partly blinded by their fears for the slavery interest, and made the mistake of identifying the capitalist interest inevitably with the national power. Partly, also, they were caught by the dead hand of their own preoccupation with states' rights theory in the past. They failed to see that the issue was now not between states' rights and the national power, but between the types of national control of business that would be developed. If, instead of following a policy of states' rights obstructionism, they had come out frankly for national legislative control of the new economic forces in the interests of the agrarian as well as the industrial groups, Marshall's much vaunted nationalism would have changed its tune.

For what it amounted to was aid and tolerance for business enterprise, both on a national scale. As between a policy of states' rights obstructionism and a policy of federal jurisdiction, it was obviously the latter that was part of the victorious campaign of history.

[1] Marbury v. Madison, 1 Cranch 137 (U. S. 1803).
[2] Fletcher v. Peck, 6 Cranch 87 (U. S. 1810).
[3] Fairfax Devisee v. Hunter's Lessee, 7 Cranch 603 (U. S. 1813).
[4] United States v. Arrendondo, 6 Pet. 691 (U. S. 1832).
[5] Chouteau v. United States, 9 Pet. 137 (U. S. 1835).
[6] Soulard v. United States, 10 Pet. 100 (U. S. 1836).
[7] Dartmouth College v. Woodward, 14 Wheat. 518 (U. S. 1819).

[8] Charles River Bridge, 11 Pet. 420 (U. S. 1837).

[9] Sturgis v. Crowningshield, 4 Wheat. 122 (U. S. 1819).

[10] Ogden v. Saunders, 12 Wheat. 213 (U. S. 1827).

[11] McCulloch v. Maryland, 4 Wheat. 316 (U. S. 1819).

[12] Gibbons v. Ogden, 9 Wheat. 1 (U. S. 1824).

[13] Willson v. Black Bird Creek Co., 2 Pet. 245 (U. S. 1829).

[14] Constitution, 4 Wheat. 316, 421, (U. S. 1819).

[15] Brown v. Maryland, 12 Wheat. 419 (U. S. 1827).

[16] Gibbons v. Ogden, 9 Wheat. 189, 194, 196, 197 (U. S. 1824).

"JUSTICE THE GUARDIAN OF LIBERTY": JOHN MARSHALL AT THE TRIAL OF AARON BURR*

By Harold H. Burton

One of the most significant trials presided over by John Marshall was the trial of Aaron Burr in Richmond in 1807. The Chief Justice exemplified the highest standards of the legal profession in his fairness, in the conduct of the trial, in the face of great public indignation against the defendant. The decision deals with several points of law other than the law of treason. One of these points was the use of the privilege of the fifth amendment.

One of the best summaries of this trial is the article by Mr. Justice Harold Burton of the Supreme Court of the United States, appearing in the *American Bar Association Journal*, here reprinted with the consent of the author and publisher.

Sharing significance with his rulings was the demeanor of Chief Justice John Marshall throughout the fabulous trial of Aaron Burr in the Circuit Court of the United States in the District of Virginia, March 30-August 31, 1807.

As the presiding trial Justice he exemplified what he meant when he had said for the Supreme Court—

> As there is no crime which can more excite and agitate the passions of men than treason, no charge demands more from the tribunal before which it is made a deliberate and temperate inquiry. Whether this inquiry be directed to the fact or to the law, none can be more solemn, none more important to the citizen or to the government; none can more affect the safety of both [*Ex parte Bollman and Swartwout*, 4 Cranch 75, 125.]

If ever there was a trial to "excite and agitate the passions of men" it was that of Aaron Burr for high treason. The penalty was death by hanging. The accused was a brilliant lawyer who had served as

---

* Reprinted with permission of the *American Bar Association Journal* and the author, from 37 A. B. A. J. 735 (1951).

a Colonel in the Revolutionary Army, United States Senator from New York and Vice President of the United States.[1] Though an Anti-Federalist, he had antagonized the idolized leader of his party, President Jefferson. While Vice President, he had killed, in a duel, the outstanding young leader of the Federalists, Alexander Hamilton. Leaving office in 1805, he was a widely known, ambitious, fearless soldier-statesman to whom fables readily attached themselves. It was rumored that he proposed not only to invade Spanish-held Mexico but to seize New Orleans and sever the Southwest Territories from the United States at the Allegheny Mountains. On January 22, 1807, President Jefferson announced to Congress that on these charges Burr's "guilt is placed beyond question".[2] That was enough for the people at large. They denounced Burr as a traitor. They demanded his prompt execution.

The Government, however, faced a new definition of treason in the Constitution of the United States. To convict Burr of treason against the United States in this instance, he must be found guilty of "levying War" against them, and this must be on the testimony of two witnesses to the same overt act. Also, he must be tried by an impartial jury of the state and district wherein the crime was committed. The Government selected as the situs of the crime Blennerhassett's Island in the Ohio River, in Wood County, Virginia, about two miles below the present city of Parkersburg, West Virginia. This brought the trial into the Circuit Court in the District where Chief Justice Marshall would preside as Circuit Justice. The hostility of President Jefferson towards the Chief Justice was well known. That John Marshall did not avoid his responsibility as presiding Justice but discharged it in the deliberate and temperate manner that this *cause célèbre* demanded was in the best tradition of the Federal Bench.

Today the case is sometimes misconceived. Chief Justice Marshall did not sit alone as presiding Justice. Joining in his rulings and sometimes making comments from the bench was United States District Judge Cyrus Griffin. The rulings of the Circuit Court as to the meaning and required proof of treason were not decisions of first impression in the trial court. In large part they were explanations by the Chief Justice of his own opinion, written for the Supreme Court, February 21, 1807, in *Ex parte Bollman and Swartwout,* 4 Cranch 75, 125. The opinions supporting the principal rulings of the Circuit Court can be found elsewhere than in the often unavailable lower court reports. They were reprinted by Cranch as Appendix B to the Supreme Court opinion just mentioned, at page 470.

The significance of the trial, however, can be fully appreciated only when seen against the background of its time and read in connection with the related litigation.

1. BACKGROUND

On leaving the Vice Presidency Colonel Burr turned to the beckoning fields of adventure in the Southwest. He announced a plan to settle lands he had purchased on the Washita River, in what is now southern Arkansas or northern Louisiana. If the momentarily expected war with Spain developed, he proposed also to lead the first expedition into Mexico. In the event of war, such a procedure on Burr's part apparently would have been welcomed by the United States. In the interest of this project, he visited the Ohio River settlements in 1805 and made plans to meet with his fellow adventurers at or near Blennerhassett's Island in 1806.

Colorful and wild rumors quickly spread about these plans. Over Burr's denials, the rumors included a story that he had conceived a treasonable plan for severing some of the Southwestern Territories from the United States and joining them to a Mexican empire of his own. General James Wilkinson, who commanded the United States Army in the Southwest, but who was at the same time a pensioner of

Spain, at first co-operated with Burr. Late in 1806, however, he suddenly reported to President Jefferson that Burr planned to attack New Orleans, seize it and lead a revolt against the United States, all of which Wilkinson proposed to resist by force of arms. It is for historians and not for us to say what degree of truth there was, or that Wilkinson believed there was, in that report.[3]

Burr's alleged treason had remained largely in the realm of rumor until General Wilkinson wrote to the President. Relying on Wilkinson, the President submitted the issue to his Cabinet and, on November 27, 1806, sent Congress a proclamation that startled the nation. It reported receipt of information that a military expedition was being organized by private persons within the United States to move against the dominions of Spain, and that such persons were collecting arms and seducing well-meaning citizens "to engage in their criminal enterprises". The President warned faithful citizens to withdraw from the enterprise or "incur prosecution with all the rigors of the law". He enjoined civil and military officers to seize the boats, arms, etc., so provided. He required good and faithful citizens to aid in "bringing to justice" all such offenders and in "giving information against them to the proper authorities".[4] The proclamation did not name anyone as the offender nor specifically charge anyone with treason against the United States. The public, however, knew that Burr was the alleged offender and jumped to the conclusion that he must be guilty of high treason or the President would not have taken such extraordinary steps to thwart his preparations. The proclamation apparently had two effects. As the President later claimed, it probably destroyed all likelihood of the success of any such treasonable plans against the United States as were reported by Wilkinson. It also convinced the public that Burr had undertaken such plans as were described. Throughout his life Burr suffered the consequences of that popular belief.

December 2, 1806, the President, in his annual message, reminded Congress of the reported expedition of private individuals against the territories of Spain. Annals, 9th Cong., 2d Sess. 11, 12. Congress demanded that the President disclose his information concerning such a conspiracy and report the measures he had taken to suppress it. He replied that his information was voluminous but that there was little in it to constitute legal evidence. He, however, detailed General Wilkinson's report of Burr's alleged treason and misdemeanor, referred to his own proclamation of November 27, 1806, identified Burr as the principal actor, and assured Congress that Burr's "guilt is placed beyond question".[5] The die was cast. The prosecution of Burr for treason became politically necessary. The unflinching adherence of the courts to their impartial duties under these circumstances deserves recognition. As the Chief Justice later said of his Circuit Court: "That this court dares not usurp power is most true. That this court dares not shrink from its duty is not less true." United States v. Burr, 25 Fed. Cas., No. 14,693, page 179, also in App. B, 4 Cranch at page 506.

A summary of the related litigation will outline the ensuing drama.[6]

II.   PROCEEDINGS BEFORE THOSE IN RICHMOND

A. November, 1806—In the Circuit Court of the United States in the District of Kentucky (Innis, J.). A federal indictment was sought in Kentucky against Burr for the misdemeanor of preparing a military expedition within the United States agaainst Spain. He appered voluntarily and the investigation collapsed. United States v. Burr, 25 Fed. Cas., No. 14,692, pages 1-2.

B. December, 1806—In the same court. Similar indictments were sought against Burr and Adair. Burr appeared voluntarily and was represented by Henry Clay. The grand jury, after hearing the evidence, not only refused to indict Burr but rendered a special report, finding that they could not "discover that anything improper or injurious to the interest of the Government of the United States, or contrary to the laws thereof, is designed or contemplated by either of them [Burr or Adair]". McCaleb, *The Aaron Burr Conspiracy*, page 163, citing Palladium, December 11, 1806.

C. *December, 1806–January, 1807. In New Orleans.* This constituted most of General Wilkinson's "reign of terror". When the Governor refused the General's request to suspend the writ of habeas corpus or to declare martial law, the General seized local military control in the name of national security. He arrested and shipped to Baltimore Bollman, Swartwout, Alexander and later Adair. He also seized others. Writs of habeas corpus were issued by local judges. To these the General made returns that he took full responsibility for the arrests and stated that the men sought were no longer in his possession. Judge Workman appealed to the Governor for help. Receiving none, he adjourned his court and shortly thereafter resigned his office.[7] At the request of the General, the Governor asked the Territorial Legislature to suspend the writ of habeas corpus. The legislature not only refused but forwarded to Congress a memorial of protest.[8]

D. *December, 1806–January, 1807. Progress of Burr's expedition.* The immediate prospect of war with Spain having been dissipated, Burr, Blennerhassett, Tyler and Smith floated down the Mississippi River with nine flatboats, manned by about six men each. They proposed to settle on the Washita. At the same time the rumor spread that Burr was coming to attack New Orleans with hundreds or thousands of men, and General Wilkinson mobilized his forces to intercept them.

December 2, Governor Tiffin of Ohio, aroused by a representative from the President, sent a warning

message to the Ohio legislature. This led to the seizure, on December 9, of some of Blennerhassett's un-
manned flatboats on the Muskingum River in Ohio.
On December 10 the Virginia militia announced that
it would investigate Blennerhassett's Island on the
following day. The expedition, being substantially
ready to leave, created further excitement by leaving
during the night. The next day the militia ransacked
the island, consumed the liquid spirits available, and
seized a flatboat with fourteen boys from Pittsburgh
aboard. The prisoners were released after brief ques-
tioning and, taking Mrs. Blennerhassett with them,
proceeded down the river.

On December 22 Colonel Burr joined the party at
the mouth of the Cumberland with two boats which
had been prepared for him by General Andrew Jackson. Passing down the Mississippi on Christmas Day,
he dispatched a friendly note to the commander at
Fort Massac. On December 29 Burr declined an
equally friendly invitation to dine at the Fort. There
was nothing about Burr's little flotilla to cause alarm
to those who saw it. Nevertheless, intense excitement
had been aroused in the Mississippi Territory by
exaggerated warnings of its approach. A detachment
of 375 militiamen was sent up the river to intercept
it. Other troops marched by land. On their contact
with Burr, he ridiculed the idea of his hostility and
volunteered to submit to the civil authorities. The
inflated monster of impending military invasion collapsed.[9] At the Town of Washington in the Territory
of Mississippi, Burr was bound over to await action
of the grand jury. General Wilkinson boasted that he
had dissipated the conspiracy and had saved New
Orleans.

E. *February, 1807. In the Supreme Court of the
Mississippi Territory.* Burr volunteered to answer any
bill of indictment. The District Attorney, after examination of the depositions submitted to him, asked the
court to discharge the grand jury. The court refused,
whereupon the grand jury filed a report favorable

to Burr and condemnatory of his accusers. The forth-rightness of this frontier document is refreshing.[10] Although no indictment was found against Burr, he was bound over to appear from day to day. At the same time a military patrol was on its way from General Wilkinson who had pledged $5,000 to cover the expenses of Burr's capture. Fearing for his life, Burr went into hiding and notified the Governor that he would submit to civil law when assured of the rights of a citizen. Attempting to flee the Territory, Burr was recognized by one Perkins and was reported to a lieutenant who arrested him. Perkins received $3,331.

F. *January–February, 1807. In Washington.* In Jefferson's response to the House of Representatives of January 22 he had stated that Burr's conspiracy contemplated two objects—the severance of the Union and an attack on Mexico. The next day the Senate, in closed session, on motion of Senator Giles of Virginia, passed a bill to suspend the writ of habeas corpus. In contrast, the House, in open session, rejected the bill 113 to 19. Going further the House almost passed, 58 to 60, what would have amounted to a vote of censure of the Administration.

At this moment, Wilkinson's military prisoners began to arrive in Washington from New Orleans. Jefferson ordered them delivered to the civil authorities and General Wilkinson's evidence presented to the courts. Alexander was promptly released by Judge Duchet for lack of competent evidence against him. Bollman and Swartwout, having been committed to jail by the Circuit Court for the District of Columbia, sought, on February 13, a writ of habeas corpus directly from the Supreme Court of the United States which was then in session. Bollman and Swartwout also sought a writ of certiorari to bring up the record of their commitment. Both writs were allowed and motions to discharge the prisoners were argued February 16, 17 and 18. Counsel appearing for the prisoners included former United States Attorney

General Charles Lee, Francis Scott Key, later to become the author of our national anthem, and Luther Martin, a leader of the Maryland and American Bars. Of the Court there were present Chief Justice Marshall and Justices Chase, Washington and William Johnson. Justices Cushing and Livingston were absent.[11] The evidence presented by the prosecution was reviewed in detail by the Court. See 4 Cranch, App. A, pages 455-469. February 21, Chief Justice Marshall announced the opinion of the Court, discharging the prisoners for lack of the proof necessary to constitute treason by levying war against the United States. *Ex parte Bollman and Swartwout*, 4 Cranch 75, 125.

General Adair and Ogden were landed in Baltimore where Judge Nicholson released them, reporting to the President that "Very much to my surprise and mortification . . . there was no proof of any nature whatsoever with them." McCaleb, *The Aaron Burr Conspiracy*, page 249, citing Nicholson to Jefferson, February 18, 1807. Adair later sued General Wilkinson, in Natchez, for false imprisonment. After eight years, he recovered $2,500 damages, which the Government paid.

III. PRELIMINARY PROCEEDINGS IN RICHMOND

The Government next concentrated upon the prosecution of Burr for treason. A determined effort was made to gather evidence by widespread use of printed questionnaires. The Circuit Court in the District of Virginia having been selected for the trial, it was necessary to find accommodations for the public at the hearings. As a result the court sat in the hall of the House of Delegates of the Commonwealth of Virginia from March into September, 1807.

A. *Counsel.* Government counsel were led by District Attorney *George Hay*, son-in-law of the future President, James Monroe. Hay was in personal correspondence with President Jefferson on every important point of policy. With Hay was *William Wirt,* then 35. He was destined to become a distinguished author and to serve as Attorney General under Presidents Monroe and John Quincy Adams. Supplementing these was *Alexander MacRae,* Lieutenant Governor of Virginia. Counsel for the accused served without compensation. They included *Edmund Randolph,* former Attorney General under President Washington; *John Wickham,* a leader of the Virginia Bar; *Luther Martin,* for many years Attorney General of Maryland, and recognized nationally as a learned and effective trial lawyer; *Charles Lee,* former Attorney General under Presidents Washington and John Adams; and as junior counsel *Benjamin Botts* and *John Baker. Burr* himself often took part in the examination of witnesses and in arguments to the court. Unlike most lawyers, he was his own best advocate.

B. *March 30, 1807.* Shortly after Burr's arrival in Richmond under military guard, Chief Justice Marshall himself wrote out, signed and issued the warrant by virtue of which Burr was surrendered to the civil authorities.

C. *March 30–April 1, 1807. Commitment.* Relying on the record in the *Bollman* and *Swartwout* cases, the prosecution asked the Chief Justice to commit Burr to jail on two charges: treason against the United States and misdemeanor in preparing and setting on foot within the United States a military expedition against Spain. After reviewing the evidence, the Chief Justice held it not sufficient to sustain commitment for treason but sufficient to sustain commitment for the misdemeanor. *United States* v. *Burr,* 25 Fed. Cas., No. 14,692a, pages 2-25. He ordered Burr committed on that charge, but released him on $10,000 bail, conditioned on his appearance at the next term of court, May 22.

D. *May 22, 1807. The grand jury.* The required

sixteen, out of a panel of twenty-four, were present and available for service on the grand jury. Burr, however, personally challenged "for favour" United States Senator Giles of Virginia, and Colonel Nicholas, a candidate for Congress, both of whom were strong partisans of Jefferson. Burr's objection to Senator Giles included the latter's recent effort in the Senate to suspend the writ of habeas corpus, indicating substantial belief in the reports to Congress on Burr's expedition. Burr offered to prove that the Senator had confirmed such beliefs by public declarations. Burr objected to Colonel Nicholas on the ground that the latter entertained a bitter personal animosity towards him. Both of those challenged withdrew from the panel. The sixteen finally accepted included some of the foremost citizens of Virginia. Two were Federalists, fourteen were Anti-Federalists. The Chief Justice named as foreman John Randolph, an Anti-Jeffersonian. In instructing the grand jury, Chief Justice Marshall followed the opinion he had written for the Supreme Court in *Ex parte Bollman and Swartwout, supra.* See 3 Beveridge, *The Life of John Marshall,* 350, 414 n., 466, 484, 506; 1 *Robertson's Reports of the Trials of Colonel Aaron Burr,* pages 31-46.

E. *May 22-28, 1807. Second motion to commit Burr for treason.* The District Attorney announced in open court that he would again move to commit Burr to jail on the charge of treason, arguing that, with the approach of General Wilkinson and the Government's principal witnesses, there was increased danger that Burr might not remain available. This motion had the earmarks of propaganda but the court ruled that if the District Attorney had something to present in support of such a motion, he had a right to do so. 25 Fed. Cas., No. 14,692b, pages 25-27. Witnesses were called as to the activities of Burr and his associates at Blennerhassett's Island. Collateral issues arose as to the admissibility of certain affidavits and as to their certification. The court ruled against their admissibility. 25 Fed. Cas., No. 14,692c, pages 27-30. The Chief Justice indicated that he hoped that no opinion would be required of him on this motion to commit for treason, prior to some action by the grand jury. When Burr agreed to double his bond, the motion was abandoned.

F. *June 9-13, 1807. The subpoena to the President.* Burr moved for issuance of a subpoena *duces tecum* directed to President Jefferson personally, calling upon him to produce a certain letter from General Wilkinson deemed material to the defense. After bitter argument, the Court ordered the subpoena to be issued. The Chief Justice stated that, while this was the Court's inescapable duty, it remained for the President to indicate in the return whether his executive duties would constitute a sufficient reason for not obeying it. 25 Fed. Cas., No. 14,692d, pages 30-38. This issue never reached its climax. The District Attorney later announced that he had the requested letter in his possession and was ready to produce it.

G. *June 15-18, 1807. Immunity of witnesses on on ground of self-incrimination.* An issue arose as to the extent to which the Court could go in requiring the secretary to Colonel Burr to state whether he, the secretary, understood the cipher letter which he had written for Colonel Burr. He declined to answer on the ground that his answer might tend to incriminate him. This resulted in a ruling that the witness could answer whether he *presently* understood the cipher, without its tending to incriminate him. The opinion states the views of the Chief Justice on the rules applicable to such cases. 25 Fed. Cas., No. 14,692e, pages 38-41.[12]

H. *June 19-27, 1807. Attachment of General Wilkinson was sought* by Burr's counsel for Wilkinson's alleged contempt of court and abuse of power in his efforts to induce witnesses to testify for the Government. The argument on this motion was interrupted by the grand jury's return of the indictments. The following day, the motion was denied. 25 Fed. Cas., No. 14,692f, pages 41-49.

I. *June 26, 1807. The indictments.* After extended hearings, the grand jury indicted both Burr and Blennerhassett not only for the misdemeanor charged, but also for treason. The indictments for treason charged that on December 10, 1806, at Blennerhassett's Island, the accused had levied war against the United States by the assembly there of a "multitude" of thirty or more people, armed and arrayed in a warlike and hostile manner. The other indictments alleged that at the same place the accused had set on foot an armed expedition against territory of the King of Spain. Two days later the grand jury returned similar indictments against United States Senator Smith of Ohio, former United States Senator Dayton of New Jersey, Tyler, Israel Smith and Floyd. Seven jurors voted to indict General Wilkinson but nine voted not to do so. Bollman, Swartwout and Adair were not indicted.

III. THE TRIAL

A. *June 26-27, 1807. Burr pleaded not guilty to the indictment for treason.* The court ordered that, inasmuch as the trial could not, without great inconvenience, be held in Wood County where the offense was alleged to have been committed, the marshal should summon forty-eight "fit persons", twelve of whom should be from Wood County, to appear in Richmond August 3, 1807, as a jury panel. From this time until the end of the trial, Burr remained committed in specially provided quarters.

B. *August 3-17, 1807. Impaneling the jury.* Out of the forty-eight persons summoned, only four were accepted as petit jurors and only one of those expressed himself as being entirely unprejudiced. After making a careful statement as to the proper qualification of jurors, the court ordered another panel of forty-eight. 25 Fed. Cas., No. 14,692g, pages 49-52. The result of their examination was no better. Finally, the accused suggested that he select jurors from those who had expressed hostility to him but to whom nevertheless he would be willing to submit his case. This implied strong faith by the accused, both in his innocence and in the fairness of the jury. It was a bold step in a capital case where there was such a popular demand for conviction. Among the jurors so chosen was one who testified that he had said that Burr should be hanged and another who had said "in the utmost spirit of levity" that he had come to Richmond with the hope of being chosen on the jury where, if accepted, he would vote to hang the defendant at once without further inquiry.[14]

C. *August 17-18, 1807. Order of proof.* Upon the appearnce of General Eaton as the prosecution's first witness, proof of Burr's hostile intentions in performing the particular overt acts charged in the indictment was objected to by Burr's counsel unless preceded by proof of the overt acts themselves. The court overruled the objection. It indicated that both the overt act and the hostile intent accompanying it were material to the proof of levying war, and that the courts should not prescribe which of the two material elements the prosecution must present first. The court added, however, that testimony relating to any plans of Burr's which, for example, were to be executed in Washington or elsewhere than in the District of Virginia, would not be an element of the particular treason charged in the indictment. While such testimony might later become admissible as corroborative of Burr's general evil intentions and thus "render it more probable that the intention in the particular case was evil," it would become admissible only "after hearing that which it is to confirm.' The testimony of General Eaton thus was permitted to be given insofar as it related directly to the overt acts charged and the hostile intent of the accused accompanying them. 25 Fed. Cas. No. 14,692h, pages 52-54.

D. *August 18-31, 1807. The crucial lack of proof.*
By August 20 the Government had not presented testimony of the presence or other actual participation of Burr in the assemblage at Blennerhassett's Island. On the contrary the evidence showed Burr's absence and his failure to participate in the assemblage. The defense accordingly objected to the introduction of any further evidence. In the absence of the constitutionally required testimony of the overt act of treason charged in the indictment, they contended that all other evidence would be immaterial. The Government recognized the propriety of the procedure. It argued, however, for permission to show that the accused had advised and procured the assemblage and that the assemblage constituted levying war against the United States.

After ten days of able argument,[15] the Chief Justice, on August 31, delivered the final opinion in the case. 25 Fed. Cas., No. 14,693, pages 55-186, at pages 159-181. He took occasion to explain and amplify the opinion he had written for the Supreme Court in *Ex parte Bollman and Swartwout,* 4 Cranch 75, 125. While it was not essential to the decision here, he indicated it to be his personal view that the constitutional requirement of levying war against the United States would be satisfied by finding the fact to be that there had been gathered at Blennerhassett's Island a military assemblage in force, with a warlike intent towards the United States and in condition to make such war. He indicated further that the evidence already before the court would justify its submission to the jury on that point, provided there were also before the court the required testimony as to the accused's participation in the assemblage.

He discussed the alleged activity of the accused in advising and procuring the assemblage. He pointed out that there had not yet been presented two witnesses to overt acts showing such advice or procurement. While not passing finally upon the point, he indicated that, to be admissible as overt acts of treason, such acts of advice or procurement should be charged in an indictment laid in the state and district where the trial would be held. No such acts of advice or procurement having been charged in the instant case, they could not be substituted for those which had been charged. Their admissibility as mere corroboration of other testimony was impossible in the absence of testimony to be corroborated.

Prosecution Fails to Prove Case

In short, the prosecution had failed to meet the constitutional requirement that the guilt of the accused be established by the testimony of two witnesses to the same overt act of the accused in levying war at a specified time and place within the jurisdiction of the trial court. The Chief Justice concluded:

> No testimony relative to the conduct or declarations of the prisoner, and subsequent to the transaction on Blennerhassett's Island, can be admitted; because such testimony, being in its nature merely corroborative and incompetent to prove the overt act in itself, is irrelevant until there be proof of the overt act by two witnesses. This opinion does not comprehend the proof by two witnesses that the meeting on Blennerhassett's Island was procured by the prisoner. On that point the court for the present withholds its opinion for reasons which have been already assigned; and as it is understood from the statements made on the part of the prosecution that no such testimony exists, if there be such let it be offered, and the court will decide upon it.
> The jury have now heard the opinion of the court on the law of the case. They will apply that law to the facts, and will find a verdict of

guilty or not guilty as their own consciences may direct. [25 Fed. Cas., No. 14,693, page 180.]

The court granted the prosecution's request to consider the court's opinion overnight. The next morning the prosecutor informed the court that he had nothing to offer to the jury, either in the way of evidence or argument. The jury retired and in a short time returned with the following verdict, prepared in a form of their origination: "We of the jury say that Aaron Burr is not proved to be guilty under this indictment by any evidence submitted to us. We therefore find him not guilty." [16]

The trial was over. The nation had reason to feel that, when administered after the manner of Marshall, Justice is the Guardian of Liberty.

[1] He had presided in the Senate, with marked fairness and competency, over the impeachment trial of Associate Justice Chase of the Supreme Court which had resulted in an acquittal of the Justice. January 2—March 1, 1805. See Annals, 8th Cong., 2d Sess. 80-675, 726-763. On leaving the Vice Presidency, he had delivered to the Senate, in executive session, March 2, 1805, an affecting farewell address marked with expressions of strong devotion to his country and its Constitution. Annals, 8th Cong., 2d Sess. 71-72.

[2] President's Message to Congress, Annals, 9th Cong., 2d Sess. 39-43.

[3] Andrew Jackson supported Burr's settlement program and refused to believe the charges of treason. He helped Burr outfit his river boats and entertained him at his home. When ordered to mobilize his militia in defense against Burr's supposedly revolutionary movements, he did so. After reinvestigating the facts, he promptly disbanded his militia.

[4] "Proclamation Against Burr's Plot", 10 Ford, *The Works of Thomas Jefferson* 301-302.

[5] "In this state of the evidence, delivered sometimes too under the restriction of private confidence, neither safety nor justice will permit the exposing names, except that of the principal actor [Burr], whose guilt is placed beyond question." Jefferson's Message to Congress, January 22, 1807, Annals, 9th Cong., 2d Sess. 39, 40.

[6] The record of the proceedings is largely available in:

(1). Robertson's *Reports of the Trials of Colonel Aaron Burr* (1808), cited by McCaleb as *Burr's Trials*. This is a two-volume publication containing, in 1135 pages, a substantially complete transcript of the record in the prosecutions, both for treason and misdemeanors in the Circuit Court of the United States, at Richmond, Virginia, taken in shorthand by David Robertson. Seee also, Coombs, *The Trial of Aaron Burr for High Treason*, condensed to 390 pages, largely omiting arguments of counsel.

(2). *United States* v. *Burr*, 25 Fed. Cas., Nos. 14,692, 14,692a, 14,692b, 14,692c, 14,692d, 14,692e, 14,692f, 14,692g, 14,692h, 14,693, 14,694, 14,694a, at pages 1-207. These contain the opinions in the several related cases. Those in the principal proceeding are in No. 14,693 and Marshall's major opinion of August 31, 1807, is at pages 159-181.

(3). *Ex parte Bollman and Swartwout*, 4 Cranch 75. This contains the opinions delivered in the Supreme Court in February, 1807, on several of the underlying issues which arose again in Burr's trial. As Appendix A, at pages 455-470, there are reprinted the documents which accompanied the President's message of January 22, 1807. As Appendix B, at pages 471-507, there is reprinted the opinion rendered by Chief Justice Marshall, as Circuit Justice for the Circuit Court in the District of Virginia, August 31, 1807. The reporter states, at page 125 note, that the opinion in the Circuit Court "elucidates and explains some passages in this opinion [of the Supreme Court in the *Bollman* case] which were supposed to be in some degree doubtful".

[7] The General soon seized this judge and another man, charging both with planning or participating in expeditions against Spanish possessions. Each was found not guilty when tried in March, 1808.

[8] ". . . no foreign enemy or open domestic foe was then, or has yet been proved to have been within any perilous distance of this city. . . . The acts of high-handed military power to which we have been exposed [are] too notorious to be denied, too illegal to be justified, too wanton to be excused." McCaleb, *The Aaron Burr Conspiracy*, page 198, citing *Orleans Gazette*, Extra, March 20, 1807.

[9] Cowles Meade, the acting Governor of the Mississippi Territory, reported to the Government as follows:

". . . this mighty alarm, with all its exaggeration, has eventuated in nine boats and one hundred men, and the major part of these are boys, or young men just from school. Many of their depositions have been taken before Judge Rodney, but they bespeak ignorance of the views or designs of the Colonel. I believe them really ignorant and deluded. I believe that they are really the dupes of stratagem, if the asservations of Generals Eaton and Wilkinson are to be accredited." McCaleb, *The Aaron Burr Conspiracy*, page 225.

[10] "The grand jury of the Mississippi Territory, on a due investigation of the evidence brought before them, are of the opinion that Aaron Burr has not been guilty of any crime or misdemeanor against the laws of the United States or of this Territory, or given any just occasion for alarm or inquietude

to the good people of this Territory. The grand jury present as a grievance, the late military expedition unnecessarily as they conceive, fitted out against the person and property of said Aaron Burr, where no resistance has been made to the ordinary civil authorities. The grand jury also present as highly derogatory to the dignity of this Government, the armistice (so-called) concluded between the Secretary, acting as Governor, and the said Aaron Burr. The grand jury also present as a grievance, destructive of personal liberty, the late military arrests made without warrant, and as they conceive, without other lawful authority: and they do seriously regret that so much cause should be given to the enemies of our glorious Constitution, to rejoice in such measures being adopted in a neighboring Territory, and if sanctioned by the Executive of our country, must sap the vitals of our political existence, and crumble this glorious fabric into the dust." McCaleb, *The Aaron Burr Conspiracy,* page 228, citing *Orleans Gazette,* February 20, 1807.

[11] . . . It appears that the Chief Justice later communicated individually with the members of the Supreme Court at some time before his Circuit Court's hearing of the *Burr* case, beginning August 3, 1807. 3 Beveridge, *The Life of John Marshall,* 480-481, and references made by the Chief Justice to the individual views of some of the Justices, expressed subsequent to the decision in the *Bollman* case. See *United States* v. *Burr,* 25 Fed. Cas., No. 14,693, at page 161, s. c., App. B, Cranch at pages 474-475.

[12] "The gentlemen of the bar will understand the rule laid down by the court to be this: It is the province of the court to judge whether any direct answer to the question which may be proposed will furnish evidence against the witness. If such answer may disclose a fact which forms a necessary and essential link in the chain of testimony, which would be sufficient to convict him of any crime, he is not bound to answer it so as to furnish matter for that conviction. In such a case the witness must himself judge what his answer will be; and if he say on oath that he cannot answer without accusing himself, he cannot be compelled to answer." 25 Fed. Cas., No. 14,692e, pages 40-41.

[14] "Miles Bott.—From the affidavits of generals Wilkinson and Eaton, my opinion has been completely made up for several months past.

"Mr. Martin.—I suppose you have only taken up a prejudice on the supposition, that the facts stated were true.

"Mr. Bott.—I have gone so far as to declare, that colonel Burr ought to be hanged.

"Mr. Burr.—Do you think that such declarations would now influence your judgment? Would not the evidence alter your opinion?

"Answer. Human nature is very frail; I know that the evidence ought, but it might or might not influence me. I have expressed myself in this manner, perhaps, within a fortnight; and I do not consider myself a proper juryman.

"Mr. Burr.—It will be seen, either that I am under the necessity of taking men in some degree, prejudiced against me, or of having another venire. I am unwilling to submit to the further delay of other 'tales,' and I must therefore encounter the consequences. I will take Mr. Bott, under the belief that he will do me justice." 1 Robertson's *Reports of the Trials of Colonel Aaron Burr*, page 426.

[15] The Chief Justice paid tribute to this argument as follows:

The question now to be decided has been argued in a manner worthy of its importance, and with an earnestness evincing the strong conviction felt by the counsel on each side that the law is with them. A degree of eloquence seldom displayed on any occasion has embellished a solidity of argument and a depth of research by which the court has been greatly aided in forming the opinion it is about to deliver. [25 Fed. Cas., No. 14,693, at page 159, s. c., 4 Cranch at page 470.] . . .

[16] Burr at once objected to the form of this "not-proven" or "Scotch Verdict" in place of a simple one of "not guilty." The Chief Justice replied that the verdict was, in effect, the same as a verdict of acquital, that it should remain as found by the jury, and that an entry be made on the record of "not guilty". Hill, *Decisive Battles of the Law*, 62.

As in each of the related proceedings, the necessary proof to sustain the charges had been found lacking when put to the final test. Thus acquitted for the misdemeanor. He was acquitted September 14, 1807. 25 Fed. Cas., No. 14,694, pages 187-201. The Government dropped its prosecutions of most of his associates. Further commitments of Burr and Blennerhassett were sought in the Mississippi Territory and in Ohio. Commitments for treason were denied. Commitments for misdemeanors in Ohio were ordered and bail was posted, but the accused apparently were never indicted.

THE COMMERCE CLAUSE UNDER MARSHALL

By Felix Frankfurter

Marshall's decisions, under the Commerce Clause of the Constitution, had a profound effect on the industrial development of this country. For this reason, the *Marshall Reader* would not be complete without an article on the Commerce Clause and its development under Marshall. The following article is taken from the Weil Lectures on American Citizenship delivered at the University of North Carolina by Justice Felix Frankfurter in 1936. It is reprinted here from the book *The Commerce Clause under Marshall, Taney and Waite* by Justice Frankfurter with the permission of the author and the publisher. The footnotes are numbered as they appeared in the book.

————

In the attempt to endow history with drama, different periods are too often conceived as duels between hostile champions. One of the classic plots in the writing of American history has been the clash of ideas attributed to Marshall and Taney. A strong central government on the one hand and states' rights on the other are the allegiances which have respectively enlisted the two sides. This kind of oversimplification of an extremely complicated interplay of forces has combined with the moral momentum which success confers upon the victorious antagonist to create the conventionalized picture of Marshall as the true believer and Taney as the false prophet. ". . . dead partisanships" Parrington shrewdly observes, "have a disconcerting way of coming to life again in the pages of their historians." [5]

This striking contrast between the significance of Marshall and that of Taney feeds on considerable truth. But its distortion fails to illuminate the real conflict in the outlook of the two great Chief Justices towards the social and economic ends to be served by our federal society, and the role of the Supreme Court in the service of these ends. Especially true is it of the problems of federal adjustment with which we are here concerned—those arising under the commerce clause—that their concrete manifestations involve stress and strain which modify the abstract principles of even the most dogmatic judge.

No judge writes on a wholly clean slate. There are compulsions and restraints supplied neither by the text of a constitution nor by opinions in the law reports. But Marshall had, as it were, the duty of creation to a degree greater than falls to the lot of even most great judges. When he was called upon to apply the commerce clause, he had available no fund of mature or coherent speculation regarding its implications. Neither the Philadelphia Convention nor the discussions preceding ratificaton of its labors generated currents of of important thought concerning the process of adjusting Congressional and state authorities. The records disclose no constructive criticisms by the states of the commerce clause as proposed to them. Their only recommendations were amendments requiring a two-thirds vote to pass "navigation laws, or laws regulating commerce," and forbidding Congressional grants of monopolies.[6] The conception that the mere grant of the commerce power to Congress dislodged state power finds no expression. At least the negative evidence permits the inference that the commerce clause was a sword available for Congressional use; it was an authorization to remove those commercial obstructions and harassments to which the militant new free states subjected one another, and to enable the community of the states to present a united commercial front to the world. The influential early commentators on the Constitution—*The Federalist* and Tucker's *Blackstone*—shed most flickering and ambiguous light on the reach of the commerce clause.[7] Nor had lower court decisions built a coral reef of doctrine, although two of the Justices on circuit, William Johnson and Bushrod Washington, had indulged in suggestive observations regarding the interaction of state and national powers.[8] And so, when first confronted with the commerce clause, the Supreme Court had to evolve doctrines without substantial guidance or restriction by previous discussion and analysis.

Temperament, experience and association converged to make it easy for Marshall to use the commerce clause as a curb upon local legislation. Valley Forge made him a nationalist; ties of friendship and shared labors in the struggle for the Constitution confirmed his faith. Local government was associated in his mind with the petty bickerings of narrow ambition and a dangerous indifference to rights of property. The need of a strong central government, as the indispensable bulwark of the solid elements of the nation, was for him the deepest article of his political faith.[9] But while he had rooted principles, he was pragmatic in their application. No less characteristic than the realization of the opportunities presented by the commerce clause to restrain local legislatures from hampering the free play of commerce among the states, was his empiricism in not tying the Court to rigid formulas for accomplishing such restrictions. His mind carried a hardheaded appreciation of the complexities of government, particularly in a federal system. Experience of men and affairs in the Virginia House of Burgesses, in Congress, as a diplomat, and as Secretary of State had reinforced a temperament to which abstract theorizing was never congenial, howsoever abstract the language in which he couched concrete results.

Gibbons v. *Ogden* affords striking proof of his effort towards the cautious direction of history.[10] The case is a thrice-told tale. The New York Legislature having granted an exclusive right to navigate the waters of the state by steam vessels, the holders of that privilege sought to enjoin Gibbons from operating his steamships between New Jersey and New York. Gibbons invoked the protection both of the commerce clause and of a license under the Act of Congress regulating the coastwise trade.[11] The right to navigate existed as a matter of international law, and the statute seems designed merely to regulate its exercise, and, specifically, to grant certain privileges to American shipowners.[12] The New York legislation did not collide with this policy of Congress. And the terms of the Constitution did not foreclose the conclusion that the mere grant of the commerce power to Congress did not debar New York from such legislation. Such was the view of Chancellor Kent in an earlier litigation affecting the steamboat monopoly,[13] and of Taney twenty years after *Gibbons* v. *Ogden*.[14] And in the opinion of James Bradley Thayer, fifty years later, it accorded both with sound constitutional exegesis and wise policy, that legislation should yield only to positive action by Congress, and not be contingent on judicial implications.[15] Indeed, such a view could have claimed support from an earlier generalization by Marshall himself, that ". . . the mere grant of a power to Congress, did not imply a prohibition on the States to exercise the same power," but that only, "whenever the terms in which a power is granted to congress, or the nature of the power, require that it should be exercised exclusively by congress," is it so.[16] On the other hand, with the knowledge that we have of the attitude of his colleagues and in view of the popular disfavor of the steamboat monopoly, it is safe to infer that Marshall could have had the concurrence of at least a majority of his Court, had he chosen to establish the "dormant" power of the commerce clause, that is, the implicit veto upon state legislation from the mere grant to Congress of power over foreign and interstate commerce.

In deciding against the monopoly Marshall was not content to place controlling reliance either on the conflict between the Act of Congress and that of New York, or on limitations upon the states implicit in the commerce clause. The concurring opinion of Mr. Justice Johnson shows how the case might have served as a vehicle for unambiguous doctrine.[17] Johnson rejected the relevance of the federal Act and rested the invalidity of the New York statute on its invasion of a field exclusively committed to Congress. For him, action by the states was foreclosed whether or not Congress had acted. In contrast to Johnson's characteristic trenchancy, Marshall's opinion was either unconsciously or calculatedly confused.

He begins with the familiar sonorous exposition of the terms of the commerce clause, which seems especially pointed towards establishing the constitutionality of the federal Coasting License Act;[18] he concludes by construing the Act as a grant of free passage over the navigable waters of the United States, which supplants conflicting state legislation;[19] in between, he indulges in a discussion of the relation of the commerce clause to the reserved powers of the states which in later history emerges as the doctrine of the "exclusiveness" of the commerce power.[20] It was logically irrelevant to Marshall's holding; indeed, he professes to dismiss consideration of the question from inquiry.[21] But it is more difficult to attribute to Marshall unconscious confusion of thought than it is to suspect that while, like Johnson, he saw in the commerce clause an opportunity to protect the national interest against state interference even in the absence of Congressional action, he was not yet prepared to transmute this possibility into constitutional doctrine.

Few problems in the unfolding of American constitutional law are psychologically more tantalizing than ascertainment of the influences which render some tentative ideas abortive and give enduring life to others. And as to the ideas that survive, it is seldom possible to discover the extent to which their consequences were intended or fortuitous. What Marshall merely adumbrated in *Gibbons* v. *Ogden* became central to our whole constitutional scheme: the doctrine that the commerce clause, by its own force and without national legislation, puts it into the power of the Court to place limits upon state authority. Of course, national self-consciousness has been with us a developing feeling, and the fluctuation of emphasis on central government or states has not yet spent its force. Marshall's use of the commerce clause greatly furthered the idea that though we are a federation of states we are also a nation, and gave momentum to the doctrine that state authority must be subject to such limitations as the

Court finds it necessary to apply for the protection of
the national community. It was an audacious doctrine, which, one may be sure, would hardly have
been publicly avowed in support of the adoption of
the Constitution. Indeed, *The Federalist* in effect
denied it, by assuring that only express prohibitions
in the Constitution limited the taxing power of the
states.[22] So audacious a doctrine eventually is bound
to provoke its antithesis. Two can play the game of
implications. By shifting the terms in the formula
of federalism, the counterpart of Marshall's doctrine
could be invoked to limit the affirmative exercise of
Congressional power: though we are a nation we are
also a federation of states, as declared by the Tenth
Amendment, and Congressional authority may therefore be subjected to such limitations as the Court
deems necessary for the protection of the independent existence of the states.[23] We shall see how
Marshall repudiated this idea.

Three years later, in *Brown* v. *Maryland*,[24] Marshall
gave powerful practical application to the possibili-
ties intimated in *Gibbons* v. *Ogden*. Immanent in the
commerce clause were severe limitations upon the
power of the states to tax as well as to regulate
commerce. To be sure, in holding unconstitutional a
Maryland statute imposing a license fee upon whole-
sale importers, the Chief Justice first construed the
federal tariff act as conferring upon the importer the
right to sell his goods in the original packages free
of local taxes, and then found the state Act in conflict with this gloss upon the federal tariff.[25] Here
again, as in *Gibbons* v. *Ogden,* Marshall reaches important constitutional results by esoteric statutory
construction. The Court's ingenuity in using legislation as an aid either in curbing or expanding constitutional powers is a great unwritten chapter in our
constitutional history. In both *Gibbons* v. *Ogden* and
Brown v. *Maryland,* Marshall so read measures of
Congress as to restrict local legislation beyond the
bounds of conflict with federal enactments.

The dependence of state authority on the range of judicial discretion which resulted from Marshall's technique of statutory construction was brought into the open in 1829, in *Willson* v. *The Black-Bird Creek Marsh Company*.[26] Here he sustained a Delaware Act authorizing a dam across a navigable tidal creek flowing into the Delaware River, although the dam completely obstructed navigation of the creek by a vessel sailing under a federal coasting license. He found that Congress could not have intended to grant rights of passage over all "those small, navigable creeks into which the tide flows, and which abound throughout the lower country of the middle and southern States." In other words, the Court would decide in any doubtful case whether the waters were important enough to national commerce so that Congress must have "intended" to guarantee the privilege of sailing over them.

The result of this sequence of cases was to make the Court collaborator with Congress in the regulation of foreign and interstate commerce, and thereby to bring before the Court questions inescapably implicating legislative policy. Policy is at stake because the actualities of life do not lend themselves to that scrupulous insulation of disparate interests which, formally at least, is the presupposition of the distribution of governmental authority as between the central government and the states. The history of the commerce clause, from the pioneer efforts of Marshall to our own day, is the history of imposing artificial patterns upon the play of economic life whereby an accommodation is achieved between the interacting concerns of states and nation. The problems of the commerce clause are problems in this process of accommodation, however different the emphasis of preference of interest, and however diverse the legal devices by which different judges may make these accommodations. Because such are the problems and such the relevant considerations for their adjustment, the constitutional labors of the Supreme Court, especially with the commerce clause, are accurately de-

scribed as statecraft. But it is an exercise in statesmanship hemmed in by the restrictions attending
the adjudicatory process. Far-reaching political principles arise through the accidents of unrelated and
intermittent cases, presenting issues confined by the
exigencies of the legal record, depending for elucida-
tion upon the learning and insight of counsel fortui-
tously selected for a particular case, and imprisoning
the judgment, at least in part, within legal habitua-
tions and past utterances.

Marshall's commerce clause decisions reflect both
his awareness of the problems of statecraft cast into
legal issues, and the tentative, experimental adjustments within the legal process whereby adjustments
without are made. We have already noted that in
Gibbons v. *Ogden* he did not choose to invalidate the
New York steamboat monopoly solely on the ground
either of its conflict with the Federal Coasting Act
or on the basis of its inconsistency with limitations
upon state power immanent in the commerce clause
itself. Hostility to monopoly easily rallied popular
support, with little heed to the effect of the decision
upon the federal equilibrium. When the immediate
results of a decision harmonize with public feeling,
the bearing of the decision upon future exercises of
power is for the moment neglected. The checkered
fortunes in the conflict between national and state
powers, as resolved by the Supreme Court, are partly
due to the fact that the respective claims have not
come before the Court in their full amplitude, but
have been entagled in specific controversies arousing
the emotions and allegiances of the moment. But
in the course of such decisions dicta are often emitted
which give momentum to a general direction for
future cases.

Doubtless what concerned the public most about
Gibbons v. *Ogden* was its desire to put an end to the
steamboat monopoly. We can only speculate why, in
reaching this result, Marshall resorted to his two
legal devices and rejected a third solution which
Webster offered in argument. Had Marshall pursued

the line of least resistance, he would have disposed of *Gibbons* v. *Ogden*, once he found a conflict between the New York and federal statutes, upon the supremacy which the Constitution explicitly gives to "the Laws of the United States which shall be made in Pursuance thereof." [27] It could not have been unwittingly that Marshall opened up much wider issues. Even the popularity of an anti-monopoly decision, however, would not have diverted attack, had he frankly avowed a broad theory of implied national supremacy with complementary limitations upon the states.

Webster, who appeared against the monopoly, had his own theory for reaching Marshall's result. His colleague, William Wirt, thus succinctly rephrased it:

> But if these police regulations of the states are to be considered as a part of the immense mass of commercial powers, is not the subject susceptible of division, and may not some portions of it be exclusively vested in Congress? It was viewing the subject in this light, that induced his learned associate to assume the position which had been misconceived on the other side. This proposition was, not that all the commercial powers are exclusive, but that those powers being separated, there are some which are exclusive in their nature; and among them, is that power which concerns navigation, and which prescribes the vehicles in which commerce shall be carried on.[28]

Marshall neither adopted his own generalized doctrine of "exclusiveness," nor did he embrace Webster's doctrine of selective "exclusiveness." Some twenty-five years later, in the case of *Cooley* v. *Board of Wardens*,[29] to be discussed later, Webster's analysis became Supreme Court doctrine. In the meantime, the theory of complete "exclusiveness" that Marshall adumbrated in *Gibbons* v. *Ogden*, although challenged, itself became doctrine, limited however in operation by a complementary doctrine to which it gave rise.

Marshall's boldness was wary. He knew the great art of consolidating a position step by step. It is legitimate to speculate that he ignored Webster's formula not because it would have failed to serve in his hands as an instrument for restricting state authority, but because its very flexibility was equally adaptable in hands bent on securing state immunity. Moreover, he may have felt that Webster's formula would reveal too obviously the large powers of discretion which judges must exercise in applying the commerce clause, and thus still further arouse jealousy of their powers. His own doctrine had at least the appearance of a more self-executing restriction upon the states. But he was not full-throated even in announcing his own theory of complete "exclusiveness." He must have felt that the time was not ripe for such contraction of state sovereignty in the name of national interest. Marshall was shrewd enough not to arouse needlessly the combination of forces against the imperceptible but steady enlargement of federal authority by making obvious the creative role of the Supreme Court in conveying to ordinary men the meaning of the Delphic language of the Constitution.

The robust English psychology of common sense whereby law is evolved case by case rather than by deduction from general principles, finds illusory application when the technique of adjudication of the common law is carried over to the statesmanship of constitutional decision. Even a decision settling an ordinary quarrel between litigants is a push, though unavowed, in the direction of one generalization rather than another. Moreover, though it is the fashion to insist that law is what courts do and not what they say, what they say has a considerable influence on what they do next. This is profoundly true of constitutional law. The impact of the concrete case is powerful not merely in securing a decision adapted to the needs of the immediate circumstances. Since the appeal is to law, the judges naturally infuse the *ad hoc* determination with justifications of more universal and impersonal validity. The wise judge is conscious of the implications of this process. He knows that generalizations are partly a projection of the present into the future, and except where he consciously attempts to determine its direction, he is curbed by his awareness of the limited scope of his prophetic vision.

Judges who have the ultimate power of adjusting conflicts within the federal system must resort to numerous legal levers of control. The interplay of political and economic forces to be adjusted demands an interplay of legal doctrines. Marshall's conception of the commerce clause as a limitation upon state powers satisfied his requirements for the national interest. Plainly enough, however, his doctrine of a completely exclusive commerce power could not be rigorously applied without changing the whole political character of the states. Marshall was, after all, a Virginian; he recognized that the effective regulation of local problems belongs to the state. And so, at the same time that he evolved from the commerce clause drastic restrictions upon state power, he also felt his way towards another doctrine, the resources of which would be available to meet the diverse local conditions of a sprawling federal society. In *Gibbons* v. *Ogden* there begins to emerge a source of authority for state legislation characterized as designed "to act directly on its system of police." [30] Because the "police power" is a response to the dynamic aspects of society, it has eluded attempts at definition. But precisely because it is such a response, it is one of the most fertile doctrinal sources for striking an accommodation between local interests and the demands of the commerce clause.

The instinct which led Marshall to give abstract recognition to limiting his broad construction of the commerce clause as a means of safeguarding state needs was confirmed by the concrete situation presented by *Willson* v. *The Black-Bird Creek Marsh*

Company.[31] The nub of the opinion is contained in a single paragraph:

> We do not think, that the act empowering the Black Bird Creek Marsh company to place a dam across the creek, can, under all the circumstances of the case, be considered as repugnant to the power to regulate commerce in its dormant state, or as being in conflict with any law passed on the subject.[32]

At the time, the laconic quality of the opinion, its stress on the absence of any conflicting federal legislation, and Marshall's omission of any reference to his full-dress exposition of the general subject of commerce in *Gibbons* v. *Ogden,* naturally suggested to some of his contemporaries a retreat from his earlier orientation towards the conception of the "exclusiveness" of the commerce power.[33] Indeed, after Marshall's death, one of his colleagues, Mr. Justice Thompson, who had shared in the decision of both the steamboat and the Willson cases, declared that the latter was "a strong case to show that a power admitted to fall within the power to regulate commerce, may be exercised by the states until congress assumes the exercise." [34] It would be interesting to have Marshall's own explanation of the relation of the Willson case to his earlier pronouncements. The supposition that the summary statement in that opinion was an implied retraction of the doctrine of "exclusiveness" is not tenable. "The circumstances of the case," in Marshall's own words, dictated the decision. Those circumstances furnish the clue to the direction of his thought. The Chief Justice noted the justification for the challenged legislation: the improvement of health and enhancement of property values.[35] Aims themselves laudable, they were also outside any context of national importance, because the legislation affected one of "those small navigable creeks . . . which abound throughout the lower country of the middle and southern states. . . ." [36] Marshall plainly implies that the Delaware statute falls outside the ban of the "dormant" commerce clause, because it is not a regulation of commerce, but of "police." State regulations of commerce were one thing; state exercises of the police power quite another.[37] But Marshall hardly furnished us a litmus paper test for distinguishing one from the other. He gave us only intimations, which Chief Justice Shaw in 1842 thus formulated:

> In considering, therefore, whether it is competent for a State to pass any particular law, we look rather to the ends to be attained, than to the particular enactments by which they are to be reached.[38]

In the early days of limited legislative activity it was not unnatural for Marshall to find that certain domains of state activity were clearly concerned with "police." In the practical aspects of contemporary legislation, he was not obviously begging the question in implying that if the effect of a statute were regulation of commerce, it would not be a "police" measure in purpose. And so it seemed not too simple or too evasive for him to look to "the end" of legislation as a means of determining its validity. As economic relationships became more interdependent, and the interaction between state legislation of every kind and interstate commerce became closer, the central inquiry necessarily shifted from the purpose of state legislation to its effect upon national commerce.[39] This condition had not become exigent in Marshall's time, and he was never called upon to canvass the elements of the problem that must be considered in determining when a state law in fact unduly burdens commerce.

Had it been given to Marshall to sharpen his coordinate ideas of the exclusive federal commerce power and the reserved state police power through the refining process of litigation, a fruitful analysis might well have eventuated. But employed by minds less sophisticated, less sensitive to the practical exigencies of government, Marshall's tentative ideas were turned into obscuring formulas whereby issues were confused and evaded. Especially applicable to constitutional law is Mr. Justice Holmes' *aperçu,* that law becomes more civilized as it becomes more self-conscious. Unless the process of adjudication was conscious of its assumptions, the legal rules regulating the commerce of the country, evolved to satisfy both the national interest and the wise claims of states, were bound to be either mechanical or meretricious. The law of the commerce clause was being made not merely by the Supreme Court. An important volume of litigation, both in the state and lower federal courts, was never reviewed by the highest tribunal. What in Marshall was the beginning of analysis, for lesser judges became tags. Judges throughout the land rested on an uncritical use of the police power, and rendered mechanical decisions in Marshall's name.[40] No formula will make great judges of little men, or automatically insure wise exercise of the wider discretion which the broad delineations of constitutional power necessarily confer. But guiding analysis and luminous generalization, either through the perception of a great leader or the gradual accretion of experience, tend to save even lesser minds from confused or mechanical judgments. Unfortunately, Marshall's formulation of his own practical insight had not gone far enough to control the direction of coherent doctrine.

He did, however, indicate two phases of the intellectual procedure to be followed in analyzing the bearing of state legislation upon the commerce protected by the Constitution. *Brown* v. *Maryland* gave us one, and the *Willson* case the other. In the earlier case Marshall insisted that substance and not form must control the Court's appraisal of state legislation.[41] What seems merely like an obviously sensible canon for statutory construction involved a major choice of attitude toward the Constitution. Certain limitations upon the taxing power of the states the

Constitution imposes explicitly.[42] Textually it is not difficult to maintain that no other withdrawals from the state taxing power were impliedly made; nor is such a conclusion without support in policy.[43] By professing merely to pierce through the form of legislation to its substance, Marshall established barriers against local encroachments upon the protected fields of commerce even by forms of state taxation which the Constitution did not expressly forbid. The Willson decision begins a wholesome emphasis upon the concrete elements of the situation that concerns both state and national interests. The particularities of a local statute touch its special aims and the scope of their fulfillment, the difficulties which it seeks to adjust, the price at which it does so. These and kindred practical considerations, in their myriad manifestations, have weighed with the Court in determining the fate of state legislation impinging on the activities of national commerce, ever since Marshall in the *Willson* case set the standard for deciding such controversies "under all the circumstances of the case."[44] To be sure, the inevitable tendency to derive a generalization from a concrete judgment has frequently led to a mechanical application of language torn from its limiting context of circumstances. In the history of the Supreme Court no single quality more differentiates judges than the acuteness of their realization that practical considerations, however screened by doctrine, underlie resolution of conflicts between state and national power.

Thus far we have been concerned with the scheme of general ideas which Marshall devised as instruments for adjudication. The specific situations which invited his judgment deserve more explicit treatment, for they constituted the chief stuff of the development of the law of the commerce clause down to this century. The central themes of this current of constitutional litigation were questions of the allowable control by the states over the business of transporting goods and persons across state lines, and the permissible extent of state taxation of business enterprise.

The enormous expansion of water transportation, especially on the western rivers, due to the steamboat, produced *Gibbons* v. *Ogden.* Connecticut and New Jersey were replying to the New York monopoly grant with retaliatory legislation reminiscent of the commercial wars between the states under the Articles of Confederation; and fear of monopoly control over the new instrument of transportation was stirring in the west.[45] In a period when the business of transportation by land was generally carried on between relatively local points, the grant of monopoly rights for the promotion of stages, bridges, toll roads and ferries was a familiar inducement offered to capital.[46] But the opportunities opened by the steam engine for developing national markets were hardly compatible with monopolistic control of the new agencies of transportation. With his vivid memory of the mercantilist conflicts under the Confederation, Marshall surely saw in the New York grant precisely the kind of threat to national free trade and harmony among the states which the Constitution was intended to avert. Water transportation after the Civil War receded in significance, but the constitutional basis of its protection served the needs of the newer instrument of transportation. The railroad was still in its pioneer stage at Marshall's death, but he had furnished an ample constitutional frame for its development.[47]

Brown v. *Maryland* was a less happy beginning for the evolution of restrictions upon state tax powers.[48] As a matter of fact, the circumstances of the case furnished a ready opportunity for curbing state taxation discriminating against interstate commerce, for the license fee which Maryland exacted from wholesalers of imported goods was required of them alone. But Marshall wrested from the case more far-reaching doctrine. He chose to discuss the case as if the Maryland tax were a non-discriminatory measure on the wholesaling of goods of whatever origin, and to hold that even such a general tax, as applied to the sale of imports, conflicted with the license to sell in 'the original package." With painful ingenuity he found this license in the interstices of the Federal Tariff Act. But not content with this discovery of a collision between the state tax and the tariff on imported goods, he dispensed with the relevance of the argument drawn from the tariff by declaring that he and his brethren "suppose the principles laid down in this case, to apply equally to importations from a sister state." The "principles" were affirmations of broad limitations, which Marshall derived not from the language of the Constitution but from the existence of the commerce clause, upon the power of states to impose general taxes upon dealings in goods while yet in the original packages in which they came from other states. In his eagerness to save national commerce from the particularism of the states, Marshall would have unduly contracted the available resources of the states' taxing power.[49] He overreached himself. His doctrine was formally rejected in *Woodruff* v. *Parham*,[50] and that, too, at a time, in 1868, when the dominant mood of the Court was nationalistic.

While interstate commerce was not to secure the protection from general state taxation which Marshall sought to win for it in *Brown* v. *Maryland,* the limitation which he neglected to impose against discriminatory state taxation afterwards became constitutional law. The failure of the Chief Justice to turn *Brown* v. *Maryland* to this use is all the more surprising inasmuch as such discrimination against interstate commerce was left unchecked by state courts.[51] Indeed, Marshall's disregard of the element of discrimination in the Maryland statute may well have stimulated resort to discriminatory taxes, and led state courts to sanction their use. The ambiguous silence of *Brown* v. *Maryland* on the issue of discrimination puzzled so penetrating a mind as that of Chief Justice Ruffin.[52] Less discriminating state court judges found no difficulty in sustaining flagrantly discriminatory taxes,[53] partly supported by some encouraging dicta in the Taney period,[54] until, in 1876, a halt was decisively called in *Welton* v. *Missouri.*[55]

Thus far we have been concerned with Marshall's use of the commerce clause as an instrument of negation. But even in so far as he struck down state legislation he did so as a means of releasing energies of national life. To be sure, these energies were to flow largely by making available opportunities for free economic enterprise. Yet the opinions in *Gibbons* v. *Ogden* and *Brown* v. *Maryland,* are not without significance in the evolution of the affirmative aspects of the commerce clause. The decisions in both cases depended on the exertion of Congressional power under the commerce clause. To be sure, in each instance Marshall sustained federal legislation directed towards relieving business from hampering state legislation. Except in the limited fields of the tariff and the hotly contested proposals of internal improvements, government was not yet thought of as a directing agent of social and economic policies. But Marshall conveyed some general attitudes towards the Constitution which readily yielded authority in support of Congressional power, when the time eventually did come for its more aggressive employment.

That counsel for the monopoly brought to bear on Marshall and his Court an enveloping atmospheric pressure in favor of a strict construction of the grants of Congressional power is familiar history.[56] Less well remembered is it that the Tenth Amendment was invoked not simply as a redundant reminder that what the Constitution did not give it withheld, but as a generating principle of restriction upon the affirmative grants of national power.[57] Marshall not merely rejected the Tenth Amendment as an active principle of limitation; he countered with his famous characterization of the powers of Congress, and of the commerce power in particular, as the possession of the unqualified authority of a unitary sovereign. He threw the full weight of his authority against the idea that, apart from specific restrictions in the Constitution, the very existence of the states operates as such a limitation:

> If, as has always been understood, the sovereignty of congress, though limited to specified objects, is plenary as to those objects, the power over commerce with foreign nations, and among the several States, is vested in congress as absolutely as it would be in a single government, having in its constitution the same restrictions on the exercise of the power as are found in the constitution of the United States.[58]

Marshall was not unmoved by the demands of moderation—the need for all sorts of accommodation in the effective working of any scheme of society, but especially of such a delicate and complicated system as ours. But his reliances were not mechanical rules of construction of legal curbs upon power, lest it be abused. For him the ultimate safeguards lay elsewhere:

> The wisdom and the discretion of congress, their identity with the people, and the influence which their constituents possess at elections, are, in this, as in many other instances, . . . the sole restraints on which they have relied, to secure them from its abuse. They are the restraints on which the people must often rely solely, in all representative governments.[59]

Marshall resisted still another attempt to misuse state lines as a barrier to the adequacy of the commerce power. It was the fashion to assume a rigid line of demarcation between the commerce over which Congress had been given authority and the "internal" commerce of the states. Physical movement across state lines was deemed the simple test. Perhaps the very narrowness of the conception of commerce urged at the bar led Marshall to sketch contours for the commerce power more generous than

later cases have always recognized.[60] In language
reminiscent of the Sixth of the Virginia Resolutions,
the Chief Justice declared:

> The genius and character of the whole govern-
> ment seem to be, that its action is to be applied
> to all the external concerns of the nation, and to
> those internal concerns which affect the States
> generally; but not to those which are completely
> within a particular State, which do not affect
> other States, and with which it is not necessary
> to interfere, for the purpose of executing some of
> the general powers of the government.[61]

Marshall thus had an organic conception of commerce. Mr. Justice Holmes' admonition that commerce "is not a technical legal conception, but a
practical one, drawn from the course of business"
would have won his full accord.[62] The wide auxiliary
powers which the "necessary and proper" clause
makes available must have been fully in Marshall's
mind;[63] and while the now familiar conception of the
"stream of commerce" was not in terms expressed by
Marshall, the phases of commerce embraced by that
doctrine were plainly covered by his philosophy.[64]

It has been fashionable to minimize Marshall's
creative talents by regarding the ground newly
broken in his opinions as essentially the work of the
great lawyers who argued before him, and particularly Webster. The latter was no mean appreciator
of his own performance, but a reading of his argument in *Gibbons* v. *Ogden* will hardly confirm his
reported boast that Marshall's opinion "was little else
than a recital of my argument." [65] Powerful counsel
of course make a difference. But not the least distinction of a great judge is his capacity to assimilate,
to modify and reject the discursive and subtly partisan arguments of counsel and to transform their raw
materials into an enduring opinion. Nor must we
overlook the fact that Marshall's opinions were undoubtedly the collaborative product of the whole

Court. In his days there was the closest intimacy among the judges. They carried their cases to their common boarding house. A man of Marshall's charm and power was bound to exert great influence with his brethren. But the idea that he dominated his colleagues leaves out of reckoning the strong personalities of some of his associates. Story had devotion to Marshall, but also vanity and views. Johnson's opinions reveal a downright character, tough-mindedness, and intellectual energy not second to that of the Chief Justice. Nor is it likely that Bushrod Washington was an echo. The novelty of the issues, the lively interest of Washington society in the Court's proceedings, the close social relations of the justices, and the ample time they had for discussion can leave no doubt that an opinion like that in *Gibbons* v. *Ogden* was an orchestral and not a solo performance.

If constitutional decisions are to be the offspring of the deliberative process, they must be a composite product of the Court. But their expression is individual. The voice of the Court cannot avoid imparting to its opinions the distinction of its own accent. Marshall spoke for the Court. But *he* spoke. And the prestige of his office, as well as the considerable deference paid by his brethren to the author of every opinion, enabled him to formulate in his own way the agreements that he and they had reached. Thus it is not accidental that the three commerce clause opinions of Marshall indulge in observations beyond the necessities of the case and outside the requirement of his own analysis.

To dismiss these phases of the opinions as mere dicta is to miss significant aspects of his achievement, and to minimize the ways in which constitutional law develops. For Mr. Justice Holmes the crucial importance of Marshall was that he was *there*.[66] Marshall must have felt it. Certainly he seized every opportunity to educate the country to a spacious view of the Constitution, to accustom the public mind to broad national powers, and to restrict the old assertiveness of the states. He imparted such a momentum to these views that it carried the Court in his general direction beyond his own time. But he had too much of an instinct for the practical to attempt rigidities which could not possibly bind the future. He wished to promote the national power, but he left open the choice of doctrine for the attainment of his purpose. And so his views were often tentative and suggestive; they conveyed cross currents of doctrine and purposed ambiguity.

Marshall's opinions are not to be judged as literary documents—they are events in American history. "There fell to Marshall," according to Mr. Justice Holmes, "perhaps the greatest place that was ever filled by a judge." [67] That Marshall seized it, the role of the Supreme Court in American history bears witness.

[5] 1 Main Currents in American Thought: the Colonial Mind (1927) i.

[6] Navigation Acts: 2 Elliott's Debates on the Federal Constitution (2d ed. 1836) 553 (Maryland); 3 id. 660 (Virginia); 4 id. 245 (North Carolina). Monopolies: 2 id. 177 (Massachusetts); id. 407 (New York).

[7] See The Federalist, (Lodge ed. 1888) No. 32, 185-187; 1 Tucker's Blackstone's Commentaries (1803) 180, 369.

[8] See Washington, J., in Golden v. Prince, 10 Fed. Cas. 542 No. 5509 (C. C. D. Pa. 1814); Johnson, J., in Elkison v. Deliesseline, 8 Fed. Cas. 493; No. 4366 (C. C. D. S. C. 1823).

[9] See 2 Beveridge, The Life of John Marshall (1916) cc. II, III. Though tinged with strong Federalist flavor, and limited in its analysis of the relation of Marshall's opinions to the development of American constitutional law, (see McLaughlin, The Life of John Marshall (1921) 7 A. B. A. Jour. 231), Beveridge's work still remains the most adequate study of the career of a member of the Supreme Court.

[10] 9 Wheat. 1 (1824).

[11] Act of Feb. 18, 1793, c. 8, 1 Stat. 305.

[12] See Johnson, J., concurring, 9 Wheat. 1, 231-33 (1824).

[13] See Kent, C. J., in Livingston v. Van Ingen, 9 Johns. 507, 578 (N. Y. Ct. of Errors 1812).

[14] See Taney, C. J., in The License Cases, 5 How. 504, 579 (1847).

[15] 2 Cases on Constitutional Law (1895) 2190.

[16] See Sturges v. Crowninshield, 4 Wheat. 122, 193 (1819).

[17] 9 Wheat. 1, 222 (1824).

[18] 9 Wheat. (U. S.) 1, 187-189.

19 *Id.* 209 *et seq.*
20 *Id.* 197-209.
21 *Id.* 200.
22 The Federalist (Lodge ed. 1888) No. 32, 185, 187.
23 See Corwin, The Twilight of the Supreme Court (1934) c. 1.
24 12 Wheat. 419 (1827).
25 *Id.* 448.
26 2 Pet. 245 (1829).
27 Art. VI, sec. 2.
28 See report of Wirt's argument in Gibbons v. Ogden, 9 Wheat. 1, 180 (1824).
29 12 How. 299 (1851).
30 See 9 Wheat. 1, 204 (1824).
31 2 Pet. 245 (1829).
32 *Id.* 252.
33 See Kellogg v. Union Co., 12 Conn. 7, 21, 25 (1837); *cf.* Low v. Commissioners of Pilotage, R. M. Charlton 302, 314 (Ga. Super. Ct. 1830); Savage, C. J., in People v. Rensselaer and Saratoga R. R., 15 Wend. 113, 135 (N. Y. Sup. Ct. 1836).
34 See Thompson, J., concurring in Mayor etc. of the City of New York v. Miln, 11 Pet. 102, 149 (1837); *cf.* 1 Warren, The Supreme Court in United States History (rev. ed. 1935) 709; 2 *id.* 27.
35 See Wilson v. The Black-Bird Creek Marsh Co., 2 Pet. 245, 251 (1829).
36 *Id.* 252.
37 Probably indicative of Marshall's trend of thought is the comment on the Willson decision in 2 Story, Commentaries on the Constitution of the United States (1st ed. 1833) 517, that if Congress has not legislated, "it would be difficult to affirm, that the sovereignty of a state, acting on subjects within the reach of other powers, beside that of regulating commerce, and which belonged to its general territorial jurisdiction, would be intercepted by the exclusive power of commerce, unexercised by congress, over the same subject-matter." There is, curiously, no reference to the Willson case or to Mr. Justice Thompson's comments on it, in Mr. Justice Story's dissent in Mayor etc. of the City of New York v. Miln, 11 Pet. 102, 152, (1837).
38 See Norris v. Boston, 4 Metc. (Mass.) 282, 292-93 (1842). *Cf.* Lewis, Federal Power over Commerce (1892) 42.
39 *Cf.* Taney, C. J., in The License Cases, 5 How. 504, 583 (1847).
40 Numerous opinions deemed analysis complete when a challenged statute was decided to have been enacted in the exercise of some state power other than that over commerce, with little or no analysis of elements of conflict between "police" legislation and restrictions upon state authority immanent in the commerce clause. See, *e.g.*, Scott v. Willson, 3

N. H. 321, 326-28 (1825); Beall v. State, 4 Blackf. 107 (Ind. 1835); State v. Fullerton, 7 Rob. 210 (La. 1844).

[41] See Marshall, C. J., in Brown v. Maryland, 12 Wheat. 419, 444, 448 (1827).

[42] Art. I, sec. 10 (2), (3).

[43] See The Federalist (Lodge ed. 1888) No. 32, 185, 187.

[44] See Willson v. The Black-Bird Creek Marsh Co., 2 Pet. 245 (1829).

[45] See argument of Webster, Gibbons v. Ogden, 9 Wheat. 1, 4 (1824): cf. Livingston v. Tompkins, 4 Johns. Ch. 415, 430 (N. Y. 1820); Livingston v. Gibbons, 5 id. 250 (N. Y. 1821). And see (1824) 26 Niles' Weekly Reg. 2, 54, 267; (1825) 28 id. 147; Lanman, American Steam Navigation (1841) 4 Hunt's Merchants' Mag. 105, 118. Cf. 1 Warren, op. cit. supra note 34, at 611, ff.

[46] Prentice, The Federal Power over Carriers and Corporations (1907) 59-64, 77-78.

[47] Compare Pensacola Telegraph Co. v. Western Union Telegraph Co., 96 U. S. 1 (1877).

[48] 12 Wheat. 419 (1827).

[49] See Story, J., dissenting in Mayor etc. of the City of New York v. Miln, 11 Pet. 102, 160 (1837), for a statement revealing the sweeping implications of Marshall's doctrine.

[50] 8 Wall. 123 (1869).

[51] See, e.g., before Brown v. Maryland, Cumming v. Mayor and Aldermen of Savannah, R. M. Charlton 26 (Ga. Super. Ct. 1816); Cowles v. Brittain, 2 Hawkes 204 (N. C. 1822); Biddle v. Commonwealth, 13 Serg. & R. 405 (Pa. 1825).

[52] See Wynne v. Wright, 1 Devereux & Battle 19, 23 (N. C. 1834).

[53] In some cases seemingly presenting the issue of discrimination, the problem was not discussed by the Court. E.g., Beall v. State, 4 Blackf. 107 (Ind. 1835); People v. Coleman, 4 Cal. 46 (1854); State v. Pinckney, 10 Rich. L. 474 (S. C. 1857). Some confuse the commerce clause issue with questions suggested by the privileges and immunities clause. See State v. Fullerton, 7 Rob. 210 (La. 1844); Shipper v. Pennsylvania R. R., 47 Pa. St. 338 (1864); Mork v. Commonwealth, 6 Bush 397 (Ky. 1870); cf. Raguet v. Wade, 4 Ohio 107 (1829). Other opinions seem explicitly to justify even taxation discriminating against foreign or interstate commerce by assertion of the absolute character of state tax power. See, e.g., Seymour v. State, 51 Ala. 52 (1874), cf. Vines v. State, 67 Ala. 73 (1880); Ward v. State, 31 Md. 279 (1869; rev'd, Ward v. Maryland, 12 Wall. 418 (1871); Davis v. Dashiel, Phillips 114 (N. C. 1867); cf. People ex rel. Attorney General v. Naglee, 1 Cal. 232 (1850).

[54] See McLean, J., in Nathan v. Louisiana, 8 How. 73, 80 (1850); and in The License Cases, 5 How. 504, 592 (1847); Woodbury, J., id. 622. Cf. Davis v. Dashiel, Phillips, 114, 117 (N. C. 1867); Ward v. State, 31 Md. 279, 285, 289 (1869);

Sears v. Board of Commissioners of Warren County, 36 Ind. 267, 275 (1871).

[55] 91 U. S. 275 (1876).

[56] See arguments of Oakley and Emmett, Gibbons v. Ogden, 9 Wheat. 1, 34, 87 (1824); *cf.* 1 Tucker's Blackstone's Commentaries (1803) App. 151-54, cited in argument for the monopoly.

[57] 9 Wheat. 1, 34.

[58] *Id.* 197.

[59] *Ibid.*

[60] *Id.* 65, 96.

[61] *Id.* 195.

[62] See Holmes, J., in Swift v. United States, 196 U. S. 375, 398 (1905).

[63] See Gibbons v. Ogden, 9 Wheat. 1, 204 (1824).

[64] *Id.* 195.

[65] Harvey, Reminiscences and Anecdotes of Daniel Webster (1877) 142.

[66] *John Marshall*: in Answer to a Motion that the Court Adjourn, on February 4, 1901, the One Hundredth Anniversary of the Day on which Marshall Took his Seat as Chief Justice. Collected Legal Papers (1921) 268.

[67] *Id.* 270.

JOHN MARSHALL AND THE LAW OF NATIONS

Edward Dumbauld

One of the significant contributions of John Marshall as Chief Justice to the jurisprudence of this country was his decisions in the field of international law. This aspect of Marshall's tenure on the Bench of the Supreme Court has been well treated by Edward Dumbauld, an active member of the Pennsylvania Bar and a Lawyer who has an active interest in legal history. This article entitled, "John Marshall and the Law of Nations", was prepared for the John Marshall symposium issue of the *University of Pennsylvania Law Review* and is reprinted here with the consent of the publisher.

––––––

"When the United States declared their independence, they were bound to receive the law of nations, in its modern state of purity and refinement," according to the opinion of Mr. Justice James Wilson[1] in an important case before the Supreme Court of the United States in which John Marshall appeared as losing counsel.[2]

What was the "law of nations" or *jus gentium* which the infant American republic thus accepted as part of its own law?[3] It was a species of universal law, based on reason and binding upon all mankind, which eighteenth century jurists did not hesitate to recognize as valid. It embraced three principal divisions: the law merchants, the law maritime, and the body of law between states which is now called public international law.[4]

In that cosmopolitan era, though it might be forbidden to cite English precedents,[5] it was not unusual for American lawyers to be familiar with Roman and civil-law doctrines. Only narrowly did American municipal law escape a greater infusion of continental principles than it in fact experienced.[6]

It was therefore very natural that in the field of *jus gentium,* where the law was professedly of more than parochial character, a very eclectic spirit should prevail.

Lord Mansfield's familiar quotation from Cicero was made in a case involving a shipowner's claim for freight: ". . . the maritime law is not the law of a particular country, but the general law of nations: 'non erit alia lex Romae, alia Athenis; alia nunc, alia posthac; sed et apud omnes gentes et omni tempore, una eademque lex obtinebit.'"[7]

And in discussing with the French minister a case pending in an American prize court, Secretary of State Jefferson thus proclaimed the universality of the law applied by such a tribunal: "It happens in this particular case that the rule of decision will be, not the municipal laws of the United States but the law of nations, and the Law maritime, as admitted and practised in all civilized countries; that the same sentence will be pronounced here that would be pronounced in the same case in the Republic of France, or in any other country of Europe. . . ."[8]

Though the universality of the law of nations was clearly perceived, as well as its dependence on the common consent of all civilized nations rather than the dictates of one or a few great powers,[9] the possibility of development and creative effort in the field of international law was equally recognized. To such progress the United States itself made notable contributions, especially in the matter of the rights of neutrals.[10] In this advancement of the law of nations John Marshall played a significant part.

Marshall's fame as expounder of the Constitution tends to overshadow his achievements in other fields of law. Yet, during his tenure as Chief Justice from 1801 to 1835, the Supreme Court rendered 62 decisions involving questions of constitutional law, of which Marshall wrote the opinion of the Court in 36; while during the same period 195 cases were decided involving questions of international law or relations, and in 80 of these Marshall was spokesman for the Court.[11]

The noted international lawyer, John Bassett Moore, the first American jurist to sit as a judge of the Permanent Court of International Justice, says of

Marshall: "He is known in other lands as the author of important opinions on questions which deeply concern the welfare and intercourse of all nations. In the treatment of questions of international law he exhibited the same traits of mind, the same breadth and originality of thought, the same power in discovering and the same certainty in applying fundamental principles, that distinguished him in the realm of constitutional discussions; and it was his lot in more than one case to blaze the way in the establishment of rules of international conduct." [12]

International law, like constitutional law, presented a new and growing field where Marshall's powerful and perceptive mind could build creatively. In the more technical and minute departments of law, such as those dealing with commercial subjects, where erudition rather than originality was required, Marshall did not excel.[13] In such branches of jurisprudence, his scanty legal education[14] had not made him the equal of his studious colleague, Joseph Story.[15]

Much of Marshall's learning in the realm of international law was derived from Thomas Rutherforth's *Institutes of Natural Law*. This digest of Grotius was one of the few law books in Marshall's library.[16] It was an influential treatise in that era, and Marshall relied extensively on its teachings.

Four epochs in Marshall's career deserve attention in appraising his contributions to the development of the law of nations. In 1797, he was a member of the XYZ mission sent to France by President John Adams.[17] Marshall was greeted with acclaim on his return from this abortive mission, in the course of which he had maintained a firm and dignified position as representative of his nation. Marshall's cogent statement of the American position in a lengthy communication to Talleyrand, the French minister of foreign affairs, and his dispatches to his own government constitute an impressive series of state papers from his pen and deserve to rank as noteworthy diplomatic documents.[18]

After Marshall's return to America and his election

to Congress in 1799, he again had occasion to deal
with a problem involving the law of nations. His
speech in the House of Representatives on March 7,
1800, on the Jonathan Robbins case was one of the
most effective addresses ever delivered before that
body.[19] John Bassett Moore thus describes the incident: "By the twenty-seventh article of the Jay Treaty
it was provided that fugitives from justice should be
delivered up for the offense of murder or of forgery.
Under this stipulation, Robbins, *alias* Nash, was
charged with the commission of the crime of murder
on board a British privateer on the high seas. He
was arrested on a warrant issued upon the affidavit
of the British consul at Charleston, South Carolina.
After his arrest, an application was made to Judge
Bee, sitting in the United States circuit court at
Charleston, for a writ of habeas corpus. While Robbins was in custody, the President of the United
States, John Adams, addressed a note to Judge Bee,
requesting and advising him, if it should appear that
the evidence warranted it, to deliver the prisoner up
to the representatives of the British government. The
examination was held by Judge Bee, and Robbins was
duly surrendered. It is an illustration of the vicissi-
tudes of politics that, on the strength of this incident,
the cry was raised that the President had caused the
delivery up of an American citizen who had been
impressed into the British service. For this charge
there was no ground whatever, but it was made to
serve the purposes of the day and was one of the
causes of the popular antagonism to the administration of John Adams. When Congress met in December, 1799, a resolution was offered by Mr. Livingston,
of New York, severely condemning the course of the
administration. Its action was defended in the House
of Representatives by Marshall, on two grounds:
first, that the case was one clearly within the provisions of the treaty; and, second, that, no act having
been passed by Congress for the execution of the
treaty, it was incumbent upon the President to carry
it into effect by such means as happened to be within

his power. The speech which Marshall delivered on that occasion is said to have been the only one that he ever revised for publication. It 'at once placed him,' as Mr. Justice Story has well said, 'in the front rank of constitutional statesmen, silenced opposition, and settled forever the points of national law upon which the controversy hinged.' So convincing was it that Mr. Gallatin, who had been requested by Mr. Livingston to reply, declined to make the attempt, declaring the argument to be unanswerable." [20]

Upon becoming Secretary of State in the closing months of the Adams administration, Marshall was again placed in a position where his official duties brought questions of international law to his notice. Negotiations with England regarding the functioning of the claims commission set up under the Jay Treaty raised questions as to the scope of the treaty provisions. Several other disputed points also required attention. A treaty provision placing in the list of contraband "whatever may serve directly to the equipment of vessels" was being applied so sweepingly by England that Marshall felt that no effect at all was being given to the word "directly." He protested that the United States deemed this construction "alike unfriendly and unjust." Another subject of controversy arose when the British ignored the requirement of international law that a blockade must be maintained effectively in order to be legally valid. Moreover, Marshall directed a strong protest against "the unjust decisions of their courts of Vice Admiralty and the impunity which attends captures totally vexatious and without probable cause of seizure." Conceding that it would be too much to expect all the commanders of naval vessels and privateers to be "men of correct conduct and habits," he stressed the importance of an upright judiciary to review the legality of their seizures. But the English courts were no better than the seamen; they seldom restored a vessel captured in violation of the law of nations and never awarded costs and damages for detention; they were "converting themselves from judges into mere instruments of plunder." The perennial problem of impressment of sailors from American vessels was likewise acute. These thorny topics occasioned Marshall's principal state papers in the field of international affairs during this period.[21]

The fourth and final stage in Marshall's official career, where it became his task to deal with matters relating to the law of nations, was his tenure as Chief Justice of the Supreme Court of the United States. To comment upon or analyze all of Justice Marshall's opinions upon questions of an international character[22] is of course impracticable here.[23] Mention must be made however of several of the most famous opinions written by Marshall which are generally considered as landmarks in the development of the law of nations.[24]

Marshall's most widely known case in the field of international law is, of course, *The Schooner Exchange* v. *McFaddon*.[25] An American vessel, which had been captured and confiscated by the French and commissioned as a man-of-war, entered the port of Philadelphia and was libelled by the original American owners, who demanded restitution of their property. In an elaborate opinion rendered on March 3, 1813, Marshall held that a public ship of a foreign state was not amenable to the jurisdiction of an American judicial tribunal.

He pointed out that "the jurisdiction of courts is a branch of that which is possessed by the nation as an independent sovereign power." Such jurisdiction is susceptible of no limitation not imposed by the nation itself. "All exceptions, therefore, to the full and complete power of a nation within its own territories" must be based on its express or implied consent.[26]

Marshall then reviewed the classes of cases where an implied consent to exemption from territorial jurisdiction is acknowledged. These include the immunity enjoyed by the person of the sovereign himself, by foreign ministers, and by armies permitted to pass through a foreign territory.[27] Should the same rule apply to ships of war entering the ports of a friendly power? Or should such ships receive the same treatment as private commercial vessels?

The Chief Justice concluded that a clear distinction is to be drawn between merchant ships and public armed ships. The latter type of vessel "constitutes a part of the military force of her nation; acts under the immediate and direct command of the sovereign; is employed by him in national objects." [28]

This famous litigation may be epitomized in the language used by the writer's teacher of international law when the case was being discussed in class: "The shipowner says 'Marshall makes a long speech about visiting sovereigns, diplomats, and troops. That does not interest me. Do I get my ship back or don't I?' and the answer is 'No.'"

Turning from exemptions from sovereign power to acquisition of sovereign power, Marshall, in *American Insurance Co.* v. *Canter*,[29] put an end to the controversy that his Federalist Party associates had been waging regarding the legality of the Louisiana Purchase during the administration of Thomas Jefferson.[30] Marshall declared that "the constitution confers absolutely on the government of the Union, the powers of making war, and of making treaties; consequently, that government possesses the power of acquiring territory, either by conquest or by treaty. . . . The right to govern may be the inevitable consequence of the right to acquire territory." [31]

The occasion for this pronouncement was presented when the insurers, to whom the owners had abandoned a wrecked cargo, claimed 356 bales of cotton which had been awarded to one Canter as salvage by a court at Key West, Florida. The court had been created by an act passed by the territorial legislature of Florida. The territorial government in turn had been established by Congress, under provisions which clearly gave it the power to establish courts having authority to award salvage, unless it could be shown that a restriction was violated which forbade legislation "inconsistent with the Constitution and laws of the United States."

The insurance company contended that such inconsistency existed, for the reason that the Florida statute vested in inferior courts of the territory a jurisdiction given by Congress to the superior courts of Florida "the same jurisdiction . . . in all cases arising under the laws and constitution of the United States" as had been vested in the Kentucky district court under prior legislation.[32]

Marshall was prompt to point out that this did not confer on the Florida superior courts *all* the powers possessed by the Kentucky court, but only such jurisdiction as arose *under the laws and Constitution of the United States.* The crucial question therefore was whether cases in admiralty and cases under the laws and Constitution of the United States were identical and to be treated as synonymous.

In holding that they were not identical, Marshall could avouch the authority of the Constitution itself, which in article III, section 2, had specifically enumerated these types of cases in separate categories, each of which independently constituted a basis for jurisdiction of the federal courts under that provision of the Constitution. He could also point to the immemorial practice of maritime nations. "A case in admiralty does not, in fact, arise under the Constitution or laws of the United States. These cases are as old as navigation itself; and the law admiralty and maritime, as it has existed for ages, is applied by our courts to the cases as they arise." [33]

Finally, Marshall disposed of the argument that Congress could not authorize the vesting of admiralty jurisdiction in territorial courts because jurisdiction over "all cases of admiralty and maritime jurisdiction" was part of the "judicial power of the United States" which article III, section 1, of the Constitution required to be vested in "one Supreme Court, and in such inferior courts as the Congress may from time to time ordain and establish." Rather cavalierly, Marshall noted that since the judges of the territorial courts held office for only four years instead or for life as required by article III, section 1, of the Constitution, "these courts, then, are not constitutional courts, in which the judicial power conferred by the Constitution on the general government, can be deposited. They are incapable of receiving it. They are legislative courts, created in virtue of the general right of sovereignty which exists in the government, or in virtue of that clause which enables Congress to make all needful rules and regulations, respecting the territory belonging to the United States." [34] The distinction which Marshall thus improvised between constitutional and legislative courts is still recognized.[35]

A dictum in the *Canter* case to the effect that all the laws in force in Florida when it was acquired by the United States, except political laws, remained in force until altered by the new government[36] was elaborated in *United States* v. *Percheman*.[37] That case upheld the title to 2,000 acres of land which the grantee had acquired under a grant from the Spanish governor of Florida on December 12, 1815. That teritorry was ceded to the United States by the treaty of February 22, 1819.

Marshall remarked that "it is very unusual, even in cases of conquest, for the conqueror to do more than to displace the sovereign and assume dominion over the country. The modern usage of nations, which has become law, would be violated; that sense of justice and of right which is acknowledged and felt by the whole civilized world would be outraged, if private property should be confiscated, and private rights annulled. The people change their allegiance; their relation with the ancient sovereign is dissolved; but their relations to each other, and their rights of property, remain undisturbed. If this be the modern rule, even in cases of conquest, who can doubt its application to the case of an amicable cession of territory?" [38]

Hence, in a transaction such as the treaty of 1819, "the king cedes that only which belonged to him;

lands he had previously granted, were not his to cede." [39]

The Spanish text of the treaty, the Court noted, contained a provision that such grants of land "shall remain ratified and confirmed." The English version of that article said "shall be ratified and confirmed." Rejecting the government's argument that the treaty contemplated further subsequent action by the United States in order to validate the titles involved, the Court construed the English text as harmonious with the Spanish.[40]

Another legal landmark involving Spanish land grants was *Foster* v. *Neilson*.[41] The issue was title to land which the United States claimed was part of the Louisiana Purchase, but which Spain had declared was within West Florida. Petitioner claimed under a Spanish grant made after the Louisiana Purchase but before the cession of West Florida and would have prevailed had the Spanish position been accepted. The Court refused to embark upon an independent investigation of the boundary dispute. Such a question was a matter for the political departments of the government. "In a controversy between two nations, concerning national boundaries, it is scarcely possible, that the courts of either should refuse to abide by the measures adopted by its own government. . . . The judiciary is not that department of the government, to which the assertion of its interests against foreign powers is confided; and its duty commonly is, to decide upon individual rights, according to those principles which the political departments of the nation have established. If the course of the nation has been a plain one, its courts would hesitate to pronounce it erroneous. . . . A question like this, respecting the boundaries of nations, is, as has been truly said, more a political than a legal question and in its discussion, the courts of every country must respect the pronounced will of the legislature." In regard to the West Florida boundary controversy, Marshall found that the legislature and the department entrusted with foreign affairs had occupied the field, and that the American government's position with respect to the disputed issue must be followed by its courts.[42]

Marshall's distinction between political and justiciable questions is still law.[43] A field in which it is particularly applicable is with regard to recognition of foreign governments.

The political character of recognition of international status was clearly stated by Marshall in *United States* v. *Palmer*.[44] He pointed out that "such questions are generally rather political than legal in their character. They belong more properly to those who can declare what the law shall be; who can place the nation in such a position with respect to foreign powers as to their own judgment shall appear wise; to whom are intrusted all its foreign relations; than to that tribunal whose power as well as duty is confined to the application of the rule which the legislature may prescribe for it. In such contests a nation may engage itself with the one party or the other—may observe absolute neutrality—may recognize the new state absolutely—or may make a limited recognition of it. The proceeding in courts must depend so entirely on the course of the government, that it is difficult to give a precise answer to questions which do not refer to a particular nation. It may be said, generally, that if the government remains neutral, and recognizes the existence of a civil war, its courts cannot consider as criminal those acts of hostility which war authorizes, and which the new government may direct against its enemy. To decide otherwise, would be to determine that the war prosecuted by one of the parties was unlawful, and would be to arrange the nation to which the court belongs against that party. This would transcend the limits prescribed to the judicial department." [45]

In *United States* v. *Klintock*,[46] Marshall found it advisable to elaborate on the *Palmer* decision. A United States citizen, having a commission from one Aury, who styled himself "Brigadier of the Mexican Republic and Generalissimo of the Floridas," took possession of a Danish vessel, upon the pretext of finding Spanish papers which he had "planted" on board the ship. Leaving the crew on a Cuban island, the captors sailed for Savannah, impersonating the Danish master and crew.

Marshall quickly disposed of the defendant's contentions. ". . . Aury can have no power, either as Brigadier of the Mexican Republic, a republic of whose existence we know nothing, or as Generalissimo of the Floridas, a province in the possession of Spain, to issue commissions to authorize private or public vessels to make captures at sea." [47] In any event, Denmark was not at war with either of those imaginary sovereignties, and the Danish vessel "was not captured *jure belli*, but seized and carried into Savannah *animo furandi*. It was not a belligerent capture, but a robbery on the high seas. And although the fraud practiced on the Dane may not of itself constitute piracy, yet it is an ingredient in the transaction, which has no tendency to mitigate the character of the offence." [48]

Captures *jure belli* were not only distinguished by Marshall from those *animo furandi,* as in the *Klintock* case, but also from those made in the exercise of ordinary territorial sovereignty for violation of the municipal laws of the local sovereign. According to this distinction, which was elaborated with Marshall's customary logic in *Rose* v. *Himely,*[49] a belligerent seizure may be made on the high seas, because war is waged on the high seas, but a seizure for the enforcement of local laws must be made within the territorial jurisdiction of the state.[50] Justice Johnson dissented[51] while Justices Livingston, Cushing, and Chase concurred separately, expressing no opinion on the question whether a seizure could be made lawfully on the high seas for a violation of municipal regulations if the captured vessel were duly brought into port without delay for adjudication. They based their concurrence in the decision on the fact that the ship had been condemned by a St. Domingo court without ever having been brought in to that place at all.[52]

However, in *Hudson* v. *Guestier*,[53] a companion case decided on the same day, Marshall upheld a condemnation pronounced under the same circumstances as in *Rose* v. *Himely*, except that the seizure had been made within French territorial waters. Here Chase and Livingston dissented because the captured vessel had not been brought into a French port for adjudication.[54] After retrial, it appeared that the seizure had in fact been made on the high seas.[55] Livingston, speaking for the Court, said that "if the *res* can be proceeded against when not in the possession or under the control of the court, I am not able to perceive how it can be material whether the capture were made within or beyond the jurisdictional limits of France; or in the exercise of a belligerent or municipal right." [56] But the decisions on the first trial and in *Rose* v. *Himely* had rejected the ground upon which the dissenting judges had wished to place the decision. Marshall now found himself a dissenter, observing "that he had supposed that the former opinion delivered in these cases upon this point had been concurred in by four judges. But in this he was mistaken. The opinion was concurred in by one judge. . . . However, the principle of that case (*Rose* v. *Himely*) is now overruled." [57]

When a ship was validly captured *jure belli,* what was the status of neutral cargo which it carried on board? Justice Marshall dealt with that problem in the *Nereide*,[58] a case involving cargo which belonged to the resident of Buenos Aires and which was shipped on an armed British merchantman. The vessel was brought into New York by an American privateer during war between the United States and Great Britain.[59] Marshall held that neutral property did not lose its immunity from capture by being placed in a belligerent armed vessel.[60] If the ship's armament, or resistance to search, prevents belligerents from exercising their right of search, no harm is done. There is no sin committed if neutral property escapes the inconvenience of search. It is in any event immune from capture; and the right of search is merely ancillary to the right of capture. The neutral property-owner is not chargeable with the ship's being armed nor its resistance; all he seeks is transportation for his goods. "He meddles not with the armament nor with the war." [61]

Rejecting the argument that a treaty between the United States and Spain[62] subjected the goods of either party, being neutral, to condemnation as enemy property if found in the vessel of an enemy, Marshall pointed out, with characteristic acumen, that the treaty merely prohibited capture of enemy property when transported in neutral bottoms. It did not provide that enemy bottoms should communicate their hostile character to the cargo they carried.[63] The object of this type of treaty provision, Marshall explained, was to enlarge, not to diminish, the rights of neutrals.[64]

Marshall again demonstrated the sanctity accorded in American courts to the pledged faith of the nation as expressed in treaties in *United States* v. *Schooner Peggy.*[65] A convention with France, signed on September 18, 1801, provided in article 4 that "property captured, and not yet definitvely condemned . . . shall be mutually restored." [66] The *Peggy* had been condemned in the court below on September 23, 1800, but an appeal was taken to the Supreme Court.[67] Marshall held that the condemnation was not definitive, since it was subject to appellate review; and that since the treaty was law of the land, the ship must be restored. Ordinarily, he conceded, the function of an appellate court is only to determine whether the judgment rendered below was or was not erroneous when rendered; but if during the appeal, a controlling law intervenes, the Court must obey it.[68]

Another notable Marshall decision dealing with captures *jure belli* was *Talbot* v. *Seeman.*[69] In that case, the *Amelia,* a Hamburg ship, had been captured by the French (who were at peace with Hamburg), and then recaptured by Captain Talbot, of the *Constitution*, an American ship. The *Amelia* was armed and was manned by a French crew when captured. The United States and France were then in a state of partial hostility, so that the recapture was lawful.[70]

The question for decision by the Court was whether Talbot was entitled to salvage. As Marshall pointed out, for salvage to be awarded it was necessary, not only that the taking be lawful, but that meritorious service be rendered to the ship by the captor.[71] Talbot contended, and the Court held, that such a service had been rendered by rescuing the vessel from the French. Normally, to recapture a neutral ship would not be such a service, because the prize courts of the nation first capturing the vessel would release it; but in the case at bar, there was proof that France would have in fact condemned the *Amelia*, even though such condemnation would violate international law.

As stated by Marshall, "the principle is that without benefit salvage is not payable: and it is merely a consequence from this principle, which exempts recaptured neutrals from its payment. But let a nation change its laws and its practice on this subject; let its legislation be such as to subject to condemnation all neutrals captured by its cruizers, and who will say that no benefit is conferred by a recapture? . . . It becomes then necessary to inquire whether the laws of France were such as to have rendered the condemnation of the *Amelia* so extremely probable, as to create a case of such real danger, that her recapture by Captain Talbot must be considered as a meritorious service entitling him to salvage." [72]

Whether the record before the Court contained adequate proof of French law was the next question to be determined. Ordinarily foreign law must be proved as a fact, which had not been done. Marshall drew a fine distinction between internal law and public law on a subject of common concern to all nations. The latter type of foreign law, important to a court of admiralty, included the French decree of January 18, 1798, which subjected to capture all merchandise produced in England or in English possessions. Marshall concluded that "this decree having been promulgated in the United States as the law of France, by the joint act of that department which is entrusted with foreign intercourse, and of that which is invested with the powers of war, seems to asume a character of notoriety which renders it admissible in our courts." [73] The *Amelia*, carrying a cargo from Bengal, an English possession, was therefore not safe from condemnation in French courts; and recapture by Captain Talbot was a genuine service which entitled him to salvage. The Court could not presume that, merely because the French decree of 1798 contravened international law, the courts of that country would refuse to execute it. [74]

An American court, however, could in Marshall's judgment be expected to display a nicer regard for the obligations imposed by the law of nations. In determining what percentage should be awarded as salvage, Marshall found it necessary to lay down the principle that an act of Congress should be construed so as not to violate international law. [75]

The source of international law was discussed in Marshall's very interesting opinion in *The Antelope*. [76] The question at issue was whether the slave trade violated the law of nations. Marshall held, contrary to a prior decision by Story at circuit, [77] that it did not, although it did violate the law of nature. [78]

Slavery arose, Marshall asserted, as one of the consequences of war in ancient times. "This, which was the usage of all, could not be pronounced repugnant to the law of nations, which is certainly to be tried by the test of general usage. That which has received the assent of all, must be the law of all. . . . If we resort to this standard as the test of international law, the question, as has already been observed, is decided in favor of the legality of the trade." [79] However abhorrent to many nations today, "that trade could not be considered as contrary to the law of nations which was authorized and protected by the laws of all commercial nations. . . ." [80]

Common consent of all nations is required to modify international law.[81] Condemnation of the slave trade by the domestic law of individual nations is not enough. "If it be consistent with the law of nations, it cannot in itself be piracy. It can be made so only by statute; and the obligation of the statute cannot transcend the legislative power of the state which may enact it." If it is neither piracy nor a violation of the law of nations, slave trading cannot subject a ship in time of peace to condemnation in a foreign forum, even if the laws of the ship's own nation prohibit the trade.[82]

Marshall praised counsel who argued the case: "In examining claims of this momentous importance—claims in which the sacred rights of liberty and of property come in conflict with each other—which have drawn from the bar a degree of talent and of eloquence, worthy of the questions which have been discussed, this court must not yield to feelings which might seduce it from the path of duty, and must obey the mandate of the law." [83]

A strain of whimsical realism akin to that exhibited in Marshall's treatment of slavery in *The Antelope* appears in *Johnson and Graham's Lessee* v. *McIntosh*,[84] a case dealing with the rights of Indians. The plaintiffs claimed ownership of lands by virtue of grants made in 1773 and 1775 by Indian tribes. The Court held that these titles were invalid. Only the government, not the Indians themselves, could dispose of lands occupied by the natives. The Indians had a right to occupy the lands which they inhabited, but "their power to dispose of the soil, at their own will, to whomsoever they pleased, was denied by the original fundamental principle, that discovery gave title to those who made it." The European nations "asserted the ultimate dominion to be in themselves; and claimed and exercised, as a consequence of this ultimate dominion, a power to grant the soil, while yet in possession of the natives." [85]

The Christian nations of Europe had developed this system of title by discovery in order to obviate conflicts among themselves in connection with their acquisitions of land from the natives. They needed to establish a rule "by which the right of acquisition, which they all asserted, should be regulated, as between themselves. This principle was, that discovery gave title to the government by whose subjects, or by whose authority, it was made, against all other European governments, which title might be consummated by possession. The exclusion of all other Europeans, necessarily gave to the nation making the discovery the sole right of acquiring the soil from the natives, and establishing settlements upon it. . . . It was a right which all asserted for themselves, and to the assertion of which, by others, all assented." [86]

Insofar as the natives were concerned, Marshall explains: "The potentates of the old world found no difficulty in convincing themselves, that they made ample compensation to the inhabitants of the new, by bestowing on them civilization and Christianity, in exchange for unlimited independence." [87]

The foregoing review of Marshall's principal decisions involving the law of nations exhibits the originality and cogency of his reasoning in that important and untrodden branch of jurisprudence. His professional prowess and proficiency as a creative genius are displayed in his work there just as in the better known field of constitutional construction. Of that work Beveridge says: "Admirable and formative as were Marshall's opinions of the law of nations, they received no attention from the people, no opposition from the politicians, and were generally approved by the bar." [88]

Perhaps the same appraisal will apply to the achievements of the present age in the realm of international law. A formative and creative period, such as evoked the genius of Hugo Grotius[89] and of John Marshall in their respective eras, confronts the legal profession today.[90] If our efforts prove equally fruitful, we can afford to forego the popular acclaim

194 THE MARSHALL READER

which falls to the lot of practitioners of less recondite skills. Let us hope, too, that our efforts to build a law-governed world will also escape the obstructive zeal of short-sighted and selfish politicians. And finally, thrice and four times blessed shall we be if we may aspire to the accolade of approval by our comrades at the bar. There, if at all, is to be found the "laurel crown."

As Justice Holmes remarked, "there fell to Marshall perhaps the greatest place that ever was filled by a judge; but when I consider this might, his justice, and his wisdom, I do fully believe that if American law were to be represented by a single figure, sceptic and worshipper alike would agree without dispute that the figure could be one alone, and that one, John Marshall." [91]

Did Marshall, like Taft, cherish ambition for the office of Chief Justice as such? Or did he, like Holmes, long to "touch the superlative"? In any event, Marshall's "intellectual power" gave him rank with the immortals.[92] In two significant branches of public law his work endures. As spokesman of the Constitution he is widely known and acclaimed. Equal glory rightly attaches to his labors for the development of the law of nations.

[1] Ware v. Hylton, 3 U. S. (3 Dall.) 199, 281 (1796).
[2] The Court held that the fourth article of the Peace Treaty of September 3, 1783, permitted recovery of debts owed by Virginians to British creditors, in spite of prior discharge of the debts by payment by defendants into the Virginia loan office on April 26, 1780, in accordance with that state's act of October 20, 1777. It was in Ware v. Hylton that Marshall argued, contrary to his famous holding in Marbury v. Madison, 5 U. S. (1 Cranch) 137 (1803), that "the legislative authority of any country can only be restrained by its own municipal constitution . . . and the judicial authority can have no right to question the validity of a law, unless such a jurisdiction is expressly given by the constitution." 3 U. S. (3 Dall.) at 211.
[3] In Respublica v. De Longchamps, 1 U. S. (1 Dall.) 111, 114, 115 (Pa. Ct. Oyer & Ter. 1784), Chief Justice McKean proclaimed that the law of nations formed "a part of the municipal law of Pennsylvania." Secretary of State Jefferson on June 5, 1793, writing to the French minister, spoke of "the laws of the land, of which the law of nations makes an

integral part." 7 The Works of Thomas Jefferson 364 (Ford ed. 1904). In The Nereide, 13 U. S. (9 Cranch) 388, 423 (1815), Marshall said "the court is bound by the law of nations, which is a part of the law of the land."

4 Dickinson, *The Law of Nations as Part of the National Law of the United States,* 101 U. Pa. L. Rev. 26, 27 (1952); 1 Crosskey, Politics and the Constitution in the History of the United States 568-76 (1953).

5 Pound, The Lawyer from Antiquity to Modern Times 181 (1953). The Pennsylvania statute forbidding citation of English post-revolutionary cases, except "any precedent of maritime law, or the law of nations," was the Act of March 19, 1810, P. L. 136. It was repealed by the Act of March 29, 1936, P. L. 224.

6 Pound, The Formative Era of American Law 107 (1938). Jefferson conceded "the superiority of the civil over the common law code, as a system of perfect justice." Jefferson to John Tyler, June 17, 1812. 13 The Writings of Thomas Jefferson 166 (Lipscomb and Bergh eds. 1904). "The lawyer finds in the Latin language the system of civil law most conformable with the principles of justice of any which has ever yet been established among men, and from which much has been incorporated into our own." Jefferson to John Brazier, August 24, 1819. 15 *id.* at 210.

7 Luke v. Lyde, 2 Burr. 882, 887, 97 Eng. Rep. 614, 617 (K. B. 1759). "Nor will it be one law for Rome and another for Athens; one thing today and another tomorrow; but it is a law eternal and unchangeable for all people and in every age." The Republic of Cicero 256-57 (Hardingham ed. 1884). Regarding this quotation, see Sutherland, *The Flag, the Constitution, and International Agreements,* 68 Harv. L. Rev. 1374, 1381 (1955).

8 Jefferson to E. C. Genet, June 17, 1793. 7 The Works of Thomas Jefferson 402-03 (Ford ed. 1904).

9 In Marshall's often-quoted words, "no principle of general law is more universally acknowledged, than the perfect equality of nations. Russia and Geneva have equal rights. It results from this equality, that no one can rightfully impose a rule on another. . . . As no nation can prescribe a rule for others, none can make a law of nations. . . ." The Antelope, 23 U. S. (10 Wheat.) 66, 122 (1825).

10 Dumbauld, The Political Writings of Thomas Jefferson xxxii (1955).

11 John Bassett Moore, *John Marshall,* in 2 The Collected Papers of John Bassett Moore 456, 458 (1944) (first published in 16 Pol. Sci. Q. 393 (1901)). Of an estimated 1106 decisions with opinions during Marshall's tenure as Chief Justice, he wrote the opinion of the Court in 519. Morgan, Justice William Johnson, The First Dissenter 176 (1954).

12 2 The Collected Papers of John Bassett Moore 458 (1944).

[13] 3 *id.* at 16.

[14] For about six weeks Marshall attended George Wythe's lectures at William and Mary College. His notebook contains about 180 pages, some of which he may have written after leaving school. 1 Beveridge, The Life of John Marshall 154, 174-76 (1916). See also 2 *id.* at 177.

[15] Regarding Marshall's intimacy with Story, see Warren, *The Story-Marshall Correspondence,* 21 Wm. & Mary Col. Q. 1 (2d ser. 1941).

[16] Ziegler, The International Law of John Marshall 9, 211 (1939). Rutherforth's treatise was published at Cambridge, England, in 1754-56. In Ware v. Hylton, 3 U. S. (3 Dall.) 199, 230 (1796), Justice Chase speaks of "the celebrated and judicious Doctor Rutherforth."

[17] War with France seemed imminent when it became known that the American mission had not been officially received, and that a loan or bribe had been solicited by the French as a condition precedent to the commencement of serious negotiations. Pinckney's irate reply, "No, not a sixpence," as it passed from mouth to mouth became the more rhetorical, "Millions for defense, but not a cent for tribute." Federalist plans for war with France received a setback when President Adams, without consulting his party colleagues, announced that he would send another mission to France if assurance were given in advance that it would be received with proper respect for its diplomatic status. Dumbauld, *op. cit. supra* note 10, at 197. 2 Beveridge, The Life of John Marshall 256-351 (1916); 2 Am. State Papers (Foreign Relations) 161 (1832).

[18] 2 Am. State Papers (Foreign Relations) 157-82 (1832). Letters written to George Washington during Marshall's sojourn in Europe also contain interesting observations on international affairs. Oster, The Political and Economic Doctrines of John Marshall 154-69 (1914).

[19] Marshall's speech is printed in Oster, *op. cit. supra* note 18, at 225-53 (1914). Regarding this debate, see 2 Beveridge, The Life of John Marshall 458-75 (1916).

[20] 2 The Collected Papers of John Bassett Moore 453-54 (1944).

[21] 2 Beveridge, The Life of John Marshall 500, 507 (1916); 2 Am. State Papers (Foreign Relations) 386-87, 486-90 (1832).

[22] See text at note 11 *supra.*

[23] A convenient digest of these opinions is Ziegler, *op. cit. supra* note 16. Topics treated by Ziegler include international status, acquisition of territory, jurisdiction, nationality and expiration, consuls, war, piracy, the slave trade, extradition and treaties. Unfortunately, there is no published collection of these cases similar to Cotton, The Constitutional Decisions of John Marshall (1905) and Dillon, John Marshall Complete Constitutional Decisions (1903). Some are found in Scott,

Prize Cases Decided in the United States Supreme Court 1789-1918 (1923).

24 International law cases decided by Marshall are discussed in 4 Beveridge, The Life of John Marshall 121-44 (1919) and in 2 Collected Papers of John Bassett Moore 459-63 (1944).

25 11 U. S. (7 Cranch) 116 (1812). This case was discussed quite recently in National City Bank v. Republic of China, 348 U. S. 356 (1955).

26 11 U. S. (7 Cranch) at 136. *Cf.* Glass v. Sloop Betsey, 3 U. S. (3 Dall.) 6, 16 (1794).

27 Modern large-scale troop movements make it convenient for the rule of Schooner Exchange v. McFaddon to be waived by treaty in some cases, so that offenses by soldiers may be punished in the local courts instead of exclusively by military tribunals of the guest army. See article 7 of NATO Status of Forces Agreement of June 19, 1951, which went into force on August 23, 1953. 48 Am. J. Int'l Law App. 86-89 (1954).

28 11 U. S. (7 Cranch) at 144.

29 26 U. S. (1 Pet.) 511 (1828).

30 Jefferson himself had been dubious regarding the constitutionality of acquiring this vast "empire for liberty." Dumbauld, The Political Writings of Thomas Jefferson 50, 144 (1955). Federalists feared that the political predominance of the seaboard states would be destroyed. 3 Randall, The Life of Thomas Jefferson 81 (1858).

31 26 U. S. (1 Pet.) at 543.

32 3 Stat. 752 (1823).

33 26 U. S. (1 Pet.) at 545. See text at notes 7 and 8 *supra.*

34 *Id.* at 546.

35 *Ex parte* Bakelite Corp., 279 U. S. 438, 450 (1929). Not being constitutional courts, such tribunals may be vested with administrative authority which goes beyond "judicial" power.

36 26 U. S. (1 Pet.) at 544.

37 32 U. S. (7 Pet.) 51 (1833).

38 *Id.* at 87. In Brown v. United States, 12 U. S. (8 Cranch) 110, 126 (1814), Marshall held that war does not automatically result in confiscation of enemy property, but merely confers upon the belligerent sovereign a right to confiscate.

39 32 U. S. (7 Pet.) at 87.

40 *Id.* at 89. The Court pointed out that in Foster v. Neilson, 27 U. S. (2 Pet.) 253 (1829), where the same treaty language was involved, the Court's attention had not been directed to the discrepancy between the two versions.

41 27 U. S. (2 Pet.) 253 (1829).

42 *Id.* at 307-09. Moreover the American position is intrinsically strong and probably correct. *Id.* at 307.

[43] See Martin, *Executive Determination of Legal Questions,* Proceedings of the American Society of International Law 53, 66-70 (1948). Some writers contend that Marshall could have relied on the doctrine of "political questions" to avoid judicial declaration of the unconstitutionality of a statute in Marbury v. Madison, 5 U. S. (1 Cranch) 137 (1803). Haines, The American Doctrine of Judicial Supremacy 201 (2d ed. 1932).

[44] 16 U. S. (3 Wheat.) 610 (1818).

[45] 16 U. S. (3 Wheat.) at 634-35. In Rose v. Himely, 8 U. S. (4 Cranch) 241, 272 (1808), Marshall said: "It is for governments to decide whether they will consider St. Domingo as an independent nation, and until such decision shall be made, or France shall relinquish her claim, courts of justice must consider the ancient state of things as remaining unaltered, and the sovereign power of France over that colony as still subsisting." This rule was followed in Gelston v. Hoyt, 16 U. S. (3 Wheat.) 246, 324 (1818), where Story spoke for the Court. See also United States v. Klintock, 18 U. S. (5 Wheat.) 144, 149-50 (1820).

[46] 18 U. S. (5 Wheat.) 144 (1820).

[47] *Id.* at 149.

[48] *Id.* at 149-50.

[49] 8 U. S. (4 Cranch) 241 (1808). "The rights of war may be exercised on the high seas, because war is carried on upon the high seas; but the pacific rights of sovereignty must be exercised within the territory of the sovereign." Hence ". . . seizure of a person not a subject, or of a vessel not belonging to a subject, made on the high seas, for the breach of a municipal regulation, is an act which the sovereign cannot authorize." *Id.* at 279.

[50] Not necessarily within the "three mile limit." In Church v. Hubbart, 6 U. S. (2 Cranch) 187, 234-35 (1804), Marshall said: "The authority of a nation within its own territory is absolute and exclusive. . . . But its power to secure itself from injury may certainly be exercised beyond the limits of its territory." The geographical scope of such power may vary with circumstances. "In different seas and on different coasts, a wider or more contracted range, in which to exercise the vigilance of the government, will be assented to." See also Cook v. United States 288 U. S. 102, 112-15 (1933).

[51] See Morgan, *op. cit. supra* note 11, at 176-77.

[52] 8 U. S. (4 Cranch) at 281.

[53] 8 U. S. (4 Cranch) 293 (1808).

[54] *Id.* at 298.

[55] Hudson and Smith v. Guestier, 10 U. S. (6 Cranch) 281, 284 (1810).

[56] *Ibid.*

[57] *Id.* at 285. *Cf.* Church v. Hubbart, 6 U. S. (2 Cranch) 187 (1804). See Ziegler, *op. cit. supra* note 16, at 74; Jessup, The Law of Territorial Waters and Maritime Jurisdiction 85 (1927). Morgan, *op. cit. supra* note 11, at 177, criticizes

Marshall's "lamentable lack of scruple concerning orderly legal procedure" in announcing as the opinion of the Court a pronouncement which only one other justice (evidently Washington) had approved. Todd, who came to the Court in 1808, agreed with Johnson. 10 U. S. (6 Cranch) at 285.

58 13 U. S. (9 Cranch) 388 (1815).

59 *Id.* at 390.

60 *Id.* at 427. Story dissented.

61 *Id.* at 428.

62 Article 15 of the treaty of October 27, 1795, 8 Stat. 146 (1795).

63 13 U. S. (9 Cranch) at 418.

64 13 U. S. (9 Cranch) at 419.

65 5 U. S. (1 Cranch) 103 (1801).

66 2 Miller, Treaties and Other International Acts of the United States of America 459 (1931).

67 5 U. S. (1 Cranch) at 107.

68 *Id.* at 110. Marshall's decision agreed with President Jefferson interpretation of the treaty, but conflicted with the opinion of Attorney General Levi Lincoln. 1 Warren, The Supreme Court in United States History 199 n.1 (1922).

69 5 U. S. (1 Cranch) 1 (1801). In the circuit court, Burr and Hamilton were opposing counsel in this case.

70 *Id.* at 32.

71 *Id.* at 28.

72 *Id.* at 37.

73 *Id.* at 38. As to proof of foreign law, *cf.* Church v. Hubbart, 6 U. S. (2 Cranch) 187, 236-39 (1804).

74 5 U. S. (1 Cranch) at 39-41.

75 *Id.* at 43-44. In Murray v. The Charming Betsey, 6 U. S. (2 Cranch) 64 (1804), Marshall reiterated this principle.

76 23 U. S. (10 Wheat.) 66 (1825).

77 La Jeune Eugenie, 26 Fed. Cas. 832, No. 1551 (C.C.D. Mass. 1822).

78 23 U. S. (10 Wheat.) at 120. Roman jurists recognized this same distinction. Dumbauld, The Declaration of Independence and What It Means Today 43 (1950).

79 23 U. S. (10 Wheat.) at 120-21.

80 *Id.* at 115. Marshall refers to the leading part taken by the United States, after attaining independence, in opposing the slave trade. Earlier attempts by the American colonies to suppress the trade had been disallowed by the crown. This was one of the grievances complained of in the Declaration of Independence. Dumbauld, *op. cit. supra* note 78, at 89 174-75.

81 See the familiar description of the international legal structure quoted in note 9 *supra.* During argument Key had asserted that "general concurrence" sufficed; universal unanimity was not necessary. 23 U. S. (10 Wheat.) at 77.

82 23 U. S. (10 Wheat.) at 122. "The courts of no country execute the penal laws of another." *Id.* at 123. This principle

had been enunciated by Marshall in Rose v. Himely, 8 U. S.
(4 Cranch) 241, 280 (1808). See also Wisconsin v. Pelican
Insurance Co., 127 U. S. 265, 290 (1888). *Cf.* Testa v. Katt,
330 U. S. 386, 389 (1947).

83 23 U. S. (10 Wheat.) at 114.

84 21 U. S. (8 Wheat.) 543 (1823).

85 *Id.* at 574. England and the United States had accepted
this system of land grants. *Id.* at 576, 580, 584. The principle expounded by Marshall has been reiterated recently in
Tee-Hit-Ton Indians v. United States, 348 U. S. 272 (1955).

86 21 U. S. (8 Wheat.) at 573.

87 *Ibid.*

88 4 Beveridge, The Life of John Marshall 144 (1919).

89 Pound, *Philosophical Theory and International Law,* 1
Bibliotheca Visseriana 72 (1923); Dumbauld, *Hugo Grotius:
the Father of International Law,* 1 J. Pub. L. 117 (1952).

90 That the American polity whose constitutional frame-
work was moulded by Marshall was in many respects itself
an international society has been emphasized by historians
familiar with that period. Warren, The Supreme Court and
Sovereign States (1924); Van Doren, The Great Rehearsal
(1948).

91 Holmes, Collected Legal Papers 270 (1920). If a second
figure were to be chosen, it would doubtless be Holmes. Or
would it be Pound, Wigmore, Williston, John W. Davis, or
George Wharton Pepper?

92 There seems to be no evidence that Marshall loved high
office as such. He did welcome as a godsend his receiving a
diplomatic appointment in 1797, but that was because he
needed the money. 2 Beveridge, The Life of John Marshall
211 (1916). His appointment as Chief Justice, Beveridge
says, was "totally unexpected," and Marshall had himself
recommended someone else for the place. 2 *id.* at 553. See
also 2 *id.* at 221, 491. In desiring to be Chief Justice, did
not Robert H. Jackson miscalculate the true nature of his own
greatness? Ought he to have wished that posterity would
number him with names such as Ellsworth, Waite, Fuller,
Chase, or White, because of the exalted station they held,
rather than with Holmes of the laurel crown?

CHIEF JUSTICE JOHN MARSHALL,

Transportation Expert†

By H. O. Bishop*

John Marshall is best remembered as Chief Justice of the Supreme Court. In addition to his great services on the bench, he served in other capacities in the government. He was one of the American Commissioners in the XYZ affair. He served in the Virginia Legislature, in Congress, as Secretary of State, in the Virginia Convention to ratify the Constitution, and in the Constitutional Convention of Virginia in 1829. In addition, he served on the Virginia Commission to survey the rivers of Virginia to determine a practical water route west. The following article summarizes Marshall's recommendations as a result of this survey. This article is reprinted here with the permission of the *American Bar Association Journal.*

The people of today only know Chief Justice John Marshall as a famous jurist—the man who "primed" the Constitution of the United States. The fact that he was greatly interested in the improvement of a transportation system from the Atlantic Coast to the Ohio and Mississippi valleys is practically unknown.

Would it surprise you to know that during the time he was serving as Chief Justice he devoted almost two months to making a thorough inspection of the route of the James River Company which had been promoted by George Washington and who was its president?

Almost a century and a quarter ago the General Assembly of Virginia named the Chief Justice chairman of a commission to make a general survey and inspection of the rivers of Virginia covering the territory from the James River to the Ohio River, which also included the Greenbrier, New and Kanawha Rivers—the early dream of George Washington and now the route of the Chesapeake and Ohio lines.

This was no summer junket for the Chief Justice. It was downright hard work with old mother earth

----

† Reprinted with the permission of the publishers from 21 Amer. Bar Assoc. Journal, 184 (1935).

* Mr. Bishop is a resident of Washington, D. C., and is the publicity representative of the Chesapeake & Ohio Railroad.

for a mattress and the sky for covering. It meant mountain climbing and wading and swimming rivers and creeks. Carrying, poling, pushing and loading and unloading boats. Meals were supplied by catching fish and shooting game. Marshall was that kind of a man. He had been brought up right. Nothing soft or fussy about him. Not a bit puny or hothoused. So tough was the work that he tells of ten days being required to cover a distance of 48 miles high up in the Alleghanies.

The New River, which plunges through a deep gorge in the Alleghanies, creating one of the most beautiful scenes in this country, is thus gently described by the Chief Justice: "The New River having to search its intricate way, and force a passage through a long chain of lofty and rugged mountains, whose feet it washes, exhibits an almost continued succession of shoals and falls, from which the navigator is sometimes, though rarely, relieved by a fine sheet of deep placid water."

Now here's a surprise for you. Even in that long-gone day the dream of steam in transportation was in the mind of that great Chief Justice. Listen to him: "Your commissioners submit with diffidence: That boats impelled by steam may be employed successfully on New River. With the capacities of this powerful agent, they are too little acquainted to speak with confidence of the use which may be made of it in the waters of Virginia. Elsewhere, it has certainly been applied with great advantage to the purposes of navigation. Neither have they that intimate knowledge of the velocity of the currents, against which vessels have been propelled by it, to compare them with that of the New River, and to hazard any decided opinion on the comparison. But they beg leave to say, that the currents of the Hudson, of the Mohawk, and of the Mississippi, are very strong; and that a practice so entirely novel as the use of steam in navigation, will probably receive great improvement, and the power itself be so diversified in its modifications, as to be applied in new and different situations, as their exigencies may require."

What a remarkable prophecy that was! How pleased Marshall would be if he could again visit the New River and see dozens of giant steam locomotives hauling 150-car trains of coal, dug from the mountains on the banks of that stream, whizzing along on their way to manufacturing plants and homes throughout the land.

In that portion of his report giving reasons for the further development of George Washington's system of transportation, Marshall makes these interesting observations: "That intimate connection which generally attends free commercial intercourse, the strong ties which are formed by mutual interest, and the interchange of good offices, bind together individuals of different countries, and are well calculated to cherish those friendly sentiments, those amicable dispositions, which at present unite Virginia to a considerable portion of the western people. At all times the cultivation of these dispositions must be desirable; but, in the vicissitude of human affairs, in that mysterious future, which is in reserve, and is yet hidden from us, events may occur to render their presentation too valuable to be estimated in dollars and cents.

"The advantages which may result to Virginia from opening this communication with the western country, will be shared in common with her by the States of Kentucky and Ohio. Considering it as a medium for the introduction of foreign articles into those states, it has claims to their serious attention.

"The proposition, that a nation finds its true interest in multiplying its channels of importation, admitting them to be equally convenient, is believed to be incontrovertible. In addition to those arguments in support of this proposition which belong to every case, the situation of the western States suggests some which are peculiar to themselves, and which well deserve their consideration.

"The whole of that extensive and fertile country, a country increasing in wealth and population with a rapidity which baffles calculation, must make its importations up the Mississippi alone, or through the Atlantic States. When we take into view the certain growth of the country, we can scarcely suppose it possible that any commercial city on the banks of that river can keep pace with that growth, and furnish a supply equal to the demand. The unfriendliness of the climate to human life, will render this disparity between the commercial and agricultural capital still more sensible. It will tend still more to retard population of that sound mercantile character, which would render some great city on that majestic river, a safe emporium for the western world.

"In times of profound peace, then, the States on the Ohio would make sacrifices of no inconsiderable magnitude, by restricting their importations to a single river. But, in time of war, their whole trade might be annihilated. When it is recollected that the Mississippi empties itself into the Gulph of Florida, which is surrounded by foreign territory; the Island of Cuba and the Coast of East Florida completely guard the passage from its mouth to the ocean; that the immense commerce flowing down its stream, holds forth irresistible allurements to cruizers, the opinion seems well founded, that scarcely a vessel making for that place could reach its port of destination.

"But the length of the voyage up the Mississippi and Ohio, must be attended with delay so inconvenient to persons engaged in commerce, as to render a shorter route, though not less expensive, more eligible. For importation of many articles, there is much reason to believe that a decided preference would always be given to the transportation through the United States, were that transportation rendered as easy as it is capable of being made.

"If the direct route through the Atlantic States would, for many purposes, be more eligible than that through the Gulph of Florida, which must often be connected with a coasting voyage to or from an Atlantic port, then the multiplication of those routes, if in themselves equal, by presenting a greater choice, and by accommodating more territory, must be desirable.

"But your commissioners are sanguine in the opinion, that the communication through the rivers they have viewed, if properly made, will possess advantages over every other, which cannot fail to recommend it to a large portion of the States of Kentucky and Ohio. All that part of the western country which draws its supplies and transports its produce through the river Ohio, and which lies east of Louisville and west of the Pennsylvania line . . . could probably use this route more advantageously than any other. . . .

"Should the navigation of James River be rendered as safe and as easy as may be reasonably expected, and the Greenbriar and New River be improved, in such manner as the object will justify, your commissioners believe they hazard nothing in saying, that the expense of transporting one hundred weight from Richmond to the mouth of the Great Kanawha, will not exceed half the price of transporting the same weight from Baltimore or Philadelphia, to the same place.

". . . The advantages to accrue to the United States, from opening this new channel of intercourse between the eastern and the western states, are those which necessarily result to the whole body from whatever benefits its members, and those which must result to the United States, particularly from every measure which tends to cement more closely the union of the eastern with the western states."

PART III.

LETTERS

OF

JOHN MARSHALL

LETTERS TO JOSEPH STORY

One of the best sources for the thoughts of a man will be found in his personal correspondence. Very few of Marshall's letters have been preserved, and only two notable collections of his letters exist. One group, now in the possession of the Massachusetts Historical Society, consists of letters addressed to Joseph Story; another group of miscellaneous letters to Bushrod Washington and others is found in the Library of Congress. Single items may be found in other libraries throughout the country.

The following letters are selected from those addressed to Justice Story published in the Massachusetts Historical Society Proceedings, volume 14, second series, beginning on page 320 and are published here with the permission of the Society.

————

The Hoñble Joseph Story.
  Salem, Massachusetts.

Richmond, May 27th, 1819.

My dear Sir,—. . . I am much obliged by the alterations you have made in the opinion in the Dartmouth College[1] case, & am highly gratified by what you say respecting it. The opinion in the Bank case continues to be denounced by the democracy in Virginia. An effort is certainly making to induce the legislature which will meet in December to take up the subject & to pass resolutions not very unlike those which were called forth by the alien & sedition laws in 1709. Whether the effort will be successful or not may perhaps depend in some measure on the sentiments of our sister states. To excite this ferment the opinion has been grossly misrepresented; and where its argument has been truly stated it has been met by principles one would think too palpably absurd for intelligent men. But prejudice will swallow anything. If the principles which have been advanced on this occasion were to prevail the constitution would be converted into the old confederation. The piece to which you allude was not published in Virginia. Our patriotic papers admit no such political heresies. It contained, I think, a complete demonstration of the fallacies & errors contained in those attacks on the opinion of the Court which have most credit here & are supposed to proceed from a high source, but was so mangled in the publication that those only who bestowed close attention to the subject could understand it. There were two numbers & the editor of the Union in Philadelphia, the paper in which it was published, had mixed the different numbers together so as in several instances to place the reasoning intended to demonstrate one proposition under another. The points & the arguments were separated from each other, & so strangely mixed as to constitute a labyrinth to which those only who understood the whole subject perfectly could find a clue.

I wish to consult you on a case which to me who am not versed in admiralty proceedings has some difficulty. The Little Charles[2] was libelled for a violation of the first embargo act in 1808. She was acquitted in the District, but condemned in the Circuit Court. After a thousand delays a question is now before the Circuit Court as a Court of Admiralty for judgement on the bond given on the property being restored. Several objections are made, two of which deserve consideration. The first is that the order for restoration was made, not in court but by the Judge out of court, not at a called court, and second that the bond was taken by the marshal to himself & not to the U. S. Upon this order the vessel was delivered, & this bond has been returned to court, but has not been acted on. Nor is there any act of the Court approving the proceeding. It is contended to be a mere act *in pais* not sanctioned by the court. That it is the unauthorized act of the marshal who might release the bond or sue upon it, and that the court cannot consider it as in the place of the vessel & so act upon it.

With great regard and esteem, I am, dear Sir, your obedt

J. Marshall.

The Honble. Joseph Story.
Salem, Massachusetts.

Richmond, July 13th, 1819.

My dear Sir,— I had the pleasure, this morning of receiving your letter of the 7th, by which I am greatly obliged. I shall at the next term decide the case of the Little Charles in conformity with your reasoning. It is, I think, perfectly sound & were this even questionable the practice of the courts ought to be uniform.

Another admiralty question of great consequence has occurred at the last term which I would carry before the Supreme Court, if I could, but as I have not the privilege of dividing the Court when alone, as the sum is only about 1500$ [*sic.*], it must abide by my decision. It is, however, one of general importance, & I must ask the favor of you to give me your views of it.[3]

A vessel belonging to the port of Richmond in Virginia was hypothecated for necessary repairs in New York & has been libelled in the District Court of this State. The District Judge condemned her, & the case is before me on an appeal. It has been agreed that New York is as much foreign to Virginia as Ireland or Guernsey to England. It has also been agreed that the power of hypothecation on simple interest is not so strictly guarded as the power of pledging the ship on bottomry for usurious interest.

From a consideration of this case I have been led to doubt what rule ought to be adopted in the United States, & to question the propriety of applying the rule in England to our situation. The foundation of the rule is that in a foreign port this exercise of ownership on the part of the master may be necessary whereas in a domestic port it cannot be presumed to be so. Now let the ports of one state be considered as foreign or domestic with respect to the vessels of another & cases may arise in which the literal application of the rule would violate its principle. It would be absurd that a vessel belonging to Amboy should be hypothecated in New York. But the same vessel at New Orlean or in the mouth of Columbia would be completely out of the reach of the owner. The necessity for exercising this power by the master would be much stronger than in the case of a vessel belonging to one side of the bay of Passimiquoddy hypothecated in a port on the other.

I do not think a republication of the piece you mention in the Boston papers to be desired, as the antifederalism of Virginia will not, I trust, find its way to New England. I should also be sorry to see it in Mr Wheaton's appendix because that circumstance might lead to suspicious respecting the author & because I should regret to see it republished in its present deranged form with the two centres transposed.

I am highly gratified by the sentiments you express & shall always feel a grateful recollection of them. The esteem of those we esteem is among the most delightful sensations of the human heart.

I had never thought of preparing an opinion in the militia case. That is committed to you, & cannot be in better hands. I shall just sketch my ideas for the purpose of examining them more closely, but shall not prepare a regular opinion. As at present disposed I do not think we shall differ.

With very much esteem & regard,

I am, dear Sir, your obedt

J. Marshal.

Mr Justice Story.
  Salem, Massachusetts.

Richmond, June 15th, 1821.

Dear Sir,—. . . The opinion of the Supreme Court in the Lottery case[4] has been assaulted with a degree of virulence transcending what has appeared on any former occasion. Algernon Sidney[5] is written by the gentleman who is so much distinguished for his feelings towards the Supreme Court, & if you have not an opportunity of seeing the Enquirer I will send it to you. There are other minor gentry who seek to curry favor & get into office by adding their mite of abuse, but I think for coarseness & maliguity of invention Algernon Sidney surpasses all party writers who have ever made pretensions to any decency of character. There is on this subject no such thing as a free press in Virginia, and of consequence the calumnies and misrepresentations of this gentleman will remain uncontradicted & will by many be believed to be true. He will be supposed to be the champion of state rights, instead of being what he really is, the champion of dismemberment.

  With great regard & esteem

I am, dear Sir, yours, &c.

J. Marshall.

The Hoñble Mr Justice Story.
  Salem, Massachusetts.

Richmond, July 13th, 1821.

My dear Sir,—. . . What you say of Mr. Jefferson's letter rather grieves than surprizes [*sic.*] me. It grieves me because his influence is still so great that many, very many will adopt his opinions, however unsound they may be, & however contradictory to their own reason. I cannot describe the surprize & mortification I have felt at hearing that Mr. Madison has embraced them with respect to the judicial department.

For Mr Jefferson's opinion as respects this department it is not difficult to assign the cause. He is among the most ambitious, & I suspect among the most unforgiving of men. His great power is over the mass of the people, & this power is chiefly acquired by professions of democracy. Every check on the wild impulse of the moment is a check on his own power, & he is unfriendly to the source from which it flows. He looks of course with ill will at an independent judiciary.

That in a free country with a written constitution any intelligent man should wish a dependent judiciary, or should think that the constitution is not a law for the court as well as the legislature would astonish me, if I had not learnt from observation that with many men the judgement is completely controuled by the passions. The case of the mandamus may be the cloak, but the batture is recollected with still more resentment.

I send you the papers containing the essays of Algernon Sidney. Their coarseness & malignity would designate the author if he was not avowed. The argument, if it may be called one, is, I think, as weak as its language is violent & prolix. Two other gentlemen have appeared in the papers on this subject, one of them is deeply concerned in pillaging the purchasers of the Fairfax estate in which goodly work he fears no other obstruction than what arises from the appellate power of the Supreme Court & other is a hunter after office who hopes by his violent hostility to the Union, which in Virginia assumes the name of regard for state rights, & by his devotion to Algernon Sidney, to obtain one. In support of the sound principles of the constitution & of the Union of the States, not a pen is drawn. In Virginia the tendency of things verges rapidly to the destruction of the government & the re-establishment of a league of sovereign states. I look elsewhere for safety.

With very much esteem & affection

I am, dear Sir, your

J. Marshall.

The Honble Mr Justice Story.
  Salem, Massachusetts.

                              Richmond, July 2d, 1823.

My dear Sir,—. . . The case concerning the securities of the cashier of the Bank goes to the Supreme Court & will probably be reversed. I suppose so, because I conjecture that the practice of banks has not conformed to my construction of the law. The Judge, however, who draws the opinion must have more ingenuity than I have if he draws a good one.

The main question respects the validity of the bond on which the suit was instituted. It was signed at different times and left in possession of the cashier, certainly, I suppose, in the expectation that he would forward it to the proper place. The plea of *non est factum* was put in among other pleas & the plaintiff proved the signature of the obligors & relied on the possession of the bond & the suit on it as evidence to be left to the jury of its delivery & acceptance.

The cause was argued with very great ability, and it was contended that this would not be sufficient in any case, but if in general, not in this case.

I held very clearly that in the case of an individual obligee the evidence would authorize the jury to infer delivery, but not in the case of the Bank of the United States.

The incorporating act requires that before the cashier shall be permitted to enter on the duties of his office he shall give bond with security to be approved by the board of Directors for the faithful performance of its duties. I had no doubt that the suit upon the bond was evidence of its acceptance & consequently of its being approved, if that fact could be established by parol evidence, but I was of opinion that it could not be so established. The board of Directors, I thought, could only speak by their record. They cannot speak or act as individuals speak or act. They speak & act by their minutes. Their approbation & acceptance of the bond could not be expressed otherwise than officially on their minutes, & no other evidence than the minutes could establish the fact. I therefore did not permit the bond to go to the jury.

The question was entirely new, & I was at first rather in favor of the plaintiffs. But in so lax a manner was this business conducted as to show very clearly that the cashier was in the full performance of his duty before the bond was executed, & to leave it very doubtful whether the breaches assigned were not committed before the bond passed out of the possession of the cashier. There was reason to believe that it had never been seen by the Board of Directors till he was removed from office, if then. It was impossible not to foresee that if the bond went to the jury questions would immediately arise on the time of its commencing obligation. The date could not be the guide because it was not executed at its date. If the time when it was signed by the last obligor should be insisted on, it was obvious that it had not then been seen or approved by the Directors, nor was it accepted by them. The delivery therefore could not be complete. If the time when it came to the possession of the Directors were to be taken, it probably never came to their possession. These difficulties produced a close examination of the point, the result of which was a perfect conviction bond. I did not doubt that the board of Philadelphia might have authorized the board at Richmond to accept the bond, but such authority ought to appear by the minutes of the board at Philadelphia.

I shall bow with respect to the judgement of reversal, but till it is given I shall retain the opinion I have expressed.[6]

With great & affectionate esteem, I am your

J. Marshall.

The Honble Mr Justice Story.
    Salem, Massachusetts.

Richmond, Decr 9th, 1823.

My dear Sir,— I had the pleasure yesterday of receiving your letter of the 24th ultimo & congratulate you on passing through your circuit in such good health & spirits. Our brother Washington was so unwell as to be under the necessity of adjourning the court at Philadelphia without going through the docket. I am still engaged at this place in a sort of dilatory way, doing very little, and still having something to do. A case was argued yesterday which I would send to the Supreme Court if I could, but I cannot. The Pilot, an American vessel was captured by pirates & converted into a piratical cruizer. She was then recaptured by one of our squadron under Commodore Porter after a sharp action. She was brought into Norfolk, libelled as prize & claimed by the original owner. The attorney for the captors abandoned the claim as prize, and asked salvage. This claim was resisted on the ground that the capture was not within the act of 1800, because that applies only to recaptures from an enemy of th United States, not to recaptures from a pirate. It was insisted too that the act of 1819 does not give salvage for a recapture made by a national ship, because although an American vessel recaptured by a merchantman or private vessel is to be brought in, yet such vessel recaptured by a national ship is not to be brought in. As there is no salvage given by statute, the claim, it was said, must rest upon general law. It was admitted that according to that law salvage is due for a vessel recaptured by a private ship, but not for a vessel recaptured by a national ship, because the nation owes protection to all its people, and it is a part of the duty of the national force to afford this protection. In the present case it was one of the objects of the expedition. It was said that the general dicta that salvage is due for recaptures made from pirates must be limited to such as are made by private ships or by the public ships of some other nation than that of the recaptures vessel.

The counsel for the recaptors relied chiefly on the general principle that by the law of nations, or by the general maritime law, salvage is due for all vessels recaptured from pirates.

The District Judge gave salvage, & the owners have appealed. I do not know that the question has ever arisen in any of the courts of the United States. Perhaps your information may be more extensive, and I will thank you to give it to me. If the case has not been decided you will greatly oblige me by your sentiments on it, as I know that you are more *au fait* on these questions than I am. The sooner I hear from you, provided you are satisfied in the case, the better.

I have read the correspondence to which you refer and regret its publication extremely. I feel great respect for Mr. [John] Adams, and shall always feel it whatever he may do. The extreme bitterness with which he speaks of honourable men who were once his friends is calculated to mortify and pain those who remain truely attached to him. A comparison of the language he applies to gentlemen of high character in Massachusetts with that which in the early part of the correspondence he applied to those who were always his enemies and gross calumniators, who cannot even now treat him with decency, inspires serious reflections. We can only say, *non est qualis erat.*

I think I can *guess,* although not born north of the Hudson, what you hint at respecting the Presidential election; but I shall be as careful not to commit my guess as you are respecting your scheme.

Farewell. Providence, I hope, will continue to take care of us. With affectionate esteem,

I am, dear Sir, your obedt

J. Marshall.

The Honble Mr Justice Story.
Salem, Massachusetts.

My dear Sir,— I have just finished the perusal of your centennial discourse on the first settlement of Salem, and while fresh under its influence take up my pen to thank you for the pleasure it has given me.

You have drawn a vivid picture, and, I believe, a faithful likeness of those extraordinary men who first peopled New England, and my feelings as well as my judgement have accompanied you in your rapid sketch of the character and conduct of their descendants. I wish the admonitory part may have its full effect on others as well as on those to whom it was particularly addressed. Some of our southern friends might benefit from the lesson it inculcates.

But I have been still more touched with your notice of the red man than of the white. The conduct of our forefathers in expelling the original occupants of the soil grew out of so many mixed motives that any censure which philanthropy may bestow upon it ought to be qualified. The Indians were a fierce and dangerous enemy whose love of war made them sometimes the aggressors, whose numbers and habits made them formidable, and whose cruel system of warfare seemed to justify every endeavour to remove them to a distance from civilized settlements. It was not until after the adoption of our present government that respect for our own safety permitted us to give full indulgence to those principles of humanity and justice which ought always to govern our conduct towards the aborigines when this course can be pursued without exposing ourselves to the most afflicting calamities. That time, however, is unquestionably arrived, and every oppression now exercised on a helpless people depending on our magnanimity and justice for the preservation of their existence impresses a deep stain on the American character. I often think with indignation on our disreputable conduct (as I think) in the affair of the Creeks of Georgia; and I look with some alarm on the course now pursuing in the Northwest. Your observations on this subject are eloquent and are in perfect accordance with my feelings. But I turn with most pleasure to that fine passage respecting the Lady Arabella Johnson. I almost envy the occasion her sufferings and premature death have furnished for bestowing that well merited eulogy on a sex which so far surpasses our in all the amiable and attractive virtues of the heart,—in all those qualities which make up the sum of human happiness and transform the domestic fireside into an elysium. . . .

I have read with much interest the character you have drawn of our deceased friend and brother, the lamented Judge Trimble. Most richly did he merit all you have said of him. His place, I fear, cannot be completely supplied. I was desirous of having the character republished in our papers, but was restrained by the flattering introduction of my name. My modesty was alarmed by the apprehension that the request for its publication might be ascribed as much to vanity as to my deep feeling for departed worth.

Most cordially do I congratulate you on the appointment of our friend Hopkinson.

With affectionate esteem, I am, dear Sir,

Your

J. Marshall.

[1] 4 Wheat. (U. S.) 518 (1819).

[2] United States v. The Little Charles, 26 Fed. Cas., 982 (1819).

[3] Selden v. Hendrickson & Pryor, 21 Fed. Cas., 1029 (1819).

[4] Cohens v. Virginia, 6 Wheat. (U. S.) 264 (1821).

[5] Pseudonym of Spencer Roane, Judge of the Virginia Court of Errors, and a friend of Jefferson.

[6] Chief Justice Marshall was reversed, by the Supreme Court in the case of Bank of the United States v. Dandridge, 12 Wheat. (U. S.) 64 (1827). The decision of Marshall is summarized in 2 Fed. Cas., 691 (1824).

PART IV.

CHIEF JUSTICE MARSHALL
EVALUATED

JOHN MARSHALL: ONE HUNDRED YEARS AFTER*

By ROBERT B. TUNSTALL

Member of the Richmond, Va., Bar

It is agreed that John Marshall's constitutional decisions have had a far reaching effect on American Government and Law but the reason for this is not obvious. The following article is an attempt to analyze those factors which contributed to his greatness. This study is reprinted here with the permission of the *American Bar Association Journal.*

To one who wears with proper pride the title of American, an invitation to Philadelphia comes with an urgent appeal. Here, where the Declaration was signed and the Continental Congresses pursued their difficult ways; here, where the Constitution had its birth and the Federal Government its adolescence; here, where the Flag was designed and the Liberty Bell rang out its reminiscent message until silenced in lamenting the very event which we are today assembled to commemorate;—this city of shrines and symbols and memories beckons with irresistible compulsion to one who believes that only in the unbroken union of past and present may we find a sure foundation for the fabric of our national life.

May I add that for a Virginian there is something beyond? For where history, like yours and ours, is measured in centuries rather than decades, men have long memories; and I cannot think it altogether fan-

---

* Reprinted with permission from 21 *American Bar Association Journal,* 56 (1935).

ciful that in this multitudinous family of States a special brotherhod exists between those thirteen that shared the privations of . . . It would be a grateful task to tell over in affectionate retrospect the many links in the chain of recollection that binds together Pennsylvania and Virginia. Not least among them would be the life of John Marshall himself. His many associations with Philadelphia, as soldier, Congressman, envoy to France, and Chief Justice, are far too familiar to you to permit my reciting them. . . . The reception on his return from the X. Y. Z. Mission, perhaps the greatest triumph in American history that has ever attended unsuccess, was a superb recognition that the transitory objective that he lost was as naught compared with what he won in upholding the Nation's honor. But that was a national and a public demonstration, when blood was hot and passion roused. To me a more touching and more intimate occasion was his visit here in 1831, when the calm judgment of the great lawyers of your bar brought to him a homage which he returned with sentiments of a kindred respect and affection. And when, four years later, he faced the end, at the place whose site we have marked today, we may be sure that he felt that he was in the house of his friends. . . .

In attempting to speak on Marshall, one finds very soon that the more strenuous the effort, the more intense the study, ever more and more deep-seated becomes the conviction that it is hard to say anything that has not been said before, and far better. The difficulty is not that one is following the same path, at however remote and respectful a distance, as Horace Binney and Joseph Story, as Edward J. Phelps and William Henry Rawle. As to that one could rest content in the humble confidence that no comparison would be drawn. The soldier in the ranks can do his stint without feeling that some one will compare him with the great captains of history.

The real hazard of repetition is otherwise occasioned. As the chief American exemplar of the most loquacious of the professions, Marshall has been the subject not only of more distinguished but of more numerous verbal tributes than almost any of our great historical figures. On the occasion of the centenary of his accession to the Supreme Court there were arranged simultaneous celebrations of the event in every State of the Union, and frequently in several places in the same State at the same time. The result was a flood of oratory, which in edited and concentrated form fills three octavo volumes. And some years later, lest any biographical detail had been overlooked, Beveridge said the last word with his monumental "Life." Verily it would seem that future novelty could be attained only through exercise of the faculty of invention.

Accordingly, in seeking a subject not altogether threadbare, I have felt that a biographical treatment must be forsworn. An attempt at appraisal is at once more inviting, more difficult, and more dangerous. When one leaves the safe harborage of fact for the open sea of analysis, the chances of faulty navigation are infinitely amplified. Certainly there can be not even the faintest of efforts towards completeness. We may not touch at all the ports to which the quest might lead. There must be some choice of destination, or we shall never arrive. Perhaps the occasion may suggest the theme.

For this is no ordinary centennial. We do not look back, with straining sight, down the long passage of one hundred years in order to recall and recapture a career that lives in history alone. Rather do we give thanks that the work of that life remains today the animating and controlling principle of our national government. To Marshall's influence time and change have brought not weakness, but only strength. And so it seems appropriate to consider just why it is that he comes down to us *sub specie aeternitatis*. What is the peculiar quality of his genius that has brought immortality to what he said, not merely to what he was? With most of our great historical characters we think of the men themselves, what they stood for, what they accomplished; but we read their words and writings with heavy deductions for obsolescence. But with few exceptions, Marshall's very words constitute what in England would be called its Constitution, and what here has given our Constitution its meaning. They are the Holy Writ of our constitutional law; though at times it may seem that, like their prototype, they afford a battleground for fundamentalism and modernism.

In the search for the secret of Marshall's enduring quality, certain obvious considerations at once present themselves. For practical purposes, he was the first of his line. To him, therefore, were first presented those basic and structural problems which inevitably followed the institution of the new government: the place of states and nations in the federal system, and the dependent questions as to taxation, commerce, and police; the function of the judiciary as the guardian of the Constitution, and the main branches of its jurisdiction; limitations upon state and federal powers, such as the contract clause and the first ten amendments. These and kindred questions lie at the bedrock of government. Their solution determines its form and character. World-wide examples attest the fact that the forms of government, and at least the *de jure* distribution of its powers, may survive while the character of its action, the actual process of government, undergoes substantial or even violent changes. When the forms have once become fixed, the powers once distributed, they are apt to remain so, with modifications of detail and practice, except so far as amendment of the fundamental law may amputate or change them. It is otherwise with the social problems which now form so large a part of the matter for decision. There the pains of the Procrustean process of amendment may often be avoided by the generous elasticity of the Fourteenth Amendment. It is not surprising, therefore, that decisions of the former type should have at least a *prima facie* capacity for survival.

Then, too, Marshall was a pioneer; and with the pioneer difficulty and opportunity go hand in hand.

As with material things, so with the written word; when the first settler has passed over the rough places, he may take what lies ready to his hand in full confidence of priority. As to matter and manner alike, the choice is free. So rich are the blessings of priority, indeed, that at times it alone seems to form the sufficient basis for permanence. "April with his shoures sote," if written by a modern poet, would hardly survive for five hundred years of quotation; and if a judge of the Supreme Court were now to declare that "we must never forget that it is *a constitution* we are expounding," it would scarcely produce the same effect as when Marshall thundered the sentence in *McCulloch* v. *Maryland*.

But it was not in mere naked priorities that Marshall's use of the pioneer's opportunities was conspicuous. For it fell to him to devise and proclaim principles, rather than merely to labor with their application; and to the declaration of these principles he brought not only an amazing foresight, but the supreme gift of phrase. There is an almost Messianic note in his great declarations as to implied powers,[1] taxation of Federal agencies by states,[2] the meaning of commerce,[3] the delimitation of judicial powers and duty,[4] and many others too familiar to justify quotation. Conceivably another pioneer might have done as well. Assuredly no other did, and so these flashes of insight and inspiration will continue to illuminate the Constitution as long as it endures.

It is, moreover, true that the period of inception of a new government is that which most urgently induces the interpretation and enforcement of the chart that sets the rules. Although the fact has sometimes aroused executive resentment,[5] the Supreme Court has never forgotten that it is not only a court, but a cordinate department of government, sustaining if it may, restraining if it must. With Marshall this consciousness was an instant spur to action. In the Bank Cases,[6] the Steamboat Case,[7] the Dartmouth College Case,[8] and many others, we may detect an almost eager insistence on the maxim of *obsta principiis*.

Having determined in *Marbury* v. *Madison*[9] that it was for the court to set the boundaries, he felt it the court's duty to mark the lines.[10] *Marbury* v. *Madison* itself, where the court followed an elaborate pronouncement on the rights of the parties with a refusal to take jurisdiction, is perhaps the stock illustration. And when counsel today are fearful as to the sufficiency of their formal procedure before the Supreme Court, they may read with envy, though I should not counsel imitation, a stipulation of counsel, not referred to in the official report, but filed with the original papers in the Dartmouth College Case, which reads in part as follows:

> "It is also agreed that no advantage shall be taken in the Supreme Court of the United States of any want of form in the proceedings, and that counsel there may add any facts, documents or records to the special verdict to be taken and deemed as part thereof or expunge any fact therefrom which in the opinion of the counsel or Supreme Court may be necessary to the obtaining a decision on the validity of the Acts of the Legislature of New Hampshire recited in the special verdict; It being the intention of the parties to submit that question and that only to the Supreme Court. . . ."

Such a willingness to come to grips with a constitutional question is far removed, indeed, from the almost tremulous approach in the *Commodities Clause Case*,[11] where the constitutional question was avoided by a construction that provoked strong dissent.[12] It contrasts, too, with cases where the court has welcomed with manifest satisfaction the relief from constitutional decision afforded by judicial legerdemain on the part of state courts of last resort in paring down a State statute to constitutional bounds.[13] But the bolder approach of Marshall is what men remember. Ruggedness is a more salient quality than ingenuity. Affirmation impresses where negation fails. It is, I think, undeniable that a period of beginnings naturally induces strong and positive judicial action. The present term of the Supreme Court illustrates the point, for the last two years have been in many respects a time of beginnings, and questions of vast moment have pressed for decision. They have received it promptly, clearly, firmly; and I can not doubt that the decisions of 1935 will go down to history as marking a salient period in the life of the Court. It is worth noting, too, in connection with the point under immediate examination, that in one case the court decided a constitutional question, not presented on the pleadings, though necessarily involved, and in another case one that perhaps might have been avoided.[14] It is this quality of decision rather than indecision that justly brings to courts their lasting fame. And so it was with Marshall.

I have described three attributes which have brought permanence to his work: its basic character, its pioneer quality, its readiness to meet the issue. They were, in a certain sense, by-products of time and occasion. They would have gone for naught without the powers of logic, advocacy, and statesmanship that Marshall brought to their support. The combination has imparted a unique character to his constructive labors. They transcend, if they do not reverse, Justice Holmes's epigrammatic description of judicial legislation. "I recognize without hesitation," he said, "that judges must and do legislate, but they do so only interstitially; they are confined from molar to molecular motions."[15] As a Constitution-builder Marshall's work was molar rather than molecular, and the spaces which his judgments fill can hardly be called interstices. They are rather gaps that could be tranversed by no spark less mighty than that of his own genius.

But genius is a word of content, not of direction. It includes, but does not point. It reflects a synthesis, not an analysis. Its existence in Marshall does not help us in our quest. It does not tell why Marshall, as Ben Jonson said of Shakespeare, "was not of an age, but for all time." Nor are we helped by an analysis of Marshall's genius that does not more than direct us to the fields in which it operated. To say that he was an acute logician, a powerful advocate, a far-sighted salesman, is to fall far short of the mark. *Vixere fortes ante Agamemnona.* Others have had these gifts, singly and in combination. And it seems almost too glib an explanation to assert for Marshall the isolation of mere superlatives. For there was something in him that infused his powers, through and through, with the quality of agelessness. Can we discover it and set it on high, for emulation or for praise?

Not altogether, certainly. We can not draw out Leviathan with a hook. But I am the more encouraged to make the attempt because I believe not only that the search, like the pursuit of all great things, will have its own reward, but that it will lead us to an explanation which, however incomplete and fragmentary, is not without its modern implications. There will be something gained if, though we may not follow the path that Marshall trod, we can at least shun the pitfalls that he avoided. The field of search we may limit to Marshall's constitutional decisions, and we may enter by the gateway of Justice Cardoza's fascinating study of the nature of the judicial process.

In that penetrating analysis he discusses its elements: philosophy, history, tradition, sociology. The proportions in which these enter the blend that forms the ultimate judgment vary from time to time, from case to case, and especially from type to type of the questions for decision. Constitutional law presents the extremes of judicial opportunity. Where the language is explicit, the precept complete, the particular situation provided for, the mandate of the Constitution represents the ultimate of imperatives. The judge has but to obey. But these conditions seldom concur in the cases that reach the courts, and so it happens, as Justice Cardozo points out, that in this field of constitutional decision the breadth and sweep of the written words afford the freest play for the constructive work of the judge. "The judge," he says, "as the interpreter for the community of its sense of law and order must supply omissions, correct uncertainties, and harmonize results with justice through a method of free decision." It is this method that, as he puts it, "sees through the transitory particulars and reaches what is permanent behind them."[16]

The "method of free decision" is the corollary of

the *"libre recherche scientifique"*—free scientific research—of the continental jurists from whom Justice
Cardozo quotes. The more literal translation strongly
suggests his "method of sociology" as the dominant
rationale of the judicial process; and at a later stage
of his study he expresses the view that in the field of
constitutional law the primacy of the method of
sociology is undoubted.[17] We need not pause on this
point, though certain recent decisions indicate that
the method may be stretched too far. But recalling
that sociology was not even a word, let alone a science,
in Marshall's day, and also recalling the different type
of questions with which he had to deal, we may appropriately, in considering his technique, dwell rather
upon the freedom of his research than upon his use
of scientific method. The preference is one of emphasis, not exclusion. We can not deny to Marshall
the use of scientific method merely because in his day
the social sciences had not risen to the dignity of
classification as such. But I may so far anticipate my
objective as to say that in my judgment a principal
basis for his enduring quality lies in the breadth and
depth of the foundations upon which his judgments
repose.

I do not, of course, refer to legal precedent. But
little was available, and he did not use that little. Nor
can I doubt that he would, if he thought proper, have
disregarded it. I mean rather what is nowadays generally called the background, though to me foundations is the better word; the sum of relevant considerations—historical, economic, governmental, or social—
which he found ready to his hand. In laying these
foundations, he permitted no bounds to the freedom
with which he selected his materials. If he did not,
like Lord Bacon, take all knowledge to be his province,
he at least took it for his storehouse. And in his selec-
tion he exercised that highest form of judicial imag-
ination that brings the sense, as Warwick says in
Henry the Fourth,

> ". . . of the main chance of things
> As yet not come to life, which in their seeds
> And weak beginnings lie intreasured."

Times change, of course, and men with them; and because of this very fact of change it comes to pass that constitutional decisions, in view of the permitted latitudes of the Constitution, may seem of all judgments the most impermanent. But the appearance is illusory. The principles remain; it is the applications that change. The principle that legislatures may regulate business affected with a public interest is not changed because the area that includes these businesses may be widened. The inherent police power is not enlarged because the occasions for its exercise may be multiplied. The power to regulate commerce undergoes no alteration because in its application it must keep pace with the racing developments of an age of speed. It is, indeed, in this very responsiveness to contemporary need that the Constitution finds its potency to endure, for otherwise rigidity of application would break down the principles themselves. "It is not," says Judge Learned Hand, "as the priests of a completed revelation that the living successors of past lawmakers can most truly show their reverence or continue the traditions which they affect to regard. If they forget their pragmatic origin, they omit the most pregnant element of the faith they profess and of which they would henceforth become only the spurious and egragious descendants. Only as an articulate organ of the half-understood aspirations of living men, constantly recasting and adapting existing forms, bringing to the high light of expression the dumb impulses of the present, can they continue in the course of the ancestors whom they revere."[18]

But fundamental principles, as distinguished from their ever widening application, achieve permanence in just the degree that the foundations upon which they rest are lasting rather than transitory. What were Marshall's foundations? No judge has ever made an equal use with him of the Constitution itself, through comparison and contrast of its provisions; and the Constitution remains. He drew largely upon history,[19] which does not change, though our knowledge and interpretations of it may; and the history that he used was largely that of which he had been a part. A large and active practice had brought him into contact with the world of affairs, and with the principles of business and economics—principles which after the turmoil of the last decade we are coming to recognize as still possessing stability and vitality. And from many sides he knew that composite of the minds and motives of men that we call human nature, perhaps the most nearly constant thing in a changing world. He had observed it in camp and field, in country and in town, in the forum and on the hustings, at home and abroad, in the simple pleasures of rural sports and in the seats of the mighty. His knowledge was not crowded into a formulary; it was none the less ready for use, in comprehensive and ordered array.

The simplest citation of its use would be "Marshall's Decisions, *passim.*" Illustrations could be indefinitely expanded. I mention a few of the more conspicuous examples. In order to derive the power of establishing and incorporating the Bank of the United States and exempting it from State interference, he appealed to history, to governmental necessity, and to social convenience.[20] Similar underlying considerations were invoked not only to free interstate transportation and traffic from the hampering effect of State action, but to vitalize the commerce clause with such power that today it remains the principal basis for government regulation of business.[21] Broad considerations of social necessity are adverted to in the Bankruptcy Cases.[22] Not only an appreciation of interstate business, but a prophetic insight into its future, led to the preservation of the free trade between States contemplated both by the constitutional prohibition against State imposts and duties and by the commerce clause.[23] History, both formal and familiar, was resorted to in his construction of the prohibition against state bills of credit,[24] which went far to save the country from the evils of a depreciated currency, and might have gone farther had not its salutary doctrines undergone some practical impairment by a later decision[25] rendered after Marshall's death. And in The Cherokee Nation

Cases[26] his exposition of the situation of the Indian tribes was so luminous as to elicit from Chief Justice Shauck of Ohio this recognition of Marshall's equipment for his task:

> "Judicial literature does not suggest another whose resources would have been adequate to the production of this opinion. It is the opinion of the philanthropist, the champion of treaty obligations, the historian of the colonies and of the Revolution, the master of the law among nations, and the father of constitutional interpretation." [27]

Inadequate as they are, these few illustrations give some conception of the freedom with which Marshall, in laying the foundation for his great judgments, drew upon available material. I venture to suggest that his example should be followed by all who are called to the supreme privilege and responsibility of judicial station. In no other wise can research be free. If he fall short in this respect, the judge does not bring to the case the light to which it is entitled. In the striking phrase of Mr. Justice Brandeis, "knowledge is essential to understanding; and understanding should precede judging."[28] But what material is available for these high purposes? Must it be material of any special type? May the judge get it for himself, or must he wait till it is brought to him? These questions were never more important than today, when social legislation urgently appeals to the social sciences for aid in its appraisal. And they are important to my thesis, for their answer goes to the root of Marshall's judicial methods.

One type of material I mention only to reject, so far as any special utility is concerned—the formidable preambles, generally styled "Declarations of Policy," which are now prefixed to almost all the great social measures that emerge from the legislative mill at Washington. Wearing, in Sainte Beuve's phrase, "the smug face of facility," apparently deriving from the cloister rather than the forum but inviting the speculation that attends the lack of an avowed paternity, these self-serving effusions range with confident and almost cosmic sweep through the course of national business, the tale of social needs, and the economic theories evolved for the occasion, while running through the gamut we hear faint echoes of Supreme Court decisions, selected, with varying degrees of adroitness, in the manifest hope of infusing some measure of constitutional validity into the acts which the declarations precede. And to what end? Close scrutiny will not discover in the Constitution any power either to legislate facts or to enact an argument. And passing this by, it is immemorial law that courts must assume the existence of any possible state of facts that would justify the legislation under review.[29] This being true, and since, as Justice Holmes has remarked, "even in the law the whole generally includes its parts,"[30] there can be no logical basis for a legislative declaration of alleged fact in order to sustain a statute, unless the so-called facts fall without the area of possibility—in other words, to put it plainly, if they are not true.

The courts have rendered lip-service to such declarations. Judges, even the most exalted, are human enough to take such grist as comes to their mill, and it is sometimes convenient to permit legislatures to assume the responsibility for their own more dubious declarations. But the thing may work the other way; and sometimes, as in the recent Railroad Retirement Case,[31] the unwary draftsman may find that in making too broad a declaration of purposes he has nursed the pinion that impelled the judicial steel. Moreover, the courts have said that they are not bound by such recitals when they are obviously mistaken,[32] or are mere prophecy, or when conditions have changed;[33] and the plain fact is that they should not be so bound at all. For of all parts of a statute these boot-strap appendages receive the least consideration by legislators or public while the law is in the making. They represent in fact little more than the draftsman's agreement with Aaron Burr that law is whatever is boldly asserted and plausibly maintained. . . .

What says the law? "The Court," says Justice Holmes in brief but comprehensive summary, "may ascertain as it sees fit any fact that is merely a ground

for laying down a rule of law."[34] In this declaration
he followed in Marshall's footsteps. I have already
declared my faith that in seeking truth Marshall would
have set no limit to the pursuit, nor would he have
permitted one to be set by counsel or witness. *McCulloch* v. *Maryland*[35] is cited as a case in which he
undertook, unwarrantably as is suggested, to decide
the so-called question of fact whether the creation of
the United States Bank was an appropriate means for
the exercise by Congress of its granted powers. But I
not not think that in that case justice would have been
furthered, or the dignity of the proceedings enhanced,
by calling Thomas Jefferson and John Taylor of Carolina to a witness-stand debate with John C. Calhoun
and your own Alexander J. Dallas. Nor does it seem
to me that the Legal Tender Cases[36] would have had
more light thrown on them by having Secretary Chase
testify to views which as Chief Justice he would have
regretted. And even in the much abused bakeshop
case,[37] it is at least doubtful whether the court would
have been better equipped to decide upon the applic-
ability of the Fourteenth Amendment after a duel of
wits between a half dozen social workers and a like
number of rugged individualists.

Yet these three instances have been treated as conspicuous examples, if not of judicial usurpation, at
least of judicial unconvincingness. I venture to suggest
that the reason for whatever unconvincingness they
exhibit was not the lack of witnesses, but the fact that
the cases all dealt with matters of opinion concerning
which men differed. All the witnesses in the world
would not have kept them from differing. It is doubtful whether they would have even supplied fresh arguments. Proof, in the sense of demonstration, was impossible; and in cases of this character it generally is.
I do not maintain that there are not many cases in
which witnesses may helpfully be called upon to
describe underlying conditions.[38] I do maintain that
whether they are called or not, the judge is free to
pursue, and should pursue, his own researches, with
or without the aid of counsel; and the researches may

include all facts which, as Justice Brandeis says again, may enrich knowledge or enlarge understanding.[39]

Broadened to a synthesis, what I have said comes to the creed that the judge must bring to his office all that he is, all that he has, and all that he can win from the garnered knowledge of the world. At too great length, as I am painfully aware, I have sought in some faint part to show how Marshall used the gifts he had and the knowledge he could gain, and to bring his example to bear upon the judicial process as it works and lives today. My parting word must be as to what he was.

It is, I think, significant that those who study Marshall the judge almost inevitably come back at the last to Marshall the man. Perhaps this tendency is especially strong in Virginia, where he lived his familiar life, where his ashes remain, and where his house is still a shrine. From letters still treasured in private possession, I shall refer to only one, which I am very sure has never seen the light of publication. It is a letter from Marshall to John Randolph of Roanoke,[40] conveying his thanks for an autographed copy of a speech of Randolph's on retrenchment and reform. The letter, while expressing a graceful sentiment and a whimsical humor, is not notable; but the significant thing is that we find upon it, in Randolph's handwriting, this characterization of his great correspondent: "That great master of the human heart."

The friendship between Marshall and Randolph, despite political differences, was a life-long one: what strikes us is that Randolph, but five years before the end of a life which had known great bitterness and but little love, should have emphasized, not the genius which he admired, but the personal charm which held him bound. Gone were the cynic humor, the sceptic mood; Marshall reached and conquered deeper things than these.

No appraisal can disregard this power. Justice Cardozo concludes his study with a reference to the subconscious forces that enter into the final judgment. In the case of the Supreme Court of Marshall's day, I do not think it strained to suppose that the influence of his intellect gained an ever self-renewing vitality through the constant and persistent force of his personality. Perhaps even more than he dominated the minds of the judges, a majority of whom were of a different political faith, he was the master of their hearts. Through this union of his powers he has made the great harmonies of the Constitution ring down the changeful years, through peace and war, through good fortune and ill. And as the Roman poet sang to his Muse, so the Constitution may say to the great Chief Justice: "That I live and serve, if mine it be to serve, is thine."[41]

John Marshall: One Hundred Years After

[1] *McCulloch* v. *Maryland*, 4 Wheat. 316, 421.

[2] Id., 431.

[3] *Gibbons* v. *Ogden*, 9 Wheat. 1, 189-90.

[4] *United States* v. *Burr*, 4 Cranch 469, 507-8; *Cohens* v. *Virginia*, 6 Wheat. 264, 404; *Osborne* v. *Bank of the United States*, 9 Wheat. 738, 866.

[5] Cf. Jefferson's attitude as to *Marbury* v. *Madison*, the *Burr* case, and others; Jackson's comment on *Worcester* v. *Georgia*, 6 Pet. 515; and the Presidential press conference following *Schechter* v. *United States*, 295 U. S. 495 (1934).

[6] *McCulloch* v. *Maryland*, supra; *Osborne* v. *Bank of United States*, supra.

[7] *Gibbons* v. *Ogden*, 9 Wheat. 189.

[8] 4 Wheat. 518.

[9] 1 Cranch 137.

[10] In *Brown* v. *Maryland*, 12 Wheat. 419, the case below was decided on general demurrer; the record not disclosing the federal question. Cf. the taking of jurisdiction in *Craig* v. *Missouri*, 4 Pet. 411.

[11] *United States* v. *Delaware* & *Hudson Co.*, 213 U. S. 366 (1908).

[12] The construction was somewhat weakened in later decisions: *United States* v. *Lehigh Valley R. Co.*, 230 U. S. 257; *United States* v. *Reading Co.*, 253 U. S. 26, 62-3; See also *United States* v. *Delaware*, etc., *R. Co.*, 238 U. S. 536.

[13] *Missouri*, etc., *R. Co.* v. *McCann*, 174 U. S. 580; *Tullis* v. *Lake Erie*, etc., *R. Co.*, 175 U. S. 348. Cf. *Smiley* v. *Kansas*, 196 U. S. 447; *Berea College* v. *Kentucky*, 211 U. S. 45; *St. Louis*, etc., *R. Co.* v. *Arkansas*, 235 U. S. 350.

[14] *Railroad Retirement Board* v. *Alton R. Co.* (1935), 295 U. S. 330 (1935).

[15] *Southern Pacific Co.* v. *Jensen,* 244 U. S. 205, 221.

[16] Cardozo, *The Nature of the Judicial Process,* p. 16.

[17] Id., p. 76.

[18] *The Speech of Justice,* 29 Harv. Law Rev., p. 618.

[19] The reference is of course to the history used in Marshall's constitutional decisions. As to legal history, he rested under the handicaps of his time. Cf., for example, *Baptist Association* v. *Hart,* 4 Wheat. 1, with *Vidal* v. *Girard's Executors,* 2 How. 127.

[20] *McCulloch* v. *Maryland, supra; Osborne* v. *Bank of the United States, supra.*

[21] *Gibbons* v. *Ogden, supra.*

[22] *Sturges* v. *Crowninshield,* 4 Wheat. 122; *Ogden* v. *Saunders,* 12 Wheat. 213.

[23] *Gibbons* v. *Ogden,* 9 Wheat. 189; *Brown* v. *Maryland,* 12 Wheat. 419.

[24] *Craig* v. *Missouri,* 4 Pet. 411.

[25] *Briscoe* v. *Bank of the Com. of Ky.,* 11 Pet. 257.

[26] *Cherokee Nation* v. *Georgia,* 5 Pet. 1; *Worcester* v. *Georgia,* 6 Pet. 515.

[27] Marshall Memorial, Vol. 2, pp. 234-5.

[28] *Burns Baking Co.* v. *Bryan,* 264 U. S. 520.

[29] *Munn* v. *Illinois,* 94 U. S. 113, 152; *Metropolitan, etc., Ins. Co.* v. *Brownell,* 294 U. S. 580 (1934).

[30] *Western Union Telegraph Co.* v. *Kansas,* 216 U. S. 1, 53.

[31] *Railroad Retirement Board* v. *Alton R. Co.,* 295 U. S. 330 (1935). In this instance the matter referred to was a statement of purposes, not a declaration of policy.

[32] *Woolf Co.* v. *Industrial Court,* 262 U. S. 522, 536; *Chastleton Corporation* v. *Sinclair,* 264 U. S. 541, 547.

[33] *Chastleton Corporation* v. *Sinclair,* 264 U. S. 541.

[34] *Chastleton Corporation* v. *Sinclair,* 264 U. S. 543, 548. He had used similar language in *Prentis* v. *Atlantic Coast Line Co.,* 211 U. S. 210, 227.

[35] 4 Wheat. 316.

[36] *Hepburn* v. *Griswold,* 8 Wall. 603; *Legal Tender Cases,* 12 Wall. 457.

[37] *Lochner* v. *New York,* 198 U. S. 45.

[38] The courts, however, have frequently refused to permit this. See *The Consideration of Facts in "Due Process" Cases,* 30 Col. L. Rev. 360, 363, and note 14. In *Adkins* v. *Children's Hospital,* 261 U. S. 525, 560, the court found such material "interesting but only mildly persuasive."

[39] *Burns Baking Co.* v. *Bryan,* 264 U. S. 504, 534. He further says pertinently (p. 533): "Much evidence referred to by me is not in the record. Nor could it have been included. It is the history of the experience gained under similar legislation, and the results of scientific experiments made, since the entry of the judgment below. Of such events in our history, whether occurring before or after the enactment of the statute or of the entry of the judgment, the court should acquire knowledge, and must, in my opinion, take judicial notice, whenever required

to perform the delicate judicial task here involved."

40 Now in the possession of Mr. William Leigh Williams, of the Norfolk Bar.

41 Hor. Carm. iv, 3: *Quod spiro et placeo, si placeo tuum est.* Forgiveness is craved for the freedom of the adaptation.

OBITUARY[1]

JOHN MARSHALL, Chief Justice of the Supreme Court of the United States, died at Philadelphia, on the 5th day of July 1835. His remains were conveyed to Richmond, attended by Mr. Justice Baldwin, one of the Associate Justices of the Supreme Court, and by Mr. Sergeant, Mr. Rawle, Jun., Mr. Ingraham, and Mr. Peters, as a committee of the Philadelphia bar.

His private virtues as a man, and his public services as a patriot, are deeply inscribed in the hearts of his fellow citizens.

His extensive legal attainments, and profound, discriminating judicial talents, are universally acknowledged.

His judgments upon great and important constitutional questions, affecting the safety, the tranquility and the permanancy of the government of his beloved country—his decisions on internal and general law, distinguished by their learning, integrity and accuracy, are recorded in the reports of the cases adjudged in the Supreme Court of the United States, in which he presided during a period of thirty-four years.

As long as the constitution and laws shall endure and have authority, these will be respected, regarded and maintained.

---

[1] 10 Peters (U. S.) v.

PART V.

QUOTATIONS
FROM
JOHN MARSHALL

Love of Union

". . . I am disposed to ascribe my devotion to the
Union, and to a government competent to its preservation, at least as much to casual circumstances as to
judgment. I had grown up at a time when the love
of the Union, and the resistance to the claims of
Great Britain, were the inseperable inmates of the
same bosom; when patriotism and a strong fellow
feeling with our suffering fellow-citizens of Boston
were identical; when the maxim, 'United we stand,
divided we fall,' was the maxim of every orthodox
American. And I had imbibed these sentiments so
thoroughly that they constituted a part of my being.
I carried them with me into the army, where I found
myself associated with brave men from different
States, who were risking life and everything valuable
in a common cause, believed by all to be most precious; and where I was confirmed in the habit of
considering America as my country, and congress as
my government."

—From autobiographical letter to Joseph
Story in 1827

Liberty and Law

"The very essence of civil liberty certainly consists
in the right of every individual to claim the protection of the laws whenever he receives an injury. One
of the first duties of government is to afford that
protection."

—*Marbury* v. *Madison,* 1 Cranch 137, 163
(1803)

". . . where the heads of departments are the political or confidential agents of the executive, . . . to act in cases in which the executive possesses constitutional or legal discretion, nothing can be more perfectly clear than that their acts are only politically examinable. But where a specific duty is assigned by law, and individual rights depend upon the performance of that duty, it seems equally clear that the individual who considers himself injured, has a right to resort to the laws of his country for a remedy."

—*Marbury* v. *Madison*, 1 Cranch 137, 166 (1803)

"It may well be doubted, whether the nature of society and of government does not prescribe some limits to the legislative power. . . ."

—*Fletcher* v. *Peck*, 6 Cranch 87, 135 (1810)

"The government of the United States has been emphatically termed a government of laws, and not of men. It will certainly cease to deserve this high appellation if the laws furnish no remedy for the violation of a vested legal right."

—*Marbury* v. *Madison*, 1 Cranch 137, 163 (1803)

"No government ought to be so defective in its organization, as not to contain within itself the means of securing the execution of its own laws against other dangers than those which occur every day."

—*Cohens* v. *Virginia*, 6 Wheaton 264, 387 (1821)

Nature of the Constitution

". . . a constitution intended to endure for ages to come, and, consequently, to be adapted to the various crises of human affairs."

—*McCulloch* v. *Maryland*, 4 Wheaton 316, 415 (1819)

"But a constitution is framed for ages to come, and is designed to approach immortality as nearly as human institutions can approach it."

—*Cohens* v. *Virginia*, 6 Wheaton 264, 387 (1821)

"The people made the constitution, and the people can unmake it. It is the creature of their will, and lives only by their will. But this supreme and irresistible power to make or unmake resides only in the whole body of the people; not in any subdivision of them."

—*Cohens* v. *Virginia*, 6 Wheaton 264, 389 (1821)

"A constitution, to contain an accurate detail of all the subdivisions of which its great powers will admit, and of all the means by which they may be carried into execution, would partake of the prolixity of a legal code, and could scarcely be embraced by the human mind. It would probably never be understood by the public. Its nature, therefore, requires that only its great outlines should be marked, its important objects designated, and the minor ingredients which compose those objects be deduced from the nature of the objects themselves. That this idea was entertained by the framers of the American constitution, is not only to be inferred from the nature of the instrument, but from the language."

—*McCulloch* v. *Maryland*, 4 Wheaton 316, 407 (1819)

"Great weight has always been attached, and very rightly attached to contemporaneous exposition."

—*Cohens* v. *Virginia*, 6 Wheaton 264, 418 (1821)

"That the people have an original right to establish, for their future government, such principles as, in their opinion, shall most conduce to their own happiness, is the basis on which the whole American fabric has been erected. The exercise of this original right is a very great exertion; nor can it or ought it to be frequently repeated. The principles, therefore, so established, are deemed fundamental. And as the authority from which they proceed is supreme, and can seldom act, they are designed to be permanent.

"This original and supreme will organizes the government, and assigns to different departments their respective powers. It may either stop here, or establish certain limits not to be transcended by those departments.

"The government of the United States is of the latter description. The powers of the legislature are defined and limited; and that those limits may not be mistaken, or forgotten, the constitution is written. To what purpose are powers limited, and to what purpose is that limitation committed to writing, if these limits may, at any time, be passed by those intended to be restrained? The distinction between a government with limited and unlimited powers is abolished, if those limits do not confine the persons on whom they are imposed, and if acts prohibited and acts allowed, are of equal obligation. It is a proposition too plain to be contested, that the constitution controls any legislative act repugnant to it; or, that the legislature may alter the constitution by an ordinary act."

—*Marbury* v. *Madison*, 1 Cranch 137, 176-
177 (1803)

"The constitution is either a superior paramount law, unchangeable by ordinary means, or it is on a level with ordinary legislative acts, and, like other acts, is alterable when the legislature shall please to alter it. If the former part of the alternative be true, then a legislative act, contrary to the constitution, is not law; if the latter part be true, then written constitutions are absurd attempts, on the part of the people, to limit a power, in its own nature, illimitable.

"Certainly, all those who have framed written constitutions contemplate them as forming the funda-

QUOTATIONS FROM JOHN MARSHALL

mental and paramount law of the nation, and consequently, the theory of every such government must
be, that an act of the legislature, repugnant to the
constitution, is void. This theory is essentially attached to a written constitution, and is, consequently,
to be considered by this court as one of the fundamental principles of society."
                    —*Marbury* v. *Madison*, 1 Cranch 137, 177
                        (1803)

Union and National Supremacy

"In our complex system, presenting the rare and
difficult scheme of one general government, whose
action extends over the whole, but which possesses
only certain enumerated powers; and of numerous
state governments, which retain and exercise all
powers not delegated to the Union, contests respecting power must arise."
                    —*Gibbons* v. *Ogden*, 9 Wheaton 1, 204-
                        205 (1824)

"This government is acknowledged by all, to be
one of enumerated powers. . . . But the question respecting the extent of the powers actually granted,
is perpetually arising, and will probably continue to
arise, so long as our system shall exist."
                    —*McCulloch* v. *Maryland*, 4 Wheaton 316,
                        405 (1819)

"The government of the Union . . . is emphatically
and truly a government of the people. In form and
in substance it emanates from them. Its powers are
granted by them, and are to be exercised directly on
them, and for their benefit."
                    —*McCulloch* v. *Maryland*, 4 Wheaton 316,
                        404-405 (1819)

"The genius and character of the whole government
seems to be, that its action is to be applied to all the

external concerns of the nation and to those internal concerns which affect the States generally; but not to those which are completely within a particular State, which do not affect other States, and with which it is not necessary to interfere, for the purpose of executing some of the general powers of the government."

—*Gibbons* v. *Ogden,* 9 Wheaton 1, 195 (1824)

"That the United States form, for many and for most important purposes, a single nation, has not yet been denied. In war we are one people. In making peace we are one people. In all commercial regulations we are one and the same people. In many other respects the American people are one; and the government which is alone capable of controlling and managing their interests, in all respects, is the government of the Union. It is their government, and in that character they have no other. America has chosen to be, in many respects, and to many purposes, a nation; and for all these purposes her government is complete; to all these objects it is competent."

—*Cohens* v. *Virginia,* 6 Wheaton 264, 413-414 (1821)

"The question is, in truth, a question of supremacy. . . ."

—*McCulloch* v. *Maryland,* 4 Wheaton 316, 433 (1819)

"The people of all the States have created the general government, and have conferred upon it the general power of taxation. The people of all the States, and the States themselves, are represented in congress, and, by their representatives exercise this power. When they tax the chartered institutions of the States, they tax their constituents, and these taxes must be uniform. But, when a State taxes the operations of the government of the United States, it acts upon institutions created, not by their own constituents, but by people over whom they claim no control. It acts upon the measures of a government created by others as well as themselves, for the benefit of others in common with themselves. The difference is that which always exists, and must always exist, between the action of the whole on a part, and the action of a part on the whole; between the laws of government declared to be supreme, and those of a government which, when in opposition to those laws, is not supreme."

—*McCulloch* v. *Maryland*, 4 Wheaton 316, 435-436 (1819)

"The framers of the constitution were, indeed, unable to make any provisions which should protect that instrument against a general combination of the States, or of the people, for its destruction; and, conscious of this inability, they have not made the attempt. But they were able to provide against the operation of measures adopted in any one State, whose tendency might be to arrest the execution of the laws; and this it was the part of true wisdom to attempt."

—*Cohens* v. *Virginia*, 6 Wheaton 264, 390 (1821)

"The commerce of the United States with foreign nations is that of the whole United States. Every district has a right to participate in it. The deep streams which penetrate our country in every direction, pass through the interior of almost every State in the Union and furnish the means of exercising this right. If congress has the power to regulate it, that power must be exercised whenever the subject exists. If it exists within the States . . . then the power of Congress may be exercised within a state."

—*Gibbons* v .*Ogden*, 9 Wheaton 1, 195 (1824)

"If the legislatures of the states may, at will, annul the judgments of the courts of the United States and destroy the rights acquired under those judgments, the constitution itself becomes a solemn mockery; and the nation is deprived of the means of enforcing its laws by the instrumentality of its own tribunals."

—*United States* v. *Peters,* 5 Cranch 115, 136 (1809)

"If any one proposition could command the universal assent of mankind, we might expect it would be this—that the government of the Union, though limited in its powers, is supreme within its sphere of action. This would seem to result, necessarily, from its nature. It is the government of all; its powers are delegated by all; it represents all, and acts for all. . . . The nation, on those subjects on which it can act, must necessarily bind its component parts."

—*McCulloch* v. *Maryland,* 4 Wheaton 316, 405 (1819)

"It is of the very essence of supremacy to remove all obstacles to its action within its own sphere, and so to modify every power vested in subordinate governments, as to exempt its own operations from their own influence. This effect need not be stated in terms. It is so involved in the declaration of supremacy, so necessarily implied in it, that the expression of it could not make it more certain."

—*McCulloch* v. *Maryland,* 4 Wheaton 316, 427 (1819)

". . . the States have no power, by taxation or otherwise, to retard, impede, burden, or in any manner control, the operations of the constitutional laws enacted by congress to carry into execution the powers vested in the general government. This is, we think, the unavoidable consequence of that supremacy which the constitution has declared."

—*McCulloch* v. *Maryland,* 4 Wheaton 316, 436 (1819)

". . . is it unreasonable that the [federal] judicial power should be competent to give efficacy to the constitutional laws of the legislature? That department can decide on the validity of the constitution or law of a State, if it be repugnant to the constitution or to a law of the United States. Is it unreasonable that it should also be empowered to decide on the judgment of a state tribunal enforcing such unconstitutional law? Is it so very unreasonable as to furnish a justification for controlling the words of the constitution?"

—*Cohens* v. *Virginia,* 6 Wheaton 264, 414 (1821)

". . . in a government acknowledgedly supreme, with respect to objects of vital interest to the nation, there is nothing inconsistent with sound reason, nothing incompatible with the nature of government, in making all its departments supreme, so far as respects those objects, and so far as is necessary to their attainment. The exercise of the appellate power over those judgments of the state tribunals which may contravene the constitution or laws of the United States, is, we believe, essential to the attainment of those objects."

—*Cohens* v. *Virginia,* 6 Wheaton 264, 414-415 (1821)

Three Branches of Government

"The President is the sole organ of the nation in its external relations, and its sole representative with foreign nations. Of consequence, the demand of a foreign nation can only be made on him. He possesses the whole Executive power. He holds and directs the force of the nation. Of consequence, any act to be performed by the force of the nation is to be performed through him. He is charged to execute the laws. A treaty is declared to be a law. He must, then, execute a treaty where he, and he alone, possesses the means of executing it."

> —From a speech in the House of Representatives on March 7, 1800 on the case of Jonathan Robins

"The wisdom and the discretion of congress, their identity with the people, and the influence which their constituents possess at elections, are, . . . in many . . . instances . . . the sole restraints on which they have relied to secure them from . . . abuse. They are restraints on which the people must often rely solely, in all representative governments."

> —*Gibbons* v. *Ogden,* 9 Wheaton 1, 197 (1824)

"It is the peculiar province of the legislature to prescribe general rules for the government of society; the application of those rules to individuals in society would seem to be the duty of other departments."

> —*Fletcher* v. *Peck,* 6 Cranch 87, 136 (1810)

"The province of the court is, solely, to decide on the rights of individuals, and not to inquire how the executive, or executive officers, perform duties in which they have a discretion. Questions in their nature political, or which are, by the constitution and laws, submitted to the executive, can never be made in this court."

> —*Marbury* v. *Madison,* 1 Cranch 137, 170 (1803)

"But where the law is not prohibited, and is really calculated to effect any of the objects entrusted to the government, to undertake here to inquire into the degree of its necessity, would be to pass the line which circumscribes the judicial department, and to tread on legislative ground. This court disclaims all pretentions to such a power."

> —*McCulloch* v. *Maryland,* 4 Wheaton 316, 423 (1819)

"Courts are the mere instruments of the law, and can
will nothing. . . . Judicial power is never exercised
for the purpose of giving effect to the will of the
judge; always for the purpose of giving effect to the
will of the legislature; or, in other words to the will
of the law."
>   —*Osborn* v. *Bank of the U. S.*, 9 Wheaton
>   738, 866 (1824)

Broad Interpretation and Implied Powers

"What do gentlemen mean by strict construction? . . . .
If they contend for that narrow construction which
. . . would cripple the government and render it
unequal to the objects for which it is declared to be
instituted, and to which the powers given, as fairly
understood, render it competent; then we cannot
perceive the propriety of this strict construction, nor
adopt it as the rule by which the constitution is to be
expounded."
>   —*Gibbons* v. *Ogden,* 9 Wheaton 1, 188
>   (1824)

"It has been said that these [enumerated] powers
ought to be construed strictly. But why ought they
to be so construed? Is there one sentence in the
constitution which gives countenance to this rule?"
>   —*Gibbons* v. *Ogden,* 9 Wheaton 1, 187
>   (1824)

"Can we adopt that construction (unless the words
imperiously require it), which would impute to the
framers of that instrument, when granting these
powers for the public good, the intention of imped-
ing their exercise, by withholding a choice of means?"
>   —*McCulloch* v. *Maryland,* 4 Wheaton 316,
>   408 (1819)

"Let the nature and objects of our Union be considered; let the great fundamental principles on which

the fabric stands be examined; and we think the
result must be that there is nothing so extravagantly
absurd in giving to the court of the nation the power
of revising the decisions of local tribunals, on questions which affect the nation, as to require that words
which import this power should be restricted by a
forced construction."

> —*Cohens* v. *Virginia,* 6 Wheaton 264, 422-
> 423 (1821)

"The government which has a right to do an act, and
has imposed on it the duty of performing that act,
must, according to the dictates of reason, be allowed
to select the means; and those who contend that it
may not select any appropriate means, that one particular mode of effecting the object is expected, take
upon themselves the burden of establishing that
exception."

> —*McCulloch* v. *Maryland,* 4 Wheaton 316,
> 409-410 (1819)

"The sword and the purse, all the external relations,
and no inconsiderable portion of the industry of the
nation, are intrusted to its government. . . . [A]
government intrusted with such ample powers, on
the due execution of which the happiness and prosperity of the nation so vitally depends, must also be
intrusted with ample means for their execution. The
power being given, it is the interest of the nation to
facilitate its execution. It can never be their interest;
and cannot be presumed to have been their intention,
to clog and embarrass its execution."

> —*McCulloch* v. *Maryland,* 4 Wheaton 316,
> 407-408 (1819)

"We admit, as all must admit, that the powers of
the government are limited, and that its limits are
not to be transcended. But we think the sound construction of the constitution must allow to the national
legislature that discretion, with respect to the means
by which the powers it confers are to be carried into

execution, which will enable that body to perform the high duties assigned to it, in the manner most beneficial to the people. Let the end be legitimate, let it be within the scope of the constitution, and all means which are appropriate, which are plainly adapted to that end, which are not prohibited, but consistant with the letter and spirit of the constitution, are constitutional."

—*McCulloch* v. *Maryland,* 4 Wheaton 316, 421 (1819)

"There is no express provision for the case; but the claim has been sustained on a principle which so entirely pervades the constitution, is so intermixed with the materials which compose it, so interwoven with its web, so blended with its texture, as to be incapable of being separated from it without rending it to shreds."

—*McCulloch* v. *Maryland,* 4 Wheaton 316, 426 (1819)

The editor would like to express his appreciation to the United States Bicentennial Commission for their permission to use the above quotations.

CHRONOLOGY OF CHIEF JUSTICE
JOHN MARSHALL'S DECISIONS

Talbot v. Seeman, 1 Cranch (U. S.) 1 (1801).
Wilson v. Mason, ibid., 45.
United States v. Schooner Peggy, ibid., 103.
Turner v. Fendall, ibid., 117.
Marbury v. Madison, 1 Cranch 137 (1803).
Clark v. Young & Co., ibid., 181.
Wilson v. Lenos and Maitland, ibid., 194.
Hooe & Co. v. Groverman, ibid., 214.
Wood v. Owings and Smith, ibid., 239.
United States v. Simms, ibid., 250.
Mandeville & Jameson v. Riddle & Co., ibid., 290.
Hamilton v. Russell, ibid., 310.
Hepburn and Dundas v. Auld, ibid., 321.
Hodgson v. Dexter, ibid., 345.

Faw v. Marsteller, 2 Cranch (U.S.) 10 (1804).
Pennington v. Coxe, ibid., 33.
Murray v. Schooner Charming Betsy, ibid., 64.
Head & Amory v. The Providence Insurance Co., ibid., 127.
Little v. Barreme et al, ibid., 170.
Dunlop & Co. v. Ball, ibid., 180.
Church v. Hubbart, ibid., 187.
Mason et al v. Ship Blaireau, ibid., 240.
Adams v. Woods, ibid., 336.
Reily v. Lamar, Beall and Smith, ibid., 344.
United States v. Fisher, ibid., 358.
Graves and Barnewall v. Boston Marine Insurance Co., ibid., 419.

Hindekoper's Lessee v. Douglass, 3 Cranch (U. S.) 1 (1805).
Hodgson v. Butts, ibid., 140.
United States v. More, ibid., 159.
Law v. Roberdeau's Executor, ibid., 174.
Wilson v. Codman's Executors, ibid., 193.
Hallet and Downe v. Jenko et al, ibid., 210.

Hannay v. Eve, 3 Cranch (U. S.) 242 (1806).
Selsby v. Young and Selsby, ibid., 249.
McFerran v. Taylor and Massie, ibid., 270.
Wilson v. Speed, ibid., 283.
Harris v. Johnston, ibid., 311.
Scott v. London, ibid., 324.

United States v. Grundy and Thornburgh, ibid., 337.
Marine Insurance Co. v. Tucker, ibid., 357.
Manella Pujals & Co. v. Barry, ibid., 415.
Maley v. Shattuck, ibid., 458.
Lawrason v. Mason, ibid., 492.

Jennings v. Carson, 4 Cranch (U. S.) 2 (1807).
Rhinelander v. Insurance Co. of Pennsylvania, ibid., 29.
United States v. Willings and Francis, ibid., 48.
Smith et al v. Carrington et al, ibid., 61.
Ex Parte Bollman and Ex Parte Swartwout, ibid., 75.
French's Executrix v. Bank of Columbia, ibid., 141.

Fitzsimmons v. The Newport Insurance Co., 4 Cranch (U. S.) 185 (1808).
Marshall v. Delaware Insurance Co., ibid., 202.
Pawling et al v. United States, ibid., 219.
Grant v. Naylor, ibid., 224.
Rose v. Himely, ibid., 241.
Hudson et al v Guestier, ibid., 293.
Alexander v. Harris, ibid., 299.
Chappedelaine v. Dechenaux, ibid., 306.
United States v. Gurney et al, ibid., 333.
Peisch v. Ware, ibid., 347.
Young v. Bank of Alexander, ibid., 384.
Stead's Executors v. Course, ibid., 403.
Higginson v. Mein, ibid., 415.
Pollard and Picket v. Dwight et al, ibid., 421.
United States v. The Schooner Betsy, ibid., 443.

Alexander v. Mayor of Alexandria, 5 Cranch (U. S.) 1 (1809).
M'Keen v. Delancey's Lessee, ibid., 22.
Tucker v. Oxley, ibid., 34.
Bank of the United States v. Deveaux, ibid., 61.
United States v. Judge Peters, ibid., 115.
Violett v. Patton, ibid., 142.
Kempe's Lessee v. Kennedy et al, ibid., 173.
Bodley and et al v. Taylor, ibid., 191.

Taylor and Quarles v. Brown, ibid., 234.
Hepburn and Dundas v. Auld et al, ibid., 262.
Yeaton v. United States, ibid., 281.
Harrison v. Sterry, ibid., 289.
United States v. Riddle, ibid., 311.
Riddle & Co. v. Mandeville and Jamesson, ibid., 322.
Yeaton v. Fry, ibid., 335.
Owings v. Norwood's Lessee, ibid., 344.

Scott v. Ben, 6 Cranch (U. S.) 3 (1810).
Field et al v. Holland et al, ibid., 8.
Maryland Insurance Co. v. Woods, ibid., 29.
O'Neale v. Thornton, ibid., 53.
King v. Delaware Insurance Co., ibid., 71.
Fletcher v. Peck, ibid., 87.
Massie v. Watts, ibid., 148.
United States v. Hall and Worth, ibid., 171.
Vasse v. Smith, ibid., 226.
Custiss v. Georgetown and Alexander Turnpike Co., ibid., 233.
Finley v. Lynn, ibid., 238.
Sheehy v. Mandeville and Jamesson, ibid., 253.
Livingston and Gilchrist v. Maryland Insurance Co., ibid., 274.
Dorvousseau v. United States, ibid., 307.

Shirras v. Caig, 7 Cranch (U. S.) 34 (1812).
Schooner Pailina v. United States, ibid., 52.
Russell v. Clarke's Executors, ibid., 69.
Sloop Active v. United States, ibid., 100.
Schooner Exchange v. M'Faddon, ibid., 116.
Welch v. Lindo, ibid., 160.
Hughes v. Moore, ibid., 176.
Sheehy v. Mandeville, ibid., 208.
Conway's Executors v. Alexander, ibid., 218.

Queen v. Hepburn, 7 Cranch (U. S.) 290 (1813).
Clark's Executors v. Carrington, ibid., 308.
Dickey v. Baltimore Insurance Co., ibid., 327.
Marine Insurance Co. of Alexander v. Hodgson, ibid., 332.
Locke v. United States, ibid., 339.
Bond v. Jay, ibid., 330.
Herbert v. Wren, ibid., 370.
Schooner Hoppet v. United States, ibid., 389.
Williams v. Armroyd, ibid., 423.
Holker v. Parker, ibid., 436.

Blackwell v. Patton & Erwin's Lessee, ibid., 472.
Oliver v. Maryland Insurance Co., ibid., 489.
Livingston & Gilchrist v. Maryland Insurance Co., ibid., 507.

Van Ness v. Forrest, 8 Cranch (U. S.) 30 (1814).
Gracie v. Marine Insurance Co. of Baltimore, ibid., 75.
Brown v. United States, ibid., 110.
The Alexander, ibid., 169.
The Merrimack, ibid., 317.
The Frances, ibid., 348.
Alexander v. Pendleton, ibid., 462.
Pratt et al v. Carroll, ibid., 471.

Meigs et al v. M'Clung's Lessee, 9 Cranch (U. S.) 11 (1815).
Sims v. Guthrie, ibid., 19.
Taber v. Perrott & Lee, ibid., 39.
Brig Short Stape v. United States, ibid., 55.
Parker v. Rule's Lessee, ibid., 64.
Polk's Lessee v. Wendal, ibid., 87.
The Mary, ibid., 126.
Clark's Executors v. Van Riemsdyk, ibid., 153.
Finley v. Williams, ibid., 164.
M'Iver's Lessee v. Walker, ibid., 173.
Thirty Hogshead of Sugar v. Boyle, ibid., 191.
Ship Societe, ibid., 209.
The Nereide, ibid., 388.

Henry v. Ball, 1 Wheat. (U. S.) 1 (1816).
The Samuel, ibid., 9.
The Mary and Susan, ibid., 25.
Thompson v. Gray, ibid., 75.
New Orleans v. Winter, ibid., 91.
The Astrea, ibid., 125.
Matson v. Hord, ibid., 130.
Taylor v. Walton, ibid., 141.
The Nereide, ibid., 171.
Walden v. Heirs of Gratz, ibid., 292.
Harden v. Fisher et al, ibid., 300.
Martin v. Hunter's Lessee, ibid., 305.
The George, ibid., 408.
Hiran, ibid., 440.
Ammidon v. Smith, ibid., 447.
Patton's Lessee, ibid., 476.

Slocum v. Mayberry, 2 Wheat. (U. S.) 1 (1817).
Greenleaf v. Cook, ibid., 13.
M'Iver et al v. Ragan, ibid., 28.
Coolidge et al v. Payson, ibid., 66.
Beverly v. Brooke, ibid., 100.
M'Coul v. Lekamp's Administratrix, ibid., 111.
The San Padro, ibid., 132.
Rutherford v. Green's Heirs, ibid., 196.

Johnson v. Pannel's Heirs, ibid., 206.
Chirac v. Lessee of Chirac, ibid., 259.
The Argo, ibid., 287.
Morgan's Heirs v. Morgan, ibid., 290.
Shipp et al v. Miller's Heirs, ibid., 316.
The Anna Maria, ibid., 327.

The Friendschaft, 3 Wheat. (U.S.) 14 (1818).
M'Iver v. Kyger, ibid., 53.
Hughes v. Union Insurance Co., ibid., 159.
Olivera v. Union Insurance Co., ibid., 183.
United States v. Bevans, ibid., 336.
The Atlanta, ibid., 409.
Evans v. Eaton, ibid., 454.
United States v. Palmer, ibid., 610.

Philadelphia Baptist Associaton v. Hart's Executors, 4 Wheat (U.S.) 1 (1819).
The Divina Pastora, ibid., 52.
Williams v. Peyton's Lessee, ibid., 76.
United States v. Holland & Allen, ibid., 108.
Sturges v. Crowninshield, ibid., 122.
Brown et al v. Gilman, ibid., 255.
McCulloch v. Maryland, ibid., 316.
M'Arthur v. Browder, ibid., 488.
Trustees of Dartmouth College v. Woodward, ibid., 513.

United States v. Wiltberger, 5 Wheat. (U.S.) 77 (1820).
M'Clung v. Ross, ibid., 116.
United States v. Klintock, ibid., 144.
Loughborough v. Blake, ibid., 317.
Blake et al v. Doherty, ibid., 359.
Handly's Lessee v. Anthony, ibid., 374.
Owings v. Speed et al, ibid., 420.
Conn et al v. Penn., ibid., 424.

Mechanic's Bank of Alexander v. Withers, 6 Wheat. (U.S.) 106 (1821).
Thatcher et al v. Powell et al, ibid., 119.
Willinks v. Hollingsworth et al, ibid., 240.
Cohens v. Virginia, ibid., 264.
Bartle v. Coleman, ibid., 475.
Bowie v. Henderson et al, ibid., 514.
Brashier v. Gratz et al, ibid., 528.
United States v. Daniel, ibid., 542.
Goszler v. Corporation of Georgetown, ibid., 593.

Newson v. Pryor's Lessee, 7 Wheat. (U.S.) 7 (1822).
Tayloe v. T. & S. Sandeford, ibid., 13.
Taylor's Lessee v. Myers, ibid., 23.
Bayley v. Greenleaf, ibid., 46.
Bouldin v. Massie's Heirs et al, ibid., 122.
Matthews v. Zane et al, ibid., 164.
Hoofnagle v. Anderson, ibid., 212.
The Gran Para, ibid., 471.
Crocket v. Lee, ibid., 522.
Bright's Lessee, ibid., 535.
The Irresistible, ibid., 551.
Holbrook v. Union Bank of Alexandria, ibid., 553.
Marbury v. Brooks, ibid., 556.

Hunt v. Rousmamer's Administrators, 8 Wheat. (U.S.) 174 (1823).
Sexton v. Wheaton, ibid., 229.
The Mary Ann, ibid., 380.
The Sarah, ibid., 391.
Johnson and Graham's Lessee v. M'Intosh, ibid., 543.
Siglar and Nall v. Haywood, ibid., 675.

Gibbons v. Ogden, 9 Wheat. (U. S.) 1 (1824)
Kirk et al v. Smith, ibid., 241.
Taylor v. Mason, ibid., 325.
Doddridge v. Thompton et al, ibid., 469.
Stephens v. M'Cargo, ibid., 502.
Peyton v. Robertson, ibid., 527.
Smith v. M'Iver, ibid., 532.
Meredith v. Picket, ibid., 573.
Osborn et al v. Bank of the United States, ibid., 738.
Bank of the United States v. Planter's Bank of Georgia, ibid., 904.

Wayman v. Southard, 10 Wheat. (U. S.) 1 (1825).
The Antelope, ibid., 66.
Elmendorf v. Taylor, ibid., 152.
Carneal et al v. Banks, ibid., 181.
Dos Hermandoz, ibid., 306.
Brent et al v. Davis, ibid., 395.
Corporation of Washington v. Yound, ibid., 406.
McDowell v. Peyton et al, ibid., 454.

Etting v. The Bank of the United States, 11 Wheat. (U. S.) 59 (1826).
Brooks v. Marbury, ibid., 78.
Harding v. Handy and Wheaton, ibid., 103.
Taylor's Devisee v. Owing et al, ibid., 226.
Armstrong v. Toler, ibid., 258.
Finley v. Bank of the United States, ibid., 304.

INDEX